The Memoir of John Baptiste Stradford

Hero of Black Wall Street

Curated by
Laurel Stradford and
Dr. Leslee Stradford

Foreword by Reverend Jesse L. Jackson, Sr.

Copyright © 2025 by Laurel Stradford and Dr. Leslee Stradford

All rights reserved. No part of this book may be reproduced, stored in a retrieval system, or transmitted in any form or by any means without the publisher's prior written permission—except by a reviewer who may quote brief passages in a review to be printed in a newspaper, magazine, or journal.

Published by
Pairee Publications
San Antonio, Texas

For inquiries, contact:
Dr. Leslee Stradford
Email: drstradford@gmail.com

Cover and Interior Design by Jessica Tilles/TWASolutions.com

ISBN 978-1-7371818-6-6

Printed in the United States

*Dedicated to all the descendants of
John Baptiste Stradford.*

To my great-grandfather, owner of the Stradford Hotel and Library on Black Wall Street in Tulsa, Oklahoma.

To my grandfather, Cornelius Francis Stradford, lawyer and founder of the National and Illinois Bar Associations.

To "C.F." Stradford, my father, who was born in Tulsa, Oklahoma, and was five years old at the time of the 1921 massacre.

To my uncle, Judge John W. Rogers Sr., Tuskegee Airman.

To John W. Rogers, Jr., my first cousin, Founder and CEO of Ariel Capital Management, who had these memoirs typed.

To Jewel Stradford LaFontant, J.B.'s granddaughter, who—without her unyielding passion to clear her grandfather's good name—spent her life in the legal profession to have his case exonerated of any wrongdoing in the Tulsa 1921 massacre in 1996.

To my sister, Laurel, who has always been a trailblazer: a writer, artist, entrepreneur in fashion and cosmetics, and a champion Stradford historian.

Acknowledgments

I would like to acknowledge Frederick Williams, adjunct professor of African American Cultural History and writer, who has worked with my sister and me over the past six years—collecting information, conducting research, and, most importantly, being a good friend and encourager—in preparing our great-grandfather's memoirs for publication.

I also want to acknowledge Jessica Tilles of TWA Solutions and Services, my outstanding editor and designer of both the book's interior and cover.

I want to acknowledge Dorian K. Carter of Ariel Capital Management, who has been a friend and source of support for more than 15 years.

I must also acknowledge my dear sister Laurel, who has been a constant companion and has never forgotten our family history. She has served as our historian and presenter at the Stradford Awards, sponsored by the Illinois State's Attorney's Office, for 35 years.

A special acknowledgment goes to my eldest sister, Carolyn Stradford-Hardy, her two children, Marion Fox and Ivan Hardy. My great-niece, Crystal Fox, who has amazed me as she has grown, and her dad, Teddy Fox And also great-nieces, Jewel and Olivia Hardy.

I also wish to thank Drs. Landi Balan and Leslie Balan for their physical and mental support throughout these many years of friendship.

I also wish to acknowledge Ernest LaFontant and the entire LaFontant family, especially Jon and Lucienne LaFontant who have been a part of my family since childhood.

Also Ronald and Juanita Temple who were instrumental in my continued academic success and as foundation board members.

A special acknowledgment to Claude Lawrence with whom I have spent the last 11 years of my life. To Arlene Wooley, Robert and Donna Jackson who have been instrumental in the care of both of our families.

And to some of the people who have been shinning lights in my life: Martha Allen, Karma and Didi Gaines-Ra, Janet Burns, Reginald Thomas, Johnny Simmons, Dr. Lorenzo Pace, Dr. Jacqueline Bontemps, Arthur Wheatley, Fan Lee Warren, Adger Cowans, David and Candace Calloway, Cara Calloway, Marsha Nedland, Victoria Rogers, ET and Lyn Williams Martin Prekop, Martin Puryear, Chris Bruce, Remi Vaughan-Richards, Milano Mellon, Julie Keys, Cash Copeland, James and Monica Grant, Bruce Byrd, Butch Woodson, Carole Ward Allen, Charles Ogletree, Classy Foat, Damerio Solomon-Simmons, Denise Malcolm, Dr. Elnora Webb, Erick Fischl and April Gornik, Frank Stewart, leslie mcfadden Patrick Banks, Ronnie Hartfield, John Torreano, Joseph, Wilson, Ken and Katherine Chenault, Khoa Ho, Laurens Tan, lonnie bunch, Napoleon Henderson, Charan Singh, Andreas branch, Polly Young, Richard Hunt, Dr. Richard Powell, Timothy Reid, and Ozell Austin

Finally, we extend our deepest gratitude to Reverend Jesse L. Jackson, Sr., for graciously lending his voice and vision to *The Memoir of John Baptiste Stradford* by penning the foreword. His lifelong commitment to justice, equality, and the advancement of African American history echoes the very spirit of our great-grandfather's extraordinary legacy. It is an honor to have Reverend Jackson's words open this memoir, framing our great-grandfather's story within the broader narrative of resilience and triumph. His contribution elevates this work, and we are profoundly thankful for his willingness to be part of preserving this vital history.

FOREWORD

*John Baptiste Stradford:
A Great Man's Legacy*

The publication of the Memoir of John Baptiste Stradford is long overdue and I applaud his two great-granddaughters, Laurel and Dr. Leslee Stradford for making it possible for the world to know the life of this great Black American.

Stradford's contributions to the history of this country are a compelling story of struggle and determination rewarded with success, only to see it all destroyed by racial hatred

He was born in 1861 in Kentucky, a slave state, grew up during the oppressive years of Jim Crow, but still managed to graduate from Indianapolis Law School and eventually become one of the most successful businessman as well as a community leader.

Of all the successful businesses on Black Wall Street, his Stradford Hotel was the most exemplary. It was considered the best hotel in the west, at that time and rivaled white hotels in quality.

With all the obstacles confronting his race during those days including the Ku Klux Klan, Stradford never backed down when challenged. He was not intimidated by anyone, regardless of race and went about building his businesses without fear of failure. Because of that attitude he had is ups and downs but ultimately succeeded in becoming one of the richest Black men in America.

All to be lost again because of racism that destroyed the most successful Black community in the history of this country.

It is my great honor to write the forward for the great granddaughters of JB Stradford. They have held on to their great grandfather's memoirs for more than 40 years.

I have known the Stradford family for decades. having worked with C Francis, Stradford Sr. in the early days of operation breadbasket. Attorney Stradford's dedication, determination and legal acumen was of great value to me. I have indeed enjoyed the company and friendship of many of the family members including his grandson John Rogers Jr. who has been a close friend for many years as well.

Indeed, I have presided over the homecoming for three members of this august family. They have all been leaders in civil rights, globally, at home, and in the White House.

In 1996 JB's granddaughter Ambassador Jewel Stradford Lafontant was able to have her grandfather exonerated from any wrongdoing and his good name restored. He had been accused of having started that race 'riot'.

Stradford left us a rich and compelling legacy to be emulated. His memoir should be a learning experience for both young and old on how to succeed during these turbulent times in America, as we continue our pursuit toward economic, social, and political equality. Finally, it will present a very different perspective of who we were during the late eighteenth and early nineteenth centuries. Not the perception of a weak, ignorant people but strong intelligent men and women equal to the task of being successful and honorable Americans. That is why John Baptist

Stradford's Memoir should be on every caring Americans reading list who appreciates the history and the culture of a great people.

Reverend Jesse L. Jackson, Sr.
Founder, Rainbow Push Coalition

INTRODUCTION

When I was only four years old, Grandma Mumsie sat my sister, Laurel, and me down and told us a story about how our great-grandfather, John Baptiste (J.B.) Stradford had been a very successful Black man, owner of a very elegant hotel in a place known as Black Wall Street. She told us how some racist men, jealous of his success, as well as that of other business owners—men and women—demolished their businesses, their homes, and killed many men, women, and children.

As I matured through my early years, teen years, and as a young adult, what Grandma told me stuck with me. I grew up knowing there was something special about my family's history, as well as the Stradford name. When I reached adulthood, my aunt, Jewel Stradford Lafontant, gave my sister and me copies of J.B.'s memoirs. A couple of years before he passed away, he wrote what he termed "the details of my life." It was a remarkable accomplishment by an exceptional man—something you will observe as you read how this man, born in a slave state (Kentucky) in 1861, became an educated schoolteacher, a lawyer, and an entrepreneur during the most harrowing times for Black Americans in this country.

What you will discover in this memoir is the story of a man who refused to succumb to the burdens of second-class citizenship in what he strongly believed was his own. During his lifetime, there were two distinct approaches of how Black Americans should respond to the oppressive forces of Jim Crow Laws—legitimized by the infamous 1896 *Plessy v. Ferguson* Supreme Court decision—as well as the brutal lynchings effectively sanctioned by every level of government, from local and state to the national level. One approach, articulated by Booker T. Washington, emphasized the importance of hard work and de-emphasized resistance to the daily injustices Black Americans experienced. The other, advanced by Dr. W. E. B. Du Bois, urged Black Americans to fight back, to no longer submit to abuse in a racist society that viewed them as less than human. What is striking about J.B. is that, while he embraced Washington's emphasis on hard work, he wholly rejected the accommodationist stance that, in his view, stripped Black men of their manhood. Instead, he supported Du Bois's radical call to fight back and to be men of courage.

Although J.B. wrote his memoir ninety years ago—and it covers a period in this country's racial history from 1861 to 1935—his experiences during that time remain relevant today. J.B. anticipated this enduring relevance when he wrote in the opening paragraph, *"If this story encourages any member of our group to greater faith in his ability to demand his rights as a citizen and to give his time and talent in the prosecution of this principle, I shall feel amply repaid for my labor and pain."*

J.B. intended his life story to be shared with the entire country. It serves as an inspiration for all Black Americans to never give up and to continue fighting the good fight. Throughout his life, he did an extraordinary amount to protect the rights of his community. J.B. always carried his gun because, during his turbulent years of fighting for survival, he knew his life was constantly in jeopardy, refusing to succumb to oppression. His memoir is also a valuable resource for white Americans, offering an alternative perspective on the Black experience, one that counters the stereotyped portrayals commonly found in books and movies during his lifetime.

One of the most compelling sections of J.B.'s memoir covers his years in Tulsa, Oklahoma—from his arrival shortly after graduating from the Indianapolis School of Law in 1899 to June 1, 1921, when a mob determined to lynch him forced him to flee. He recounts his determination to build a hotel of exceptional quality, one that would rival the best Black-owned hotels in the United States. Regarded as one of the most elegant in America, The Stradford Hotel opened in 1918.

He describes how traumatic that single day—June 1, 1921—was for all his "group," as over 7,500 white Tulsans obliterated the prosperous Black neighborhood. Racists specifically targeted him because he was both a leader in the community and its most successful businessman. J.B. was the wealthiest entrepreneur on Black Wall Street.

Immediately following the destruction, a grand jury convened and indicted him. By that time, however, he had already left Tulsa and was living with his brother in Independence, Missouri. When the Tulsa authorities attempted to extradite him, his son—my grandfather, Corneluis Francis Stradford, Sr.—rushed to Independence, posted bail, and brought him to Chicago. J.B. could never go back to Tulsa because of the indictment.

Years later, his granddaughter, Jewel Stradford, and great-grandson, Cornelius Toole, worked tirelessly to have him exonerated—and succeeded. Long after his passing, Oklahoma Governor Frank Keating exonerated him at a ceremony in Tulsa on October 18, 1996, and proclaimed the date "Stradford Family Day" in the State of Oklahoma.

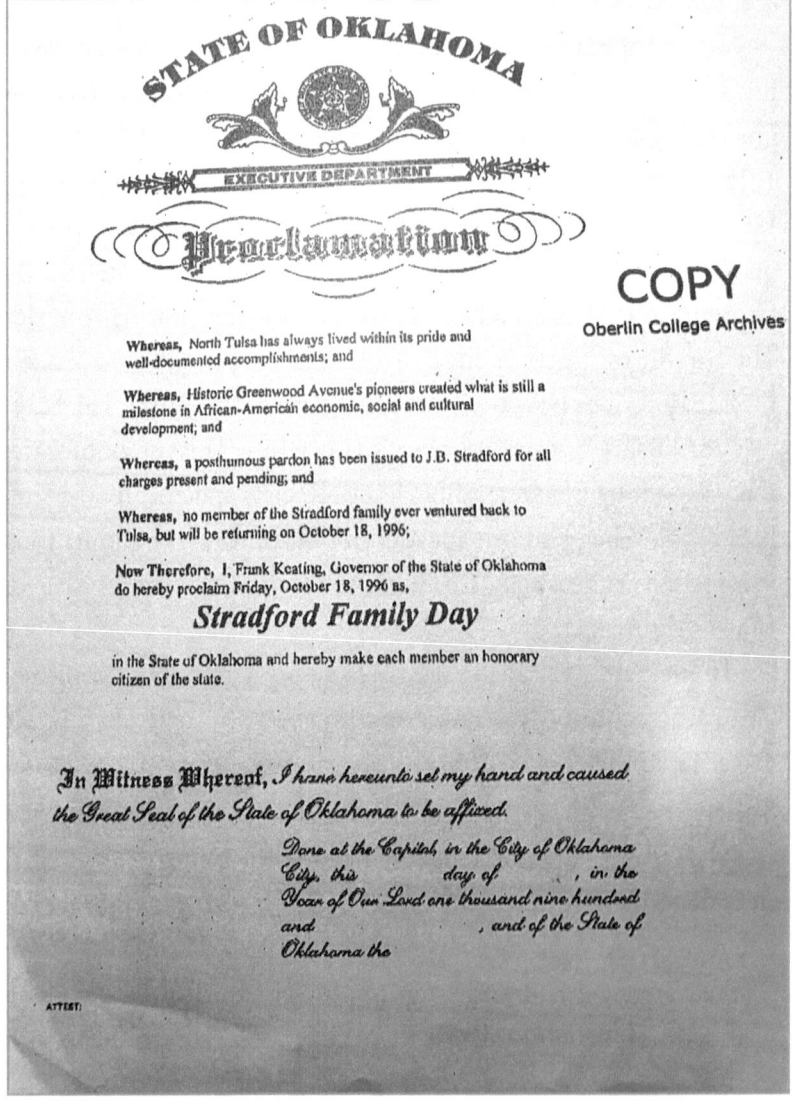

Jewel Stradford LaFontant, with her son, John W. Rogers, pictured in the frame.

Curators' Note to Readers

This memoir has been preserved in its original voice and authentic historical context. Written in the 1920s, the narrative reflects the language, perspectives, and cultural attitudes of that era. The author's distinctive voice—his manner of expression, vocabulary choices, and storytelling style—remains unchanged from the original manuscript.

While minor spelling and grammatical corrections have been made for clarity, no alterations have been made to the content, tone, or character of the author's words. The social attitudes, terminology, and viewpoints expressed herein are those of the author writing in the early twentieth century and should be understood within that historical framework.

This document stands as an authentic witness to one man's extraordinary life journey, told in his own words and in the vernacular of his time. Readers will encounter not only a remarkable personal story but also a genuine artifact of American literary and social history, preserved with all its original power and authenticity intact.

Chapter 1

I am simply giving the details of my life, which have always been opposite to the standard and ideal of the American people relative to their attitude toward our group. If this story encourages any member of our group to greater faith in his ability to demand his rights as a citizen and to give his time and talent in the prosecution of this principle, I shall feel amply repaid for my labor and pains.

I don't feel that this book would be complete if I failed to give a short biography of the life of my father, who I believe was one of the grandest men that has ever lived or died for honesty, pride, chastity, and morality. He had no superior. He was respected by all in the vicinity in which he lived and a leader in all enterprises connected with our group.

Born in Woodford County, Kentucky, on June 1, 1814, a slave, of his early life I never heard him talk much. According to the story he told me, he was a fine specimen of physical manhood, weighing 190 pounds and standing 5 feet 9 inches high. He was, indeed, a very comely person, and as he grew, he became the

Caesar Stradford, father

favorite of the family. His master, being a pro-slavery man, and his daughter, his mistress, was an abolitionist. In spite of all the objections to teaching the slaves, she determined to teach him to read and write.

She bought him a book and arranged the place to secretly give him lessons without the consent of her father. After each lesson, he would take the book and put it in his hat. When plowing, he would wait until he got to the far side of the field, and there he would spend a few minutes studying the lesson which had been assigned him by his teacher.

In the early mornings before the time came to go to work and in the evenings, he would utilize his available time in preparing the lesson which had been assigned to him. This process was continued long enough to enable him to read and write. And his writing was a facsimile of that of his master's. His young mistress was very kind to him on account of his bonds.

In those days, there were night patrollers or, as the slaves called them, "padder-rollers." And they were paid to catch and whip any slaves found off his master's plantation without a pass. In most cases, when he wanted to leave his master's plantation, he wrote his own pass and, at times, passes for his fellow slaves. And at no time were his passes ever questioned.

My father was owned by a man named Henry Moss who was very kind to his slaves and made my father the head man, that is, the overseer on the farm, and treated him with great kindness and leniency on account of his effective, efficient service. Although being exempted in a great measure from many hardships through which his fellow slaves had to pass, he early decided that he would not allow no man, not even his master, to whip him. He also decided that he would never marry a slave woman for the reason that he had seen so many husbands sold to go down South and taken away from their wives and children. The wailing and mourning of the broken-hearted wives and mothers, and the bereaved children, whose lamentations out of the depths of their hearts ascended to the gates of Heaven, to be slightly brushed aside without the least consideration. And as he said, "I wonder if there is a just God who rules the destinies of men, who only lends a deaf ear to the persecutions of an enslaved people."

His young mistress married a man by the name of Pow Hattan Woolridge, who was a friend to the Moss family. This man, Woolridge, disliked my father on account of the liberty accorded to him by his master and had taken pains to inform my father of his dislikes. As the years rolled by, on account of business reverses, his master became bankrupt and had to sell not only all his slaves, which numbered over two hundred but also his farm. He apprised my father of the situation and told him that as he was a part of the estate that came to him through his wife, he would have to go to his young mistress, the wife of Pow Hattan Woolridge, the man he hated. So, after making ready, he was sent down into the Green River country in Kentucky to his new master, Mr. Woolridge.

After arriving at his new home, he went to his new master and told him, "I have been sent here by Mars Henry to serve you as your slave. I will always be faithful to your duty, ready at all times to do your bidding, whatever it is, but I won't stand to be whipped by you and no other man."

He knew what his feelings were for him, and he had prepared himself for the inevitable. He carried along with him a dirk, carefully concealed in a scabbard under his shirt, for 12 months to kill him. At the expiration of that time, having done the work of two ordinary men, he went to him and said, "Mars Pow Hattan, I want you to sell me up the river or down the river or wherever you can find a sale for me because I won't stay with you any longer." So, as he was an heirloom, Pow Hattan agreed to send him back to his former master. In a few days, he was sent back to his old homestead. When he arrived, he met his former master who was glad to see him and welcomed him back to the place of his birth.

About two years after his return home, he married my mother, a free woman, and he set about to provide a place for her to live. He bought a house and lot in an alley between Morgan and Lexington Streets, Versailles, Kentucky, and paid for it by working overtime at night on his master's farm and also neighboring farms.

In those days, and especially in that vicinity, corn, wheat, and hemp were the staple products. In the corn harvest, they paid $0.10 a shock. For cutting and shucking corn, they paid about the same. A shock of corn consisted of 16 hills square, and after he had finished his tasks for his master, he would cut or shuck 10 or 12 shocks every night for himself during the hemp-breaking season. His task was to break 150 pounds each day, and all over that amount, he would get extra pay. He was called one of the best hemp-breakers in the neighborhood. His average was 400 pounds per day. After having paid for his property, he thought that if he could get a piece of property and deed it to his wife and children, he felt that he could buy himself. At that time, his master's financial circumstances were very pressing, and he was compelled to sell most of his slaves on account of the agitation of freeing them.

Taking advantage of this situation, my father went to his master and proposed to buy himself, offering this argument in defense of his proposition. "I have a wife and three children whom I love. I have bought a home for them and am caring for them by working overtime, and they are as dear to me as my life, and I am willing to lay down my life for them. I know you are negotiating a sale for me, and I know that in a few days, I will be torn from my family, never to see them anymore. Won't you give me a chance to buy myself?"

His master replied, "Caesar, if I sell you now, I can get the cash for you. I fear that within a few years, that you will be free, and I will lose the cash which I can now get for you."

My father replied to his master, "I have served you for 40 years of my life. I have led the slaves to work and have kept them busy from sunup to sundown. You have given me high praise for my services, and the interests which I have taken in your business. You have never called me to any task except I was ready and willing to do your bidding. I have zealously guarded your interests in every way. And for the interests which I have taken in your welfare, I am appealing to you out of the depth of my heart, and for the sake of my wife and children, to set the price you want for me, and give me a chance to pay you. And if in any event I should be liberated before the debt is paid, I will pay you every dollar which is left unpaid at the time of my liberation. You have known me all of my life. You know that I am honest and trustworthy, and for this, I give you my solemn promise. I will pay you."

His master fixed the price at $500.00, issued to him his free papers and took his note for the payment of the debt.

Several years later, in 1863, the Emancipation Proclamation declared the slaves free. My father had not finished paying for himself. A great many of his friends advised him not to pay the balance of the debt because the proclamation had exempted him from the debt. He replied that he had given his solemn promise to his master, and he would pay every dollar of the debt even though he was free, and he did it, and it took him several years after freedom to finish paying the debt.

After marrying, his master gave him one night each week to visit his family, and after he bought himself, he was at home each night. He ceased working for his master on account of the distance his farm was from town. He made his living by gardening and working by the day on farms and any other work he could find to do. The house that he bought for his family consisted of four rooms: two on the first floor and two on the second story. The lot was surrounded by a high board fence, and in that yard was our playground. We were forbidden to play in the street under penalty of being punished.

By the death of my mother, my father was left with eight children: four boys and four girls. In those days, it was the custom of the Colored people, when they had more children than they could support and even with a great many, when they were able to support them, to bind them out to some of the whites who needed help, until they were 21 years of age. The compensation was room, board, clothing, and a horse, saddle, and bridle when they became of age. This transfer of the child was almost as bad as slavery. You could seldom find a very few, kind and generous-hearted guardians among them and a very few ever stayed to get the horse, saddle and bridle. Relative to his children he said, "I will never bind one of them out. I have a house and lot for them to live, and by the help of God, I will feed, clothe and educate them."

My sister, Alice, being the oldest, acted in the place of a mother. My brother, Benjamin, the oldest of us, helped Father to support us by working each day with him in the field or anywhere he could find employment. At that time, there were no public schools, but he sent us to private teachers and kept us in school until we all learned to read, write, and cipher. He was a faithful worker, no task too hard, no undertaking too arduous for him to perform in the pursuit of giving support to his children. He believed in not sparing the rod. He was a hard taskmaster, very severe on his children. Our backyard was our playground, our orders were to play in it, and not in the alley, and if we were reported to be out in the alley playing, we were sure to be whipped severely. He was a devout Christian and reared us in the fear and admonition of the Lord. He taught us by example, as well as by precept, and his teaching has largely demonstrated itself through every member of the family.

Here, I will mention some of his teachings. On the wall, going up the steps to the second floor of the house, hung a large chart containing the Ten Commandments in rhyme, which were as follows: "Thou shalt have no other god before me; Before me no idol bend the knee; Take not the name of God in vain; Dare not the Sabbath profane; Give to parents honor due; Take heed that thou no murder do; Abstain from words and deeds unclean; Steal not for thou art by God seen; Thou shall not commit adultery; Thou shall not covet thy neighbor's wife, etc.; Thou shall not bear false witness, etc."

This chart hung on the wall for many years, and we were drilled in the very elementary principles of it until it became a part of us. And I have fashioned my life in a great measure by the teachings received from that chart. He also taught us never to associate with anyone who had served a term in prison; also, not to associate with half white people. He claimed that they had no race and compared them with mules and said that they had no nation. He sent us to the Sunday school regularly in order that we might learn more about Jesus.

In 1885, burdened by the years of hard work and oppression, he gave up the struggle and fell to the sleep that knows no awakening.

It has been an inspiration to me to know that my father, under such adverse circumstances, a slave, could buy property, buy himself, and secure a little education. It has spurred me on to greater and bigger achievements.

I shall now proceed to write the memoirs of my life from my earliest existence to the present.

In 1865, when the soldiers were mustered out in Kentucky, a few of them came to our house to board. I can't say how many. I can remember one of them by the name, Doug Sherry, who when he had finished his meal, would put a box in his chair and set me up to the table to eat my meal. In addition to what my mother had prepared for the meal, he gave me some little hard biscuits to eat, which they called "hard tack." I can remember how I enjoyed eating them. I can remember how big it made me feel for him to put me up to the table in his place and tell me someday I would be a great man, and I have done my best to make his prophecy come true.

The next incident I very clearly remember—my mother was one of those honest-hearted women who would air her grievances before her children, not thinking, no doubt, that the children would think of avenging her adversary. She had a white neighbor by the name of Mrs. Schultz, who would steal her chickens. Instead of going to Mrs. Schultz when she knew she took them and demanding reparation, she would wait until Father came home at night and tell him in the most pathetic way of her losses until she aroused the vengeance of the children. Mrs. Schultz had chickens, and they came into our yard every day, and they were never molested. One day, I saw one of Mrs. Schultz's chickens come into our yard and a thought came to me to kill the chicken and take it to my mother as the custom was. I picked up a stone and pointed the index finger on my left hand, and at the same time, threw the stone and down came the chicken. I ran and grabbed the chicken and in triumphant joy, carried it into the house to my mother and said, "Oh, Mama, here is one of Mrs. Schultz's chickens I have killed for you."

She did not even as much as smile, but gave me a very black look and said, "Take that chicken and throw it back over the fence and then come to me and I will teach you not to take anything which is not yours."

I threw the chicken back over the fence and went back to my mother. At that time, I was 8 years old, but I was very large for my age. She took me into the smokehouse where we smoked or cured our meat and proceeded to give me an unmerciful beating. She threw me down on the floor and put her foot on my head, took the clothesline and, with her foot on my head, she whipped me just like she would have killed a snake, having my head pinioned on the floor with her foot. In spite of her efforts to hold it, I would extricate it. She forbade me to take my head from under her foot and the oftener I extricated it, the harder she whipped me. The policy in those days, of the parents, was to make their children subservient to their will, and they generally whipped the children until they tamely submitted even under the most severe punishment. She put forth every effort to bring about that state of affairs, but not so in this case. The pain was so great, the only objective I had was to get my head out from under her foot.

By this time, she had rubbed the skin off the side of my head, where she had her foot upon and the side which was on the floor was also bruised and bleeding. After she found she could not get perfect obedience, in this case, she ceased to beat me and left me in the smokehouse, not realizing the condition I was in. Both sides of my head were swollen out of recognition. My eyes were bloodshot, and I was hardly able to get into the house. There was a closet under the stairs which we used for soiled clothes and rags, etc., so I crawled into it, and there I remained until Mama's passion subsided. And then she called me to her, but I failed to come. She came to the door and told me to come out, and not until then did she realize my condition. She called our family doctor, and he dressed my wounds. He found that my neck had been very badly strained, and I had been handled too roughly for a child of my age, and it would be necessary for her to give me the best of attention, or the injuries might prove fatal.

So, Mama, as we called her, became somewhat alarmed and gave me the very best of attention during the week of my sickness. When my father came home that evening, he found me in bed and after Mama had told him what she had done to me, he became very indignant and told her she should have had that beating instead of me. "You pour out your grievances before your children by telling them how other people treat you, until you arouse their hearts to revenge. Feeling that they would have your approval, they do something to avenge your adversary, and you try to kill them for doing something you caused them to do.

And from now on, tell your troubles to the policemen and not to your children, and you won't have to beat them half to death for doing something to get even with your enemies."

This beating has made a lasting impression upon me in more ways than one. Not only from the standpoint of my mother's desire to bring me up an honest and upright man, but for every lick she hit me, she felt it was for my own good, and I am really convinced if more corporal punishment was used in rearing the youth of today, our jails, penitentiaries, and reformatories would not be crowded to the overflow. But also, the words which she spoke to me when she said, "Take that chicken, throw it back over the fence and come back to me and I will teach you not to take anything which is not yours," I can truthfully say that from that day up until now, I have been scrupulously honest in all of my transactions with my fellow man.

As I have said before, our playground was our backyard, and we were restricted to that alone, and my father picked out the boys and girls whom he allowed to come in and play with us. We had some very high-class neighbors, and as a matter of fact, their children were permitted to be our playmates. We seldom ever had any brawls. My oldest sister was the custodian of the playground and any infractions of the rules, she would report to Father, and he would punish the violator or see to it that, if it was the visiting children who had violated the rules, their parents would punish them. If not, they were barred from the playground. On our ground, we had what we called an "acting pole," a swing, and sufficient space to play marbles. I learned a great many acrobatic stunts with the view to excel in everything in every way. I learned to play marbles and was the best player in

Versailles. We played what we called "for keeps." If we won our competitors' marbles, we kept them. I won all of the boys' marbles every day, day after day, until I had more than 2,000 marbles of all descriptions, crystals.

In those days, we called them "aggies," "scotch papers," "white peas," "scotch peas," both large and small. I had more marbles than the man who sold them. And from this batch of marbles, I received my first lesson in business. My father was a great egg eater, and I thought, as the boys were spending their nickels buying marbles, they could buy them from me at a reduced rate. I not only accepted nickels, but I sold more of them for eggs than I did for money. I never thought where the boys got the eggs, but I do know that I received more eggs for marbles than it took to supply the family. And to the extent, I felt that I was helping a little to support the family. The money I gave to Father, and he said that I was quite a help to him.

In the early history of our playground, we had quite a few agreeable and affable playmates. Later on, a new neighbor moved into the neighborhood by the name of Henry Rankins. He had a brother by the name of Sid who was a little older than I. He was admitted as one of our playmates. He was a little bully and had most of us afraid of him. He chose me to pick on, and every morning when he came, he would play around for a while, and then he would begin to pick on me. He would put a chip on his shoulder and dare me to knock it off and then put it on his head and dare me to knock it off, which I refused to do. He would then put the chip on my shoulder and knock it off, and also on my head and then knock it off, and I would not resent it. After he found that he could not get a fight out of me in that way, he would stick his fist under my nostril and say to me, "Smell your master's fist." This procedure continued for some time. My oldest sister had noticed the incident several times, and she decided to call the attention of our father to it. So, one evening after we had eaten supper, she came into the room where Father and I were, and told him what Sid Rankins had done to me, how he had placed chips on his shoulder and head and dared me to knock them off, and how he had stuck his fist in my face and said, "Smell your master's fist," and she wanted to know what should be done about it.

My father, looking over his eyeglasses at me, said, "You devil, did you allow that boy to treat you that way?"

"Yes, sir, Papa. You told me not to fight."

"Well, if that boy comes here anymore and you allow him to treat you that way, I will beat you half to death."

That was just what I wanted him to say. The boys all imposed on me, and I thought I had to stand it, for I would much rather stand for them to impose upon me than to violate his orders for he would never whip me with my clothes on because he said that he did not want to wear them out. And he whipped unmercifully.

The next day, Sid came and began to pick on me again. And when he attempted to put his fist into my face, I knocked it away.

He then asked me, "What do you mean?"

I told him not to do it again, if he did, I would make it hot for him. So, he attempted it again. I struck him, and we clinched. I threw him down and proceeded to give him a sound flogging. We fought for some time before he cried, "Nuff." And when he did, his nose was bleeding profusely, his eyes were blackened, and he was so disfigured that he was unrecognizable. He went home and told his father that all the Stradford boys had jumped on him and beaten him unmercifully. His father came with him in great haste to our playground and demanded to know why all of us had beaten his boy.

I was the spokesman. I said, "Uncle Henry—" We always called people older than we, "Uncle Henry" in those days. "I whipped Sid by myself. No one helped me, and I can whip him again."

He then asked Sid, "Did he whip you?"

And he said, "No."

His father said, "Jump on him," and he obeyed his father's command.

We clinched. There was a ditch on the side of the alley that led the water into the sewer. I rushed him over to that ditch and threw him into it and fell on top of him. The ditch was just wide enough for me to get each of my legs on either side of him and I had him pinioned in such a manner that he could not extricate himself, and so I proceeded to beat his head and face with all my power.

Finally, a most pitiful wail came from him saying, "Oh, Daddy, take him off!"

The fight was over, and I had won twice.

His father said, "I will teach you not to lie to me," and took him and put his head between his legs and almost wore out a strap that he carried in his pocket for that purpose.

That was my first fight. Since that fight, I have engaged in scores of others with almost equal success. Years after this, my first competitor married my cousin and a great many years passed before I saw him. In 1893, I went to the World's Fair in Chicago, and while there, I learned from my sister that he was living there. I went over to see him and was, indeed, glad to see him. He entertained me in great style. We talked about the doings of our childhood and the scenes around the town. He finally asked me if I remembered the whipping which I gave him when we were boys. I told him I did, and that I could whip him again.

He said, "I guess you can for you are much larger and also younger than I am, and besides, I have been sick for a long time, and you have never been sick a day in your life. At any rate, 50 years ago, you were my conqueror, and I see no reason, from all appearances, that you are not the same man today that you were as a boy, physically 50 years ago, relative to your prowess."

And even today, I have no friend who I regard with more devotion than this man whom I vanquished 60 years ago.

Prior to the death of my mother, I had never attended any school. She had taught me my ABC's, and I had learned to spell a little. After her death, my father decided to send me to school. There was a private school, conducted or taught by a woman named Mrs. Washington. Her education was quite limited. She could read and write and knew very little of any of the other branches of study. But she was a woman of very strong Christian character with a loving disposition, and at the same time, strict in her rules which pertained to the conducting of the school. She was interested in the advancement of the pupils. To any of the pupils who were not able to grasp the work, she would always give all the spare time she had to make them understand their lessons. She had an adopted son, Theodore by name, who had the dropsy. He and I were the most mischievous boys in school. We were in the same class, as a rule, and we stood at the head of the class. If he was not at the head, I was. For some time, it was tit-for-tat as to which stayed at the head the more. My first book was *McGuffey's First Reader*, and after we had mastered it, our teacher gave us the second reader and the *Blue Spelling Book*. In those days, when the pupil had gotten over as far as Baker in the spelling book, he thought he had learned it all. And when asked how far over in the book you have gotten, it would be his great pride to say that "We have gotten over to the word, 'Baker.'"

The school was largely attended. In fact, there were too many children for one teacher to keep order in the school. Theodore and I were very mischievous. We were always doing to make the children laugh, throwing balls of paper, making faces, and sticking pins in some of the other pupils. We were bright pupils, always knew our lessons and always first to do some funny trick to cause laughter in the room. Whenever the teacher caught us, she would larrup us with a long switch, but as soon as her back was turned to us, we would do something else to have a little fun. Seemingly, it was inherent in us to make fun. Finally, one day, Theodore and I had a fight. And I gave him a sound beating. That afternoon, his mother, the teacher, kept us in and had several of the pupils to remain to tell what they knew of the fight. Most of the pupils testified in my favor, and as I think of it now, what they said in my behalf was enough to convince any unbiased mind that I was justified in doing what I did to Theodore. Knowing his condition and seeing his blackened and swollen eyes, which I had given him as a present, the love which she had for her boy prohibited her from giving me a square deal, so she dismissed the other pupils, and kept Theodore and me in. She said that I had no right to treat Theodore like I had treated him, and that she was going to give me a good whipping.

She got the strap and told me to get down on my knees. I obeyed her. She then told me to put my head between her legs and when I had done it, she began to whip me. She had not been at her task very long before I tried to get my head out from between her legs. I turned and twisted my head until I could get in position to bite her. She relinquished her grip a little, and I grabbed her with my teeth on the inside of her leg, and I bit her as hard as I could. She cut all kinds of capers trying to get loose. Finally, she cried, "Turn me loose. I will not whip you anymore." And when turned loose, she proceeded to beat me over the head with her hands and fists. I ran out of the room and went home to my father. She followed me home and told my father how I had mistreated Theodore and how when she attempted to whip me, I had bitten the blood out of her leg, but I don't think she showed the place to Father for in those days, women were more modest than now. After she had told Father how unruly I had been, my father gave me another whipping in her presence and warned me to mind my teacher or else. After that incident, my teacher never attempted to whip me again. She was always kind and affable to me.

In my arithmetic class, I was the best and the teacher always made me a criterion for the rest of the class on account of my accuracy in the work. These are some of the experiences which I had with my first teacher.

Another event in my early life I remember as well as if it happened yesterday. In 1868, Grant and Colfax ran for the presidency of the United States, and their opponents were Seymour and Blair. Our group was allowed to vote without molestation on that day. For them it was a holiday, and the town was full of people, both black and white. The election passed off quickly without any casualties, and after the polls closed, the election officers had to count the votes so that they could be announced from the county seat of government which was Versailles, Kentucky. In those days, it took some time to deliver the result from the remote precincts to the town. While waiting for the returns, the people would build bonfires in the street and have a jolly good time. We were not allowed to go outside of the playground, but on this occasion, a great many of our playmates had come to hear the returns from the election.

Chapter 2

Our playground was just one block from the courthouse, and we could hear every word the crier said. When the returns came in, he would read aloud from the courthouse steps, "Grant and Colfax, Seymour and Blair." Each time the returns from the precincts came in, he would repeat the same, "Grant and Colfax" so many votes, "Seymour and Blair" so many votes. This was done until all of the precincts in the county were heard from. At that time, I was seven years old. Four years later in 1872, I listened to the same procedure, confined to the same playground that had been given us by our father at the death of my mother. This time, the candidates were Grant and Wilson, Greeley and Brown, and all through my life, those candidates' names have been ringing in my ears like a bell, and no other candidates' names can I remember so distinctly as I do theirs. And this has taught me that the things which we learn in our childhood become a part of us, and through life, we go without any fault of ours, having joined to us as members of our bodies, the things which we learned in early childhood.

The slaveholders taught their children that they were better than the slave children, and we were not their equals, and we should not have the rights and privileges guaranteed to us by the Constitution. When the foreigner comes to this country, the first thing he learns is to despise and discriminate against our group. He teaches his children the same principles which engender ill will, hate, animosity, and a desire to avenge our oppressors for injuries done to us by them.

The race question in this country is a very menacing proposition, and in a few years, it will become more menacing. Fifteen million American citizens, deprived of the rights of American citizens, their members mobbed, lynched, burned at the stake, hunted like wild beasts, and murdered with impunity and deprived of their property without due process of law will not stand such dishonor always. There will be sure to come a day of reckoning, and this government will pay the cost until it changes its attitude toward our group. The motto of this government, "Good will to all and malice toward none," is nothing more than sounding brass and tinkling cymbals and should be rewritten to read, "Good will to white people and malice toward black people." What we need in this country, the only country in the world that will burn a human being to death at the stake, is more of the teachings of the fatherhood of God and the brotherhood of man.

Children of all groups play together, day after day, and if they are allowed to follow their instincts, there would never be any race question. When the parent ceases to poison the mind of the child with the venom of race, prejudice, the happy medium will be reached, and all men, regardless of race or creed, will recognize a man as a man, and all of that. We, as a race, are suffering and have suffered the persecutions imposed upon us by our fellow citizens until it is almost unbearable. And we are diligently looking every day for a Moses to come out of our ranks to deliver us from under these bonds. It may be Oscar DePriest or some other representative we elect to Congress to represent us, but if not one of our group, then some man who believes in the principles of Lincoln, who would dare to see to it, that all the laws of this country, relative to citizenship are enforced, even though it takes the shedding of blood in every instance to uphold the majesty of the law. When that state of affairs exists, a black man or any other man will be as safe from murder, rapine, and destruction of his property in Mississippi, as he would be in the Capitol at Washington, D.C.

After having developed into a great marble player, my father allowed us to play out in the alley, where there was more room. I continued to win all the marbles, and my trade increased. Boys came from all parts of the town, both white and black, to play with us. The rivalry between the boys and me was very acute, and the crowd at times was so large that the city marshal would disperse us, and finally, he would not let us play without interference from him. He would slip up on us some time before we saw him, and he would slap and kick those he could catch, but he took pains not to kick the white boys.

Several of the white boys were excellent marble players and came every day to play with me but could not accomplish their purpose. And so, they agreed among themselves that since they could not beat me, they would take my marbles from me. I was not only the king marble player but was the king physically of all the boys who played with me in the alley. One day a white

Young JB Stradford (left), other unknown

boy about my size whose name was Charley Moore, a son of one of the aristocratic families of the town and one of the closest competitors, claimed I had cheated him and demanded me to return his marbles. I refused to do so, whereupon he told me that if I did not give them back to him, he would take them away from me. In reply, I told him that I had not cheated him, and if he thought he could take my marbles, he was sadly mistaken, and there was nothing between me and him to prevent him from trying to take them. In those days, we were taught that everything the whites did was right, and whatever we did was wrong, and the unwritten law was "Nigger, don't fight or hit a white person." And, no doubt, this boy thought that I would give up my marbles without a struggle. So, he grabbed me, and, in the tussle, I threw him to the ground and began to beat him. We fought for some time before he cried for help. Ben Ridgely, one of his friends, who in after years became editor of the magazine called *The Truth*, of Louisville, Kentucky, came in to help. My brother stopped him and told him to let us fight and not to interfere. Other white boys came running in, and we had a free-for-all. It lasted until my sister came to the door, being attracted there by the noise we were making. She seized a broom and ran to the fray. She used it to good effect, and the white boys were soon routed, and we were left, for the present, masters of the situation.

The white boys were not satisfied with their defeat. They went up in town and solicited the older boys to come back with them to get revenge for what we had done to them. In a short time, they came back with as many as 12 or 15 in the company. In the meantime, my father had come home from work, and when they started to come in the house, my father said, "Stand back, don't come into my house." They stopped at the door and told my father what we had done, and they wanted me and my brother. Father told them, "If you come into my house, you will come in over my dead body. If my boys have mistreated you, I will punish them. Give me a chance to investigate it."

They all knew my father very well, and said, "Uncle Caesar," as they called him, "We want an investigation now." Just at that time, the town marshal appeared on the scene and dispersed the crowd and told my father he would protect us. He told Father to keep us indoors that night, and he would see to it that nothing would happen to us. Mr. Edwards, the marshal, was a deacon at the white Baptist Church, and Father was the sexton of the church and had been for years. During their connection with the church, he had become very much attached to my father and had befriended him in many ways. He was a devout Christian and believed in the brotherhood of man and the fatherhood of God. If he had not, I don't think this story would have ever been written.

So, he went back uptown and told the crowd that if they went back down there to molest us, he would put all of them in jail and see to it that they would be prosecuted. He had the reputation of being a hard man on law violators and had proven to the citizens of the town that he never faltered in doing his duty as an officer. Everything passed off quietly that night and on account of the assurance of the marshal, we felt that the matter had blown over. And so, the next day, we went out on the street as usual. My brother went up in town, and in passing a group of boys, Ben Ridgely, of whom I have spoken before, emerged from the bunch and said, "Here is one of the black S.B.s." He picked up a brick, and with all his might, he threw it at him. My brother caught the brick in his right hand and hurled it back at the fellow. It struck him just above the eye, and he fell like a piece of beef to the sidewalk. My brother ran home and hid under the bed. They took Ben to the doctor to dress his wound, and by that time, a mob had formed. Providentially, the town marshal and the sheriff got on the scene in time to save us again. They rushed into the mob, throwing them back, demanding them to disperse, and with pistols and blackjacks in their hands, they struck them over the head when they failed to obey orders. They arrested one of the fellows who was persistent in his cries to incite the riot by saying, "Let's mob that nigger." After the excitement died down, things went along alright for a while, but it gave us this reputation that we would fight white people. Ben Ridgely, editor of *The Truth* in Louisville, Kentucky, will testify to that.

From that incident, I have learned two lessons. First, if the officials who take the oath will fearlessly enforce the law and let that solemn and binding obligation be the paramount issue of their tenure in office, there would be no more rioting, no mobbing, no more outlaw societies, establishing governments to correct the failures, as they think, of the established regime. Secondly, I learned that the man who will fight back at all times will always have the respect of those with whom he comes in contact.

As an illustration of that fact, I will relate an incident that occurred to me many years ago. My father hired me out to a farmer who lived five miles from town. I would leave every Monday morning and walk to my work. One morning, as I was on my way to work, I saw approaching me a very large, vicious-looking brindle bulldog, seemingly taking his time. I was late that morning and was walking as fast as I could. I was expecting every second to see the dog get out of the path and give me the right-of-way. But instead, he did not seem to notice me and kept right on in the middle of the path. When I thought I was near enough to him, I quickly stepped out of the path and gave him the right-of-way, feeling that at any moment, he might attack me. Had that been a little or even a big dog, which showed a streak of cowardice, I would have shuffled my feet on the ground and yelled at him, and he would have scampered away in a hurry and left me master of the situation. I have found that in going through life, the man who demands his rights at all times and resents insults and other offenses, even if he plays the bulldog at times, will fare much better than the man who is spineless and is afraid that he may hurt someone's feelings by demanding his rights as a man.

My first sweetheart, contrary to my father's teachings, was one of my playmates, a blue-eyed, half white girl, who was as pretty as a speckled pup. Her father was the toll gate keeper out on the Lexington Pike, and her mother was his common-law wife. They had lived there for many years and reared a family of eight children. We were classmates in school and as much as possible, playmates on the school ground, and after school dismissed, I would go home and leave my books and steal away from the other children and overtake her and go almost to her home with her every evening. She was the sweetest girl I have known, and I loved her. I have often heard it said that children's love at that age is "puppy love," and they did not know what true love meant. I am free to confess that if the love that I had for that girl was "puppy love," I don't desire to know what real love is. Children in those days were more modest and reserved than in these days. We never thought of the familiarities then as they do now. We never kissed, only when we were playing such games as "Walking on the Green Grass," or "Old Mr. Brown," or other such games as those.

To my best remembrance, I don't think I ever kissed any girl except her in all of our plays, and I don't remember her kissing any other boy except me. Her soul was so pure, sweet, and angelic that I felt that I was the most happy boy on earth. How well do I remember that I could not express my love in words to her, but

I would write verses to her which would express my feelings for her. I will now write a few of them which I shall never forget:

"Roses are red, violets are blue, sugar is sweet, and so are you."

"Come, Darling, let us wander to that shady bow that yonder there we will sit and talk of love until the stars grow dim above us."

"Will you always love me just as you do now?"

And a great many other verses which I can't repeat now.

This courtship continued for years, until the Ku Klux Klan forced her father and mother to sever their connection, and he sent the mother and children to Chicago to live. I did not hear from her for a number of years, but the impression that we made on each other was lasting. And after we had grown up, we renewed our courtship. At that time, she was working out in service in Oak Park, Illinois. We corresponded for some time, and finally, we were engaged. I went to Chicago in 1881 to fill the engagement, but by some misfortune, I was unable to find her and left Chicago very much disappointed. She vowed that she would never marry if she did not marry me, and she remained single until she became an old maid. After my disappointment in Chicago, I determined to finish my education. And in the autumn of 1882, I matriculated in the preparatory department of Oberlin College in Ohio, and I never saw her anymore until after I was married. I have been married twice, and I have loved neither of my wives more dearly than I loved her.

Another event in my life, which is impressed upon my mind just as a scar on one's body, and that was the treatment which was meted out to our group in 1870. The white people of the South banded themselves together in a society known as the Ku Klux

Klan, for the purpose of terrorizing and intimidating our group to prevent us from voting. The 15th Amendment to the Constitution had been passed, giving our group the right to vote. Quite a few of the states were given over to the rule of our group. A great many Northern politicians called "carpetbaggers" went South and made themselves political leaders with a few Southerners who supported our group's cause. They resorted to everything to accomplish their purpose. The law was that any man convicted of a felony was deprived of his citizenship. The members of our group were arrested for minor offenses, thrown into jail, convicted of felonies, and sentenced to the penitentiaries for a term of years. The prisons were teeming with men of our group. One evening before the election, they would parade the streets with white robes on and go into the quarters of our groups. And they would not only strike terror to the hearts of the people by their ghostly appearance, but they would take some of the most intelligent ones of some of their leaders, whip and sometimes castrate them, and more often, kill them as a warning to keep us from the polls.

Just before the election of 1872, when Grant (President Ulysses S. Grant) and Colfax (Schuyler Colfax—17th Vice President of the United States) were elected, there was an edict that came from the Imperial Wizard of the Invisible Government to kill every leader among our group on a certain night. On said night, the Klan robed themselves for the fulfillment of the edict and went out to slaughter. They would go to those leaders' houses and call them to the door in the wee hours of the morning and kill them like they would a mad dog. This incident struck terror into the hearts of our group so that they would leave home and stay in the woods at night or any secret place they could find. On this same night, when all of our leaders were killed, they came to our house and asked for my father. He was not there. There was a man by the name of Tom Seller, manufacturer of the Sellers Buggies, who was a member of the white Baptist Church of which my father was sexton, and he came to our house early that night and told my father what was going to happen. He told him to come up to his house and go into the cellar, and stay until the next morning, and nothing would happen to him.

So, father stayed in that cellar every night until the danger passed. This terrorism struck deep into the hearts of our group, to such an extent that the intimidation had its desired effect. Our group ceased to be a part of the body politic, and in those states where our group ruled, their power faded away as the mist before the sun; and from that time until now, the right of suffrage has been denied to us practically all over the South. After the passage of the Force Bill, President Grant put the militia into the South to enforce this bill. And they were kept there until the election of President Hayes (Rutherford B. Hayes, 19th President of the United States), who was defeated by Tilden (Samuel J. Tilden, who won the popular vote, but lost to Rutherford B. Hayes) in 1876. I shall not go into detail of Hayes' seat as president, but will say that on account of the liberal Republicans believing that the South should have more liberal treatment, that through some political skullduggery, by giving the presidency to Hayes in exchange for turning over the reigns of the government back to the Southern states. In consequence of that trade, the National Guards were removed from the South, and that ended the carpetbag rule. We were left to the mercy of the former masters, who were more cruel, more oppressive, and more bloodthirsty.

When we were chattel, they placed a value upon us, and they guarded that value, just the same as they would a good horse, cow, or jackass. But once we were of no monetary value to them, for no cause, they would mob, kill, rape, and burn at the stake with impunity. I believe in the immutable laws of God. Whatsoever a man or race soweth, that shall he reap; and I also believe that man or race may, in the evolution of time, mend his ways before it is too late, if he so desires. What a happy medium or a state of brotherly love would be attained if this nation would change its attitude toward our groups and give us equal rights before the law, and let there be no exclusive privileges for anyone.

It has also been said that a house divided against itself cannot stand. This house is very much divided. No one can tell how long it will stand. We have men of wealth, honor, of high degree, of distinction, who are smarting under these conditions, who are ready to resort to any trickery to bring about a change; men who rank high in the political affairs of this government, who would turn traitor at the first opportunity to better their condition, and nothing is being done to alleviate the situation. Reading from a German viewpoint, an article in the *Herald and Examiner*, "We will have to fight Japan on her own soil." This prophecy may never come true, but suppose it does, or some other great unforeseen incident occurs? What a great consolation in the awful mystery of human life, that we could march to the fray in one accord, with one purpose, to defeat our adversary. You fooled us once when this government entered the World War. It sent out its spellbinding orators to induce us by their fiery eloquence to go to war and fight for universal democracy. We went; you carried your American prejudice over to France and denied the soldiers some of the privileges which were given them in that country. When the war was over and everything was made safe for democracy, the soldiers were sent back to their former places of abode. They found things or conditions worse than they were before they left.

While in France, he learned that the ideal woman was not the ideal woman because she was white, but that a woman was a woman, and all of that, regardless of her color. Numbers of those brave boys who had gone to France to fight for universal democracy came back from the fray in France to their homes and lost their lives for disobeying orders not to be seen on the streets again in their uniforms. Disobeying this order, they were shot down and murdered like dogs on the street with impunity. This government condones such treatment, and that is the democracy we fought for in France.

As a member of this oppressed race, I ask, "How long, oh Lord? How long before this oppressed group of ours shall be liberated from our bonds?"

My first job was given to me by a white lady by the name of Mrs. Sally Macy. She employed me at $.50 per week to drive her cow to and from its pasture, which was about a mile from town. I also had to milk her and do the chores about the house. This lady had six children, Robert and Gus, who were trainers of trotting horses and had on their strings such noted horses as Woodford Chief, Maud Mace, and Aldine, which were sold to Vanderbilt for a mate to Maud III. The girls' names were Miss Fanny, Miss Kate, Miss Emma, and Miss Willie. They treated me very kind. They were much older than I, except Miss Willie, who was very fond of me, and we played together whenever I had time to play. I would help Miss Sally to get breakfast, and then she would have me go in and wake the girls up to come to breakfast. After breakfast, I would take the cow to the pasture. Then I would go to school, and each evening after school, I would go to the pasture and drive the cow home and feed her with bran. One afternoon, I had a fight in the pasture with a white boy who lived out there in the woods near Macy's training stable. I gave the boy a good beating, and as it happened, Gus Macy saw me flog him, and he came running over to where I was and began to beat and kick me unmercifully. He told me that I should never strike a white boy. I told him that if I were a man, he would not beat me like that, and told him when I got to be a man, I would get even with him. I never liked Gus Macy after that. I reported him to his mother. She sympathized with me and lectured him for what he had done to me. On account of their kind treatment of me, I was very much devoted to the family and especially to Miss Willie, who called me her nigger, and whenever I went to Versailles to visit my relatives, she expected me to come to see her. I did several times, but the last time I went to see her, I told her that if she did not stop calling me nigger, I would not come to see her anymore.

She said, "John, you know I don't mean any harm. It is just our custom to call you niggers here. You know I have always treated you with the greatest consideration and kindness, and you must not stop coming to see me when you visit your old home." The last time I went home, I did not go to see her, and when she found out that I had been home, she went down to my sister's home and told her to tell me that when I came back home to visit, I had better come to see her.

My next job was with a cattle buyer. He had two horses, one for himself and the other one for me. My duties were to help him clean the horses, feed them, and keep the stable clean. It was all new to me. I had never ridden a horse before or done anything along that line. One morning, while I was feeding them, one of the horses stepped on my foot. I have never had such pain in all my life, and it seemed an hour or more before I could extricate my foot. Those who have had their foot pinioned under a horse's hoof know what it all means. I rode the horses to the watering trough to drink, and a great many times, he threw me upon the horse with only a halter to guide him. In those days there were coaches and the driver drove four horses and sometimes six. They had long whips to whip the horses to make them keep step with the leaders and carry their part of the load. One morning, as I was coming from the watering trough with only a halter to guide the horse, a stagecoach driven by a man named Mote Hall, overtook me and with his long whip, struck the horse I was riding with such fury that the horse ran away with me. All that I could do was to cling on to the horse by holding his mane. He took a beeline to the stable as fast as he could go. And when he got to the door of the stable, he suddenly stopped. I went up in the air over and over and landed on my back on the ground. When I came to myself, I was at home in bed, and the doctor was in attendance, dressing my wounds. After that incident, I never again rode a horse without a bridle.

My employment with Mr. Evans was the most thrilling of my life, and a great many times, fraught with great danger. He would take me with him whenever he went to buy cattle, and a great many times, the cattle would be wild and dangerous. After buying them, we would have to round them up and drive them to town for the market. How often have I seen those wild bulls go together seemingly in a death struggle and fight for almost an hour before we could separate them and get started again for town? Mr. Evans, with his long whip, was a fearless man. He would take his whip in hand and ride right up to the fighting bulls and use his whip to a great effect in separating them. In one of these spectacular fights, one of the bulls knocked the horse down in his effort to get to the other bull. And Mr. Evans barely escaped with his life. But he remounted his horse and renewed his attack on the bulls until he had separated them.

On court day, one of the cattle was running wild, and the people were all running to places of safety. Mr. Evans stepped out from the crowd when he saw the wild cow approaching, just in time to grab her by the horns and throw her to the ground and hold her until she was tied. That was the most thrilling incident I ever saw in my life. I stood in awe looking to see Mr. Evans gored to death by that cow.

He paid me $1.00 per week for my services. I continued with him until school took up, and I went back to school. In those days, the county furnished a three-month term of school for Colored children and from the time it closed until the time it opened again, we had forgotten in the nine months' vacation, all we had learned in that three-month term. Our schoolteachers in those days were very inefficient as a rule. They could read, write and spell very well, but as for arithmetic, few of them knew very little of the fundamental principles of it, although they taught in their way that subject. A few in our class were very apt in that branch, and we progressed very rapidly. I had some experience in mathematics. I had many a marble to sell. My father was a hemp breaker, and I would ask him every night when he came home how many pounds of hemp he would break each day, and I would put it down on a piece of paper and I would add it and tell how many pounds he had broken that week and the amount of money he had made that week. And he called me his banker. At seven years of age, I demonstrated by my answers to questions in arithmetic that I was mathematically inclined. So, we succeeded very well in our work. Whenever a difficult problem came up in our class, the teacher would leave it to me to give the answer, and whatever answer I gave was taken as correct. And all through my school life, arithmetic was one of my hobbies.

Another one of my hobbies was spelling. I got more real inspiration to excel than in any other branch of learning. We stood in a line on the floor to spell. We were called to the class by our numbers, beginning with first, second, and third, and so on until we were all lined up in a row. The teacher would then begin at the head and pronounce the words to be spelled. If the head of the class missed or failed to spell it, it was passed to the next pupil. And if he failed, it would be passed on until someone spelled it. And the one who spelled it would come up and take the place of the one who first missed it. Sometimes the word would pass all the way down the class and go back to the one who first missed it, and then the teacher would spell it for us, or we would all have to come the next day prepared to spell the word or write it on the blackboard. There were a great many good spellers in the class, and so the teachers made a rule that any pupil remaining at the head of the class one week would, on the following Monday morning, go down to the foot of the class. This method finally was changed and the pupil at the head was allowed to retain his place at the head until he was turned down by another pupil.

There were about three of us in the class, close rivals, who seldom ever missed a word, and when either of us got to the head of the class, they stayed for a long time. My father was very proud of my spelling ability on account of my staying at the head of the class so much and told me that if I would stay at the head of the class four weeks longer, he would give me a suit of clothes. I felt overjoyed at the prospect of getting a new suit. So, I determined to acquire that suit. I studied the lessons every night. I studied them down and I studied them up until I knew them perfectly well. On Friday of the fourth week, I was still at the head of the class. The lesson that we had for that day had the word "vehicle." In my study of the word, I called it "vehicle" and pronounced it that way. When the class was called, I was satisfied that I knew every word and could spell every word in the lesson, and felt that I would get the suit my father had promised me. During the recitation, the word "vehicle" came to me, and I told the teacher that word was not in the lesson. She said it was and ordered me to spell it. I again said it was not in the lesson. She said, "Next," and the girl who was second in the class, Anna Hicks, spelled it and turned me down. Oh! How I bellowed and cried. I broke completely down, and the teacher sent me home, and I did not get over the shock for several days.

When my father came home that night from work and was informed what had happened to me, he said it was too bad that I had failed to win the new suit of clothes. He said, "I told you that if you came home the fourth Friday at the head of your class, I would give you a new suit. So, you failed to do so. I am just going to be as good as my word." I begged him to give me the suit on the grounds that I had stayed at the head of the class four weeks and had not missed the word and did not attempt to spell it, for I did not see it in the lesson. But he said, "The word was in the lesson, and your teacher gave it to you to spell, and you did not spell it. So, she gave it to the one next to you, and she spelled it and went to the head of the class. And you are now second; therefore, you are not entitled to the suit, and I will not give it to you."

In all my life, I have never had such a sore disappointment. The shock made me sick. My teacher insisted upon my father giving me the suit, and everyone who knew of the incident did so, but it had no effect upon him. He believed in living up to every obligation he made and the fulfillment of every promise. I must say that his life has been copied by me from the teachings he has imparted, not only by precept but also by example.

In my early training in school, we had only three months' schooling until I was about 15 years of age, but during those early years in my life, we would have school at home every night. My oldest brother was one of the advanced scholars, and he was our teacher. And instead of standing still, we were able to make the grade. After the state legislature had passed an act providing five months of school for us and giving the patrons the power of electing three trustees in each school district to serve three years, these trustees would have the school census to find out how many children of school age were in the district. After ascertaining the number of children, they would multiply the number by the prorate allotted to each child, thereby ascertaining the amount of money appropriate for their district. They also had the power to employ the teachers.

Whenever the amount of money was insufficient to pay a teacher, the trustees, a great many times, would take the responsibility upon themselves to raise the deficit. And in cities or towns where there were a great many children, the amount would be sufficient to pay two teachers at a fixed salary for seven months, and very often, the trustees would raise enough money, in addition to the allotment, to extend the term of school eight months. After the legislature had extended the term of school to five months, we had a better grade of teachers, and the school was placed on a higher basis.

The examinations were more rigid. The questions and answers were prepared by the State Board of Examiners and sent to the County Board of Examiners to be used in the examination of their teachers. We had only a few of our group able to pass the examination, so it was necessary to have teachers come from Ohio, Indiana, and other states to supply the demand for teachers. For several years, our teachers were very efficient, and the work in school was done with a system and very accurately. The advanced pupils, some of them finishing the eighth grade, and some of the old teachers were also finishing the same grade, felt that they ought to be reinstated in the school as teachers. The fact is, they were not prepared; not one of them could pass the examination to teach. The superintendent, a typical Southern man, did not wish it necessary for our teachers to know as much as the white teachers, and a great many of them knew more than he knew, in an educational way, and the fact that he disapproved of the Northern teachers teaching the children, the ways of the North, that all men were created equal, to be impugned, and should have the same rights and privileges as any man, white or black.

In quite a few of the districts, he compelled the trustees to hire some of the old teachers and also some of the eighth-grade pupils to teach. Most of the teachers were women and could not make the third-grade certificate in an examination. I knew teachers who had made first-class certificates who were turned down by the superintendent for one of his favorites on the ground that he believed in home talent, and the teachers he could not use as a tool, did not keep their jobs very long. He would domineer the trustees and the teachers in a way that was tyrannical. I shall not go into the details of all of those women teachers, holding their jobs without qualifications, but will say that it demoralized our school system all over by not having qualified teachers.

    I attended two terms of a five-month school and five terms of a three-month school, which made 25 months of public instruction altogether. During the five-month terms of my attendance in school, I assisted the teacher in teaching the primary grades very often and also the arithmetic class. It was the custom of my father that just as soon as we grew large enough, he would take us with him to work on the farms or hire us out to someone who needed a boy to work. I was a very handy boy and could always make a few dimes nearly every day, and especially on Saturday. I would go up in town and stand around on the street waiting for someone riding a horse to come up and let me hold his horse. He would give me the reins of the horse's bridle to hold the horse until he called for it, and many a time, I stood on the street nearly all day, waiting for the owner of the horse to come and take it. Sometimes he would give me as much as $0.75, and other times, I would get $0.10, $0.25, and $0.50, which I would give to my father. I also got jobs to clean up stores in the morning for the proprietors of the stores and they would pay me $1.00 per week, and on rare occasions, $1.25 per week.

My father hired me out to work on the farm for a man by the name of Mr. Woolridge at $6.00 per month. At that time, I was 12 years old. He taught me how to plow, to drop, to thin and hoe corn and also how to bind wheat.

Chapter 3

And in harvest time, I made a hand in binding wheat and in all the other farm activities. I stayed all week on the farm, and on Saturday, I would go to my home in town to stay over Sunday. I worked for this man from early cropping time until school took up. During my stay on his farm, my father insisted on him paying me more for my services. He said that the scale of wages for men was $8.00 a month, and the man had to give greater service than I gave; the man had to feed the stock and had to stay on the farm all the time except a few hours on Saturday afternoons. Of course, he furnished a cabin for him and also fuel. I received for my services during my stay with him a total of $36.00, all of which I gave to my father. He would ask me each time I got my pay how much I wanted out of it, and I don't remember at any time that I asked for more than a nickel or a dime.

One of the teachings of my father was that I belonged to him until I was 21 years old. And that was so firmly embedded in me that I had no desire to change the condition. He further said that everything I made belonged to him, and I was very zealous to make money and give it to him, and there never was a time that I failed to accept any kind of job to earn some money for him. He was very strict in enforcing the rules that he made to govern our conduct. Our oldest sister reported to him every infraction of the rules when we could not influence her by begging her not to do so. His method of punishment was severe. He would not whip us with our clothes on because he said he would wear the clothes out. So, when he got ready to whip us, he would say, "Take your shirt off," and most often all your clothes. Sometimes, he would whip with long switches and sometimes with a strap, and nearly every night in the week, my brother Will and I would get unmerciful beatings. We were both very unruly boys.

I shall here relate some incidents. Our orders were to play in our own backyard. Sometimes we would slip out and go to play with other children. On one occasion, we were playing marbles in a lot not very far from our house, and as usual, I was winning all of the marbles. There was a large tomboy girl who played with us. As a rule, when I won her marbles, she would take them away from me. This time, she had supplied herself with some very pretty marbles, among them, she had aggies or crystals. She finally lost all of her marbles and then traded her taw for so many marbles and lost them. After we broke her, she tried to borrow marbles to keep on playing, and when she could not borrow anymore, she got mad and broke the game up.

After breaking it up, we all straightened away. But she caught me and asked me to give some of her marbles back. I refused to do so, and she said, "I will take them from you." She was much larger and stronger than I was, but as I was not afraid of her, I gave her a battle as long as I could keep her from getting hold of me. I had a chance to whip her, but she kept rushing me until she got me firmly in her grip. I punched her in the nose and did my best to keep her from throwing me down. She finally threw me down, and after she had taken all the wind out of me, she sat on my head and took all of my marbles from me. Then she let me up. She had given me a good beating. When I got up, I ran to a rock pile and picked up a rock. She started toward me and told me to drop the rock and continued to come to me. So, I took aim with my left index finger and threw the rock, which struck her just above the left eye.

She fell to the ground like a log. I took to my heels. I ran home, got into the house unnoticed by anyone, and got under the bed. She was taken to the doctor, who dressed her wounds, and then they sent her home. She lived with a white family by the name of Scott, whom she had been bound out to, and they were very kind to her and treated her as one of the family. After Mr. Scott had found out who had struck her, he got the town marshal and came down to our house looking for me. My sister told them that I was not there and had not been there since the fight and that they had been looking for me and could not find me. They insisted that I was there. She told them to come in and search the house. They came in and looked around a little and then went out. Had they been listening intently, they could have heard my heart beating, for it was making such noise as the ticking of a clock.

I remained under the bed a short time after they left, then I slipped out and went to my grandfather's and stayed there until Father came home that night. As soon as he came, my sister told him what had happened, and she had not seen me since the fray. Mr. Scott and the marshal came and told Father what I had done and agreed with my father that if he would whip me, they would take no further action in the case. After dark, I came home and found my father there. I knew I was going to get a severe beating, and I was shaking like a leaf with fear. After he had eaten his supper, he called me in and got my side of the case. He then went to see the girl, and she corroborated my statement. He came back home and told me that he had promised the marshal that he would whip me for what I had done, but he felt that I was justified in defending myself against the girl. He said he would not whip me for that. But he said, "You know, that it is my orders for you to play in your own backyard. Why did you go out to play without permission from your sister?" I had no excuse to offer. He said, "Pull your shirt off." He went out and got some switches, came back, and after lecturing me some more, he began to whip me. My back was sore from the last whipping, and I begged and begged him to let me off this time, and I would never go out to play again. But he said, "I know you won't." My plea fell on deaf ears, and he continued to whip me until my back was as raw as a piece of beef.

I did not go out to play for several days. My sister kept my back greased to keep the shirt from sticking to it. That night, while whipping me, several people were standing on the outside of the house in the street. They said, "Uncle Caesar, don't kill the boy. You have whipped him enough." He said, "Get out from in front of my house and tend to your own business, and you won't have time to meddle with mine." And so, he continued to whip me until he was satisfied that he had amply punished me for my disobedience. I can honestly say that I was never bothered with that girl anymore. She became my best friend on the playground and would take up for me whenever any trouble came up. And years afterward, I had left home, married, and had a family, and had forgotten the girl, I went back home on a visit with my wife. She came to see me, and I did not know her. She pointed her finger to the scar on her forehead and asked me did I remember that scar I put on her head. Like a flash, it came back to me. I grabbed her hand and shook it most friendly, and we sat down and chatted most pleasantly over the happenings and scenes of our childhood.

Another incident, which I feel will be of some interest to those who read these memoirs, I will give account of. I had a job in a private family by the name of Thornton. We called Mrs. Thornton, "Old Miss." My duties were to take care of the horse and cow and drive the cow to and from the pasture. A boy by the name of Harry Carol, older and larger than I was, had the same kind of job in the family of the Honorable Joe C.S. Blackburn. We both rode to and from the pasture on horseback. There was a public watering trough. The stream came out from a cave between two hills and furnished plenty of water for the use of the town. On the hottest day, we could go down to the spring or to the town pump, and there, imbibe a cold drink of water.

This boy Harry was overbearing. Whenever I took a place at the trough, and if he felt that he did not want me in that place, he would ride around to where it was an attempt to make me move. We had several fights, and as he always came out on top, I shunned him as much as possible. I told my oldest brother how he treated me. He was a much better fighter than I was. He said he would teach me how to whip him, and I said I would be very glad. He asked me how or what was his way of fighting. I told him. "Well," he said, "That is easy. When he grabs you the next time, put your left arm around his neck and put your finger in his eye, and at that same time, bite him on the side of the face and pull as if you were trying to pull his eyes out. Be sure you don't turn your hold loose."

In a few days, we met at the big spring again to water our horses and cows. He again began to rough it over me and told me what he would do to me if I did not do what he told me to do. I told him I would fight him again before I would do what he told me to do. He jumped off his horse and told me to get off. I jumped off my horse and ran right up to him and grabbed him around the neck with my left arm, put my finger in his eye, and began to bite him. He tried to get loose, but I held him vicelike. I was trying to pull his eye out at the same time I was biting his jaw as a dog would. He hollered so loudly and pitifully that half the town folks came running down to see what was going on. I was afraid to turn him loose. I knew he could whip me. So, the town marshal took him away from me; his eye was pulled out, and his cheek was bleeding very profusely. He was a pitiful-looking sight. The marshal put me in the little jail and kept me there until night.

When Father came, he had me turned out. I don't know what arrangement he made with the marshal, but I do know that he did not whip me. I can see him in my mind's eye now as plainly as I could see him then. When that pleased smile came over his face and he laid his hand on my head and said, "Don't let anyone impose on you; always take your part but be sure you are right." What he said on that occasion made this impression on me. He did not say white or black, but said, no one, and I took that, the meaning in its broadest sense and from that day until the present,

I have in all cases where I have had a ghost of a show resented every wrong or insult which has been directed at me.

It was some time before Harry's eye and cheek got well. But after that engagement, I never had any more trouble with Harry. We were good friends after. The last time I saw him was in Louisville, Kentucky. He had a family and invited me down to take dinner with him. While eating, he told his wife of how he used to whip me nearly every day until that last day when he met his Waterloo. She enjoyed it very much. I have not seen him since.

Another incident that I feel is worth mentioning. In those days, there were no YMCAs or bathing beaches or rivers near for swimming purposes for the boys. There were a few ponds within a radius of several miles where we used to swim. The pond that Colored boys used was called "McGee's Pond." Some of us went out there every evening to swim. The white boys decided to run us away from that pond. And so, one evening, when I was not with our boys, the white boys came and ran our boys away. When we heard of what had been done, my brother and I got a gang together and went out to the pond. When we got there, we found the white boys in the pond swimming. We went right up to the bank of the pond, undressed ourselves, and jumped into the water. The white boys came out when they saw us jump into the water, and with rocks in their hands, ordered us out.

We came out and put on our clothes, and then they ordered us to beat it. I said, "Wait a minute. Let's talk this matter over. We have been swimming out here all summer, and you boys have had Ashmore's Pond. We want to know by what authority you come to take our swimming place?" The spokesman for them said that they were going to take it without authority. I said to him, "You can't take it without a fight, because we are not going to give it up. There is no use of all of us fighting. Maybe some of us would be seriously hurt," for boys in those days fought with rocks, and we had a brave set of boys who could throw hard and straight. So, I said to them, "Pick out your best man and we will pick ours and we will let them fight. Whichever one whips, his gang will have a right to the pond." It was also agreed that no one would be allowed to take a part in the fight and that the contestants would fight until one of them cried "Enough."

After a short caucus, they selected the boy to defend them, and I volunteered to defend our gang. The white boys got on one side of the path, and our gang on the other side. I stood on the edge of the path in front of my gang and the white boy stood on the other side of the path in front of his gang. The white boy was somewhat larger than I, but I did not think that counted for much. The signal was given, and he rushed me and hit me several times until I found out he could "out-knock" me as we used to say. Then I ran in and clinched him. I threw him to the ground, and he rolled me off, and I rolled him off and got on top of him. In the first part of the fight, the white boys had all the best of it, and they cheered vociferously, and when I got on top of the boy the second time, our boys cheered to the echo. After I had pinioned him down to the ground, I commenced to beat his head and face with my fist. In the struggle, he came out from under me again, and I got on his back and snatched his hands out from under him and got on him again. We were both bloody and were fighting like tigers. I pinned him to the ground again and beat him so fast on the head and face that in a short time, he cried, "Enough."

I got off him, and we both went down to the pond and washed the blood from our hands and faces. And according to our agreement, the white boys went to town, and we stayed and finished our swimming exercises. After this fight, we were never bothered by the white boys anymore, and we bathed in that pond, unmolested, during all my childhood. By winning this fight, I was hailed as the Sampson of our gang, and it had a great deal to do with the treatment we received from our white citizens in Versailles, Kentucky.

Another incident that happened nearly every day when we played marbles, wrestled, and boxed. Very often, white men would come down to see our sport, and they would make purses for the one who would run the fastest. I am sure I never won a race, and seldom ever won a place in the race. I was a very poor runner. They also would give purses for the best fighter with our bare fists. Sometimes the purse would be as small as $0.10 and we would make a ring and go into it and fight until one knocked the other out or said "Enough." In these fistic encounters, I was defeated only once, and that was by my cousin, who was much older than I, to be exact three years older. But I was larger than he was. I had been bragging about being a better boxer than he was and did everything to get him to box with me. He told me that he did not want to hurt me and not to keep on challenging him to box. The boys were anxious to see us box, and I was very anxious to box with him.

The boys would taunt and tease him and tell him he was afraid to fight me, and so one morning we were all on our playground. And some white men came down who were lovers of the sport and offered $0.50 to the best boxer and $0.25 to the next best.

I was selected as one of the boxers, and as I was considered the best, none of the other boys would box me. They insisted that my cousin, Cornelius Stradford, go in the ring against me. He was sore with me anyway because I was always after him to box with me and told him he was afraid to box me. So, he agreed to fight me. In those days, we did not have any gloves to box with; we used our bare fists.

The ring was made. I was sure I could whip him, and I was so glad that I had gotten a chance at him because he had always said that he did not want to hurt me and advised me to box with boys in my class. Everything was made ready, and the word was given to go. I rushed at him, hitting with all the power that I could command, and the boys were all cheering me, but I could not deliver one blow effectively. He would sidestep my rushes and duck my blows. In those days, when we went into the ring, there were no stops until the fight was ended. After having led the fight with rushes and wild swinging, I began to get tired and eased up on my rushes. My cousin weighed about 90 pounds, and I never dreamed that he had a chance. We continued to fight for some time in that manner. Feeling that I had him going, I made another mad rush at him. He sidestepped me and gave me a punch right in the temple.

The fight ended. I went down like a rock to the ground. I guess the boys all cheered him for his feat, but I was forced to confess that I did not hear them. When the blow was delivered, we were near a brick building, and I thought that the building had fallen upon me. They picked me up. Standing there in a dazed condition, I asked what had happened to me. They said that Cornelius had knocked me down and out, and I had just realized what had happened to me. After the fight, they gave me my end of the purse, and I went home very much aggrieved on account of my defeat. My cousin was a jockey; he was the head jockey of General Abe Buford, who owned such noted horses as Inquirer, McQuitter, Nellie Gray, and many other nationally known horses, and he had brought many a one of this stable over the tape first.

He had learned to box scientifically. He had been a jockey for years, and had learned to be tough, and he was tough—you can prove that by me. He would come home to see his people once a year. On one occasion, after he came home on a vacation, he came down to see our family. When he came, he shook hands with us on account of being so glad to see us. My father said to me, "Son, can you take him?" And I said, "Yes, sir, Papa," and he said, "Go to him." I grabbed him and, in the scuffle, I threw him. And I never saw my father more pleased than he was on this occasion. My cousin was not satisfied and wanted me to wrestle again, but my father would not let me wrestle him again. In a joking way, he told him that I was too good for him, and he advised him to get in his class if he wanted to wrestle. My father was very proud of me on account of my ability to clean up all the boys anywhere near my age. After a year or so, I was able to defeat my cousin in boxing and wrestling.

In 1875, my oldest brother, who was eight years and five months older than I, went to St. Louis, Missouri. After residing there for one year, he came back to see us. I was in my 15th year. When he came and greeted us all, my father said to me, "Son, can't you take him?" And I said, "Yes, sir, Papa." At that time, my brother had a very nice pair of pants that were too small for him, and he told me that if I threw him, he would give me the pants, and when he made the promise, my father said, "Go to him." I ran up and grabbed him, and we tussled for a short time. I threw him to the ground, and he turned me and got on top of me. Father said that I had won the pants and would not let me wrestle him again. My brother claimed it was a dog fall and would not give me the pants unless I wrestled again. Father refused to let me do so, and so he never gave me the pants. My father was a very cold and unemotional man, but he could not help showing great emotion and warmth for me because I had taken the place he occupied among the boys and men in his early life. He was without equal in knocking, kicking, and wrestling, and he could not find words to express his real feelings and admiration for me.

Under the charge of my second teacher, I had a classmate named George Wilson. He was much older than I, and thought, on account of my age, that I ought to consider him my superior. We were close rivals in our lesson, and more often, I had better recitations than he had. In our arithmetic class, when any question came up that the class could not answer, the teacher invariably called on me to give the solution for it. George Wilson had the problem and had given his solution for it, and claimed it was right. When I gave another answer, he said my answer was wrong and he was tired of having to take whatever I said as final. At recess, he took me to task for the answer and said, "You think you're smart, and if you ever give another answer to any problem of mine, I will give you a good beating."

I told him that I did not give the answer voluntarily, but the teacher called on me to give the solution. "You ought to blame the teacher and not me. I can't afford to disobey her, for if I did, my father would whip me." But he said, "If you do it again, I will beat the devil out of you." George was a boy who wanted everything his own way, regardless of circumstances, and would not listen to reason. He disliked me because I could beat him in our lessons, and also because he felt I was a favorite of the teacher. I told the teacher what George had said, and she kept him in the following evening and warned him not to do anything to me.

The next day, he told me that he was going to whip me whenever he caught me off the school grounds. I was a little afraid of him, and every afternoon, when school dismissed, I would go out of my way, several blocks, to keep out of his way. Finally, one afternoon, he caught me coming home the back way, and he ran right up to me and said, "I got you now," and he began to fight me. I did not want to fight him because I thought he could whip me, but I had no alternative. I had to fight. I found out very quickly that he was not a good fighter; he was awkward and could not hit very hard. So, I waded right into him, knocked him down, jumped on top of him, and gave him a severe beating, much to my surprise.

I have no doubt that there was a crowd of more than 100 people watching him get a good beating. I had many a fight, but this one was the greatest surprise of my life. He was game and could stand a lot of punishment, and we fought for nearly an hour when he finally cried out, "Enough." After the fight, there was no malice between us. In our childish simplicity, we played together, recited our lessons together, and we never had any more misunderstandings. There are lots of things we could accomplish that we fail to do, if at the opportune time, we tackle the thing with all of our might and do it. Our success lies in our ability to do things. If we doubt ourselves, in business or any other undertaking, there will not be very much accomplished.

At the age of 13, my father hired me out to a family by the name of Nuckols, who lived four miles from town. For $6.00 per month, I was not only the factotum around the house, but I had to work on the farm after I had finished my duties around the house. One of the duties that I had to perform, which I did not like, was the bathing of Old Miss's feet and legs every morning. I shirked it every time I could. She had rheumatism or dropsy in her feet; I know that her feet and legs were very large. I told her that I did not like that job, and I wished she would get someone else to do it. She told her husband that I had sassed her and refused to bathe her legs and feet. He did not give me time to say anything but called me a black rascal and began to whip me. He gave me several licks before I could get away from him. When I got away, I started for home, ran out in the cornfield, and hid myself. He called his boys and started them on the hunt for me, but they could not find me, and late that evening, I showed up at home.

After telling my father the circumstances, he told me that I should have told him before I protested to her, and he would have told me what to do. So, he sent me back the next morning early and told me to go in and tell "Old Miss" that I was sorry that I had done wrong, and I would do her bidding in the future without a protest. I obeyed the order, and "Old Miss" forgave me, and I took up my duties as before and seemed to please all of the family. All the servants went to town every Saturday evening to buy their necessities and have a good time. The owner would furnish the horse and spring wagon for transportation free. In those days, the people would have what they called "Moonlight Feasts" every Saturday night to entertain the people who came in from the country, and also for those who were in town. These "Moonlight

Feasts" were held on the lawns, and as a rule, they were beautifully lit up with Japanese lanterns. They had tables, chairs, refreshment stands, and a post office where you could deliver and get notes from your sweethearts and beaus.

On this particular night I came to town, my friend, Dan Barnum, told me that he had just come by the place where they were holding the "Moonlight Feast" and he saw my girlfriend and his there. We decided to go up. Dan was a very bashful boy, and so was I. We had never been bold enough to talk to our girls in public, and he did not feel that we would be able to talk to them this time. Dan suggested that we get a half pint of whiskey and drink it between us, and that would take away our bashfulness. I asked him how we could get it. He said that he could get a man by the name of Sharp McKinney to get it for us. The cost of the whiskey was $0.25 per half pint. I gave him $0.15 and he put in $0.10. He took the money and gave it to Sharp, and he bought the whiskey for us. We gave him a drink, and the rest we drank.

Dan drank first and said he had his part and gave the bottle to me. I told him that I could not drink that much and gave the bottle back to him, and told him to drink some more, which he did, leaving about one-fifth of the contents in the bottle. I drank it, and it made me beastly drunk. I don't remember anything that happened from the time I drank that whiskey until the following morning. I woke up in my room, upstairs in the cabin on the farm where I worked. If I saw my girl, I do not remember. If I went to the "Moonlight Feast," I do not remember. I don't remember when I was put in the spring wagon, which carried me back to the farm. I don't remember anything that happened while on my way to the farm. I do remember that before I lost consciousness,

I went home. My father was there, and I sassed him and left the house before he could catch me. I also remember how all the men looked to me. I thought I was as large as Gulliver, and all men looked like gnats and flies to me. I could take my hand and, with one stroke, could kill a thousand of them without exertion. The last thing I remember was standing on the corner and noticing all the houses moving toward me. And I was waiting for our house to move by. I stood in motion as if I was going to catch a streetcar. Finally, our house came along, and I made a dash to catch it. I guess I caught it; I don't know whether I did or not. But I do know the following morning, when the bell rang for us to get up and get ready for work, I did not hear it.

The other servants went to work, and when the boss missed me, he came down to the cabin and made me get up and help do the work. He saw my condition and told me to go to the cabin and lie down. I was drunk from Saturday night to the following Wednesday morning. I don't mean that I was helplessly drunk, but I did not have my right mind. One of my duties was to drive the carriage for the family, and on Tuesdays, I drove the family to Midway, Kentucky. Mrs. Nuckols sat on the front seat with me, and when she saw that I did not give half of the road to the vehicles approaching, she would take the lines out of my hands and drive herself. I remember she called me several times a drunken little puppy. When I came to myself, I told her how I happened to get into that condition. She sympathized with me and advised me not to ever take another drink of liquor, and I can truthfully say that I have never been drunk since.

I was 16 at that time, and for more than 50 years, I have never taken a drink of liquor as a beverage. From that drunk, I learned a

Young JB Stradford

valuable lesson. If I wanted to feel that I was as strong as Samson and had all the world under my feet, subject to my order, and that I was rich as John D. Rockefeller and Henry Ford combined, all I would have to do was to get another drink. When I was in that condition, I wanted to fight, and I knew it would be only a question of time before I would reap what I justly deserved, for lunatics and bullies are soon caught and put where they ought to be. I stayed in the employment of that family until after the crops had been garnered, and then I went back to school.

After I had shown my father that all of my interests were centered on him in a financial way by giving him all of the money I made so cheerfully, he agreed to give me one-half of the money I made. He knew that I was very saving and said that he would give me a chance to put my money in the bank. I always believed in having something to do, a job of some kind; if I could not get my price for the work, I would take the other fellow's price. So, I always had something to do. My brother, William, did not like to do hard work, and when he did, he would not give Father his money unless he was compelled to. In harvest time, we would leave home and go out into the country to help harvest. Sometimes, we would go out on Lord Alexander's farm, the man who owned Longfellow and Ten Broeck and many of the best racehorses that this country has ever produced. We also went to Mr. Emach's. I made a hand binding the grain and received what the men received, sometimes as much as $2.00 per day, and sometimes one dollar and a half a day. My brother would pile the bundles and receive about half as much as I got for my work.

Sometimes we would be gone for weeks before coming back home. I would bring back home sometimes as much as $25.00

and give it to my father, and he would give me part of it. But my brother would never give but a very little of what he made to him, and very often, he would whip him very severely for his failure to give him the money he made. Father gave us food, clothing, and sent us to school and demanded what money we made to help keep up the family. He never allowed the girls to go out into service. They stayed at home and kept house for us. They took a day out to go to school and what we made helped to dress them and keep them looking respectable, but William said that we were his children, and it was his duty to feed and support us, and he would not give him his money.

I am very sorry to say that he had malice in his heart against his father. After we had gotten whipped very severely for some infraction of his rules, William came to me and proposed to run away from home. He said that although he gives you half of what you make, if we run away, you can have all you make for yourself. He further said, "You know you work nearly all the time, and you won't have anyone to beat you as Father does." So, we agreed to run away. We set the day to leave and kept it a secret. I began to save my money for our escapade. On the appointed morning, William was ready and came to me and said, "Let's go." I had never stayed away from home a night in my life, and I had a place to eat three times a day. I had never had to look for a place to sleep or eat, and I asked William where we would sleep at night or where we would get our meals. He said, "Damn that, as for me, I can sleep under a tree in the woods and will beg for something to eat before I will remain here any longer. You have money and you can pay your way." I told him that I would rather stay at home and take the treatment he gave us than run away. So, he said, "You are a dirty coward, and have gone back on your agreement, so stay and take this punishment. I am gone."

When he turned to leave me, I cried, "Oh, Will, don't leave me," but he paid no attention to my appeal and went his way.

I was very much aggrieved on account of his going, and I cried as if my heart would break. That night, when Father came home, my sister Alice told Father that William had run away, and that I had been crying all day and was grieving myself to death. I went in to see him and told him how much I was affected by him going and that I had $10.00 that I would give to him if he would go find him and bring him back home. He took the money, hired a horse and buggy, and went to Lexington, Kentucky, where he was reasonably sure he had gone. We had a cousin by the name of Wilkins Allen in Lexington, and William went directly to his home.

When he had related the circumstances to him, Wilkins told him he could not stay there and that he was going to take him back home. There was a funeral procession leaving Lexington for Versailles the following morning, and Wilkins drove the hearse. He put Will on the seat with him and brought him back home. When I saw him, I ran to him and threw my arms around him and rejoiced to the uttermost. On the same day, Father went to Lexington to look for him, he was told by Wilkins' wife that Wilkins had taken him home.

When Father came home, I begged him not to whip him, and he said he would not. But he lectured him and told him what he would do if he ran away anymore. The facts in the case were that he did not like to work. If he could get something easy or a piddling job, that was his ambition. Any man or boy who fails to take his place among men and depends upon himself for the maintenance of himself and those who are dependent on him for their support, and also in ordinary circumstances to support, defend, and protect himself socially, economically, and financially, in my mind, is a miserable failure.

From the time that the lamp of reason dawned upon me, I have shown business acumen. I have always believed in doing something. I have never been an idler. When other boys had nothing to do, I was working, and what I made, I saved. As I stated before, when my father agreed to let me keep one half of the money I made, less $2.00 per week for board and room, I was 15 years old and up to that time, I had never received more than $0.25 a day for my work, except in harvest time, and I don't remember ever getting as much as $0.50 a day, but at the age of 17, I had $72.00 in the bank. I was very proud of my $72.00 and was striving to make it $100.00 and then invest it in some property or something that would yield me an income. I had a cousin who had served in the Civil War. He had contracted a cold, and it had fallen into his eyes and had made him almost blind. And in order to save his sight, his physician said that he would have to go to Cincinnati and have his eyes operated on. Father did not have the money to defray the expenses, and so he asked me to lend him the $72.00 so that he could take him to Cincinnati and have his eyes operated on. I did so, but the operation did not have its desired effect, and instead of having my money in the bank, my father owed it to me.

On account of my reputation for being an honest, trustworthy, and faithful servant, I was recommended to a Jew who had a large department store as a porter. I applied for the job, and he employed me to work for him and gave me $4.00 per week. My duties were to clean the store, deliver bundles, and when all the clerks were busy, I waited on anyone who would use my service. I learned the cost and also the selling prices of the goods. The prices were not written in figures, but in letters, so that the purchasers could not tell what the article cost.

Being apt in learning and neat in my work, my employer took a liking to me, and when he found out that I was trying to educate myself, he gave me books and also taught me. He gave me lessons in grammar, arithmetic, and spelling. I remained in his service for one year, and I can truthfully say that was one of the most fruitful and profitable years of my life. He was very kind and generous. In addition to my wages, he gave me enough clothes to keep me from buying any clothes during the time I was in his employ. During one of his reduction sales, he added a lot of cheap articles which were placed on the counter and were sold for, from $0.05 to $0.25 each.

During this sale, the store would be crowded with customers, and I was one of the clerks. A boy by the name of Will Tanner bought an article from me, and the following morning brought it back and asked me to exchange it. I told him my orders were not to exchange anything. He insisted that I could exchange it, and the proprietor would not know anything about it, but I told him that I would not go against my orders. He told me that if I did not exchange it, he would get even with me whenever he caught me out of the store. I did not pay much attention to him. I was so much larger than he, and he knew I could whip him. Several days passed, and I did not see him. I was sent out to deliver a package containing silk to make a silk dress. That package was valued at $30.00.

I was going down Morgan Street and just as I got to the alley that led down to the big spring, Bill Tanner and Howard Black stepped out of the alley in front of me, and Bill said, "Now, I got you." He had two rocks, one in each hand, and he rushed right into me and struck me on the head with the rock, and before I could get my hands on him, he struck me again. Just as the second blow was delivered, I clinched with him and at the same time, I caught the hand in which he held the rock. In a short time, I had the rock, and then I threw him down and began to beat his head with it. I saw a much larger rock lying beside us, and I picked it up, intending to finish him if I could. Just as I raised it to strike the fatal blow, the sheriff caught my arm and stopped the blow. At that time, I was bloodthirsty, and had the sheriff not interfered, I am sure I would have killed him. I am happy to say that since that time, I have rejoiced many times that I did not do what I intended to do.

The sheriff arrested us and put us in the holdover, and my boss came down and had me released. The valuable parcel of silk goods that I went out to deliver was picked up by someone and carried back to the store the next morning. I failed to report the loss of the parcel after I had been released because, after I had been struck on the head with that first stone, I did not remember anything I had or where I was sent. When the boss was informed of the loss of the parcel, he questioned me relative to not reporting it. I explained to him the best I could, but not to his satisfaction, and so he discharged me for not reporting the loss of it. The year that I spent in his employment will long be remembered by me.

During my stay there, I succeeded in winning the good will of all the clerks in the store, and the contact which I had with the patrons and public at large gained for me an enviable reputation as a boy who was honest, trustworthy, genteel, polite, and entitled to the respect of both white and black people.

Chapter 4

During my confinement on our playground, besides playing marbles, I learned to play several other games, namely, bushel checkers, pyramid, and checker pool, which is called "Spanish Pool." For those games, checkers was my favorite game. I became very efficient in it, and it was not long after I began to play before I was considered the champion boy player of Versailles. The best checker players, desirous to see me, would have me come to their homes and play with them. Lawyers, doctors, and merchants all said I was a wonder and that if I continued to play, I would be the champion of the world. My nearest rival was my oldest brother. He taught me how to play, and on account of my age, he hated for me to beat him.

In 1875, he went to St. Louis to live, and while there, he practiced a great deal in order to beat me. When he came back on a visit to see us in 1876, he brought a checkerboard with him, and Father gave us permission to play at home. That was the first time in our lives he had ever permitted us to play any kind of game at home. He told me that he had come back to beat me at playing checkers, and I told him that I did not know about that. But I was willing to give him a chance, and so we started to play. In the first series, I beat him. We played every day and almost all day long in order to settle, beyond a doubt, which was the better of the two. He finally yielded to my superiority and said, "You are better." Then I told him I would teach him to be as good a checker player as I was if he would promise that after he had become as good or better, he would not boast over me and tell me I was nothing but a scrub checker player. He agreed to my proposition. I had learned several book games, namely, "The Old 14th," "The Single Corner," and "The Goose Walk," and I knew just where he fell down in his plays, which made him easy pickings for me.

The first lesson which I gave him was to show him where he made the wrong plays in the game which he had lost. After showing him several times, he, being an apt pupil, soon learned how to defend his position and make the game a draw. Then I taught him all the other openings and finishes I knew. When we played after I had taught him all I knew, I would say, "Now, go for yourself. Beat me if you can."

The contest became very bitter. Some days he would beat me and some days I would beat him. In fact, I did not know which of us had the better of it. He claimed he could beat me, and I claimed I could beat him. He would tell everyone that he could beat me and boast of his superior ability over me to my chagrin. The very thing he agreed not to do if I teach him, was the very thing he did. I told him that under the agreement, he had no right to boast over me and tell everybody that he was a better player than I was. I told him that any honorable man would live up to his agreements. I said, "If you could really beat me, and you know you can't, you would give me the benefit of the doubt as you agreed." On account of his arrogance, I sorely regretted that I ever gave him a lesson. But this incident only spurred me on to greater achievements in the game of checkers. I resolved that I would not cease in my quest for checkers until I had made him a mere pigmy in the game compared with me. After his vacation, he returned to St. Louis and remained there for several years before he came back home, which I shall say more about later on in my memoirs.

My father, being a devout Christian, reared his children in fear and admonition of the Lord. Every night before retiring, he would have family prayers, and on Sunday mornings, prayer before breakfast. He was hardly ever with us on any other morning except Sunday. Sunday was the day that the Lord hallowed, and he taught us to dress up on that day and refrain from all work and go to Sunday School.

Our family was Baptist, and as a matter of fact, we attended the Baptist Sunday School for years and were active in all the affairs of the school. I was elected secretary of the Sunday School and retained that office for a number of years. I resigned after the pastor, Reverend C. Smothers, upbraided me in public for what I said in my paper on the subject, "Who was the first Christian martyr?" In speaking of John the Baptist, I said that John was neither a Christian nor a martyr. At that time, he was conducting a revival, and the people were very deeply affected on account of the interest which was being shown by the number of confessions and also the number going up to the mourner's bench. Before I had finished my paper, Reverend Smothers rose from his seat in the pulpit and said that he did not want me to make such false statements in my paper, as such statements would detract someone from the narrow way and ordered me to sit down. I refused to sit down, stating that I had the right to defend my side of the question. He insisted that I sit down. I appealed to the superintendent, and he said, "For the sake of harmony, take your seat." I left the building and resigned from my office as secretary of the Sunday School.

While an active worker in the Sunday School, I enjoyed the work very much. I was a close Bible student of the New Testament scriptures and I learned more and more about the life and character of Jesus. Our superintendent, on the first Sunday of each month, would give prizes to the pupil who could recite the most verses. Some of the pupils would recite chapter after chapter of verses until they had recited hundreds of verses verbatim et literatim to win the prize. Then what I learned in that Sunday School had a great influence on me later in life, which caused me to accept Jesus as the Bishop of my salvation. In concluding this narrative, I will say this much for our preachers. A great majority of them do not believe it is necessary for a minister to be highly educated.

They will tell you that God sent them to preach and will put into their mouths what He wants them to say. This class of preachers, instead of being a benefit to our group, is a detriment, and today, in this Northland, there are more of this type of preachers than there are of prepared men. There should be a standard of preparation for a preacher. Doctors, lawyers, dentists, and schoolteachers all have to pass an examination to practice their profession. Why not preachers? Whenever the preachers are made to qualify in the same manner as other professional men, and when that requirement is made effective, there will be the dawn of a new day for our group, and ignorance will vanish from among us as the mist vanishes before the sun.

After finishing my second five-month term in the public school and having had the privilege of assisting the teacher when she had more work than she could do, I felt that I was qualified to teach regardless of qualifications. I knew the superintendent believed in home talent and would give those of us who applied for a teacher's position the preference over Northern teachers.

In the summer of 1880, my brother returned home from St. Louis. While in St. Louis, he learned the barber's trade. There were no barbershops in Versailles for our group, and so he rented a room from my father and opened a barbershop. He took me as an apprentice to learn the barber trade. He had not only learned the barber trade but had gone to night school and prepared himself to teach. There were two schools that we decided on getting; one was the Versailles which had funds sufficient to pay a teacher a fair salary for five months, which we agreed, he would teach on account of his age and experience; and the other one I decided to take because of my age and the fact that the fund was not enough to pay the teacher more than $90.00 for three months. We went to the superintendent and made our applications for said schools. And in the meantime, we made our applications to the trustees, and the superintendent recommended us to the trustees. And jobs were assured. We took the examination at the stated time and both passed. He received a second-grade certificate, and I was awarded a third-grade certificate.

Our schools began on the first of September. Prior to the opening of school, we were associated every day in the barbershop. He was doing whatever work that came in, and I would lather the men's faces and comb their hair before he had shaved them. My first lesson was learning to sharpen a razor. He taught me how to hold the razor and, when placed upon the hone to begin sharpening, saying as I dragged the razor to keep time with the movement, "From heel to point, heel to point, heel to point." That was kept up until I had finished the practice. This exercise was given not only for the purpose of learning how to sharpen a razor, but also to get the proper wrist action, which is very indispensable in the art of shaving. We kept a checkerboard in the barbershop, and whenever we did not have anything to do, we played the game of checkers. During the time he was away, I had left no stone unturned in the quest for checker knowledge to place him in the class where he belonged. I learned a few new moves and the old games; I had learned the variations that would defeat the old-line positions. I was very careful in my deliberations to know the position after each move. He seldom ever won a game, and I was again his acknowledged master. He told me of a man in St. Louis by the name of J.T. Smith who could beat him playing checkers, and he wanted me to go with him to St. Louis to beat him.

Up until this time, I had never been more than 12 miles from home. But on account of going with him, I had no fear of my safety, and so I agreed to go at the close of his school. On the first Monday in September 1880, our schools opened. My school was five miles out in the country, and I had to walk to it every Monday morning and back every Friday afternoon. My board and room cost me $8.00 per month. My schoolwork was very pleasant, and my average attendance was about 12. My daily attendance was about 15. In the organization of the school, I followed the rules laid down in the Teachers' Guidebook. I was punctual in my duties as a teacher, and I demanded obedience and perfect order in the schoolroom.

During this three-month term, I enjoyed myself very much. My association with the pupils was of the most pleasant nature, and my relationship with the parents was most cordial. At the end of the term, we had an exhibition which I thought was a very unique affair. All of the neighbors turned out to witness what the children could do in speech making, songs and dialogues. The parents took pride in dressing their children very nicely for the affair. Prior to the time I taught at this school, I thought in terms of a half man, because my father had firmly impressed it upon my mind that I belonged to him until I was 21 years of age, and I would not be a man until then. But after I had assumed the responsibility of a grown-up man, I began to think like a man and act like a man. I took pride in meeting with parents and visitors of the school and discussing with them matters pertaining to schoolwork and topics in general.

I really felt my importance as a teacher. I don't think any greater change could have come over anyone in such a short time. One of my friends said that I had the "big head" and needed an iron band around it to keep it from bursting. I felt that what he said was a compliment rather than a criticism. Up until that time, I had never accompanied a girl to church. Every Sunday night, my brother and I would escort our girls to church. It was nothing new to him, but for me, it was very embarrassing. We did not sit with them in church, but when the collection was called for, we would go over to where they were sitting and give them money to take up to the table to give in the collection. I wore my best clothes every day, kept my shoes polished, and my hair dressed every day.

No one could hardly realize that such a change could take place in anyone in such a short time. My father was not willing to give up his authority over me, and several times while teaching, he would give me a black eye, which I carried to school with me, and very often my girl would make fun of me for permitting him to treat me in that manner.

In the foregoing, I mentioned that my father borrowed the $72.00, which I had saved to take his nephew to Cincinnati to have his eye operated on. He not only borrowed my money but also borrowed my overcoat to wear. We were about the same size. After he had gotten to Cincinnati, one evening while we were all together in the sitting room, I said that Father had the nerve to ask me for my overcoat to wear to Cincinnati and that I ought not to have loaned it to him for the reason that I came home from school last Wednesday night to see my girl, and it was raining, and I got wet as I could be. My feet were soaking wet, and I asked him to lend me his new shoes to wear that evening, and he would not do it. On the following Sunday, he came home, and my sister, Betty, whom we called his parrot, told him what I had said about my overcoat after he had asked her what had transpired or happened while he was away. He felt that I should be whipped for what I had said.

On the following Monday morning, I got up early and was dressing myself, getting ready to go to my school. He came into the room where I was and told me what I had said. He then ordered me to take off my shirt; he was going to whip me. And he wanted that to be the last time. In a defiant manner, I said, "You have whipped me your last time." When I finished my saying, he dropped his switches and rushed at me, struck me with his fist, and continued to try to strike me, but being a good boxer, I blocked his blows, and as soon as I could get away from him, I ran out of the back door. He followed me. The hoe was standing by the side of the smokehouse, and he grabbed it and, at full speed, chased me around the smokehouse several times. I could run faster than he, so I turned the corners. I would stop and wait until he got near enough for me to be on my way out of danger.

Finally, I decided not to run any farther, and so I stopped suddenly just around the corner he was approaching. When he turned the corner with the hoe uplifted, I grabbed him around the breast and squeezed as hard as I could. He dropped the hoe, but I was holding him so tight that he could not hurt me.

Just at that time, my oldest brother came out on the scene and said, "John, don't fight your father."

I said that I was not fighting him, but that I was damn tired of him beating me up, and with that, I turned him loose and ran as fast as I could. He picked up a brick and threw it underhand at me. It missed me and struck my eldest sister in the foot, and inflicted a severe wound. I did not get a chance to get my clothes, and so I went uptown without a hat or coat. My brother came to me and told me that Father had gone out and for me to come and get ready to go to my school.

I went home, got ready and left with the intention of not going back to live there. On the following Friday, I came in from my school and I did not go home. My father sent my oldest brother for me and told him to tell me to come home. I told him to go back and tell Father that only on one condition would I come home and that was he would have to promise not to attempt to whip me. My brother delivered the message, and he promised not to whip me. I went home and from that day on our relationship was most cordial. I knew I was his favorite boy, and he was proud of me. He often said that I had been more help to him than all of his children, but he was of the old school. He believed in corporal punishment upon me. He thought that it was his duty to soundly whip us for the least infraction of any of his rules or any disobedience. To tell the truth, we were what they called, "bad boys." We were very determined or, as they called it, "bullheaded." The things we were told not to do were the very things we took pleasure in doing, and the things we were told to do, were the things which we would not do. There were very few nights in a week that we did not get unmerciful whippings.

One of our duties was to keep a supply of water in the water bucket. We took our turn about supplying it. When my time came to get the water, I would try to put it on my brother, William. As a rule, our sister would most often call the one whose time it was to get the water. She called me and told me to get a bucket of water, and I told her that it was not my time to bring the water. She insisted that it was, and I told her that I would not get it. It was near time for Father to come home. When he came, he found the bucket empty. He asked why the bucket was empty, and she told him that I had absolutely refused to get it, saying that it was William's time. At the time, Father came home, I was out at play. When I came home, he did not say anything to me about refusing to get the water. I thought, everything had passed off unnoticed. Early the next morning, before I awoke, he came to my bed, took me by my foot, pulled me out of the bed and began to whip me with the butt of a switch until I was almost unconscious. He said, "Hereafter, when you are told to bring a bucket of water, do it, whether it is your time or not." This was the only whipping I ever got in my life that did me any good. I was a good boy for several months; I was very prompt in all my duties, and there were no charges preferred against me for a long time. I have heard it said by many that whipping a child does no good, but I firmly believe in the old Bible doctrine, "Spare the rod and spoil the child." As I have said before, I believe my father was one of the grandest and most noble men that has ever lived; every lick he gave me, he thought it to be for my own good, and I further believe that if he had not been so hard on us, our career in after-life would have been one of crime and immorality.

He reared seven out of eight children to manhood and womanhood, three girls and four boys. Not one of the boys has ever been arrested for any crime, petty thieving, or any violations of the moral code and not one of the girls has had the finger of scorn pointed at her for any immoral act. They were all married honorably and have eschewed the evil things of life. It gives me great pleasure to say that in all my life, I have not heard one word, derogatory to their character. They always had company when they went out at night. Father would send one of the boys along with them whenever they went out to any public gathering or private home. When they were allowed to have beaus to escort them, Father would send one of us along with them and tell us to walk behind and not butt into their conversation, and we did as instructed. There was no kissing or spooning when they parted. When they got home, they said goodnight and went into the house.

One other incident which happened during my boyhood made a lasting impression upon me. The Honorable J.C.S.

Blackburn was running for Representative to Congress on the Democratic ticket. The Honorable William Cassius Goodloe was the candidate on the Republican ticket. Bills had been circulated all over the country advertising the meeting. It was announced that a Colored man, Reverend Stansberry, would be one of the speakers. On the day set for the speaking, the town was crowded with members of our group and also with white people. At two o'clock, the meeting was called to order. The courthouse was filled to overflowing and the yard was also filled. Reverend Stansberry was the first speaker on the program. After being introduced, he discussed the issues of the campaign and stated very concisely our interests in the issues at stake and then appealed to us to support the Honorable William Cassius Goodloe.

I had never heard a Colored man speak publicly before. I thought it was the greatest speech I had ever heard. At the end of his speech, pandemonium reigned among our people, and it was some time before order could be restored. The next speaker was Mr. Goodloe. He discussed the issues of the campaign and talked mainly to white people. He was a great orator, a nephew of Henry Clay, and when he had finished his speech, he received the applause of all the Republicans. The next speaker was Joe Blackburn. He was a resident of the town and very popular among the citizens of Versailles.

I saw him leave his residence many a day and start downtown. He would shake hands with every white citizen he met and take a drink with all of them before he got to the hotel. When he arose to speak, he said, "Fellow Democrats, I came here today to address Democrats and not Republicans and niggers. If it takes the vote of a nigger to elect me to Congress, I would rather not have the office." He further said that a nigger had no rights that a white man was bound to respect. The Democrats cheered vociferously. I listened very intently to his whole speech and from it, I learned what little respect the Southern crackers had of our group and vowed that day that if any cracker violated any right of mine, I would resent, if necessary, with my life. Ever since that day, I have been diligent in seeing to it that every infraction of my right has been combated, as you will see further on in these memoirs.

My last teacher was quite efficient in his schoolwork. He had been a student in Oberlin College, Oberlin, Ohio. He knew that I was ambitious and was seeking a higher education. He advised me to attend Oberlin College. He told me it was the best place in the world to get an education. I made up my mind that I would go to Oberlin as soon as I could make enough money to go and pay the first term's tuition and my board for the term, which was three months. My oldest brother encouraged me to go and said he would help me with all that he could. After my school closed, I stayed in the barbershop. I had learned to do fairly good work. When my brother's school closed, he persuaded me to go with him to St. Louis, saying that I would have a better chance of making money there than at home. His real reason, however, was that he wanted me to play checkers with the man who had beaten him. I first asked my father for permission to go to St. Louis, and he gave his consent.

In a short time, we arranged our affairs, and on the 8th of March 1880, we arrived in St. Louis. I had never been 20 miles from home before in my life. My brother, being acquainted there, secured a very respectable place for us to stay. We both had a little money, and before going to work, we decided to spend a week sightseeing and visiting friends. We had a very enjoyable time. I was so amazed at the many beautiful parks, buildings and the many large boats which were running up and down the river; also, the water tower and Eads Bridge, which spanned the river. After taking in a great many places of interest, we then began to visit friends, relatives and acquaintances. We were invited out to dinner and tea, and I certainly enjoyed myself to the greatest degree.

On the following day, my brother made an appointment for me to meet J. T. Smith, the man who had been beating him playing checkers. When we met, my brother introduced us and said, "I have brought my brother from Versailles, Kentucky to beat you playing checkers."

Mr. Smith was a very affable, jolly, and agreeable man, and after the introduction, he jokingly said, "You have come to get the same medicine which I have been giving your brother."

I replied, "I don't know about that, but no man has contended with me but to his own destruction."

We then sat down at the table and began to play. The tally sheet was arranged to read "St. Louis vs. Versailles." The number of games to be played, 13. Versailles scored the first game, St. Louis the second and third, and when the series ended, Versailles won seven, St. Louis, four, draws, two.

My brother rejoiced in the greatest degree over my success and said to Mr. Smith, "Oh! Vengeance, thou art sweet."

I played with him a great many times after that, but he never beat me a sitting. I played with a great many of the best players in the city and found only one whom I considered better than I was.

After our week of sightseeing and visiting was over, we started out to seek employment. We both got employment as barbers. I went to work in a Colored barbershop for a man named George Tegas, who was a good friend of my brother. He gave me a good chance to make good, but this trade was not sufficient to guarantee me a living wage. The first week I worked there, I made $2.50, which was not enough to pay my expenses. My room rent was $1.50 per week, and it left me with $1.00 on which to board.

I stayed in that shop one month and the most I made any week was $4.50. And that week, I quit the job. I got employment at the Cotton Compress at $1.50 per day. I had not been there very long before I contracted a severe cold, and on account of it, I had to quit the job. As I think of it now, the cotton was stored down in an underground basement. The place was lighted with dim gaslight, and it was exceedingly damp and cold. Each one of us had a cotton hook and a truck, and we worked in gangs. We would run our trucks up to the bale of cotton and stick the hook into it, and pull it over on the truck, and then truck it away to some other part of the building. It was a very hard job, and they worked as though their lives depended upon it, running and singing all day long. I stood it as long as I could.

When my cold got better, and I was able to work, I looked for another job. The next job I got was in an iron foundry. I had to handle pig iron and also a great many old sows. It was the hardest work I had ever done. I told my brother that I could not stand such hard work, and he advised me to quit it, so I did. Up until this time, I had been in St. Louis for about two months and had made very little progress and felt that I would never make a sufficient amount of money to accomplish my purpose at the rate I was going. Every morning, I would take the morning paper, "The Globe Democrat" and look in the want-ads for help wanted. I saw an ad which I thought would suit me very well. I answered it. I found a middle-aged man who was the proprietor of the house, sitting at his desk. He had a kindly expression and was seemingly full of warm respect for me. He asked me how long I had lived in St. Louis. I told him. He asked me for references. I told him that I did not know anyone that I could give him for reference, but if he would give me the job, I would guarantee him satisfaction. I asked him how much the job paid. He then explained the nature of the job and what it paid. In the first place, he paid $4.00 per week. There were five or six boarders in the house who paid $1.00 per month each for shining their shoes and that it was my duty to run errands for all the guests and to be the factotum about the place. I told him that I could not accept the job until I brought my brother up to see him, and he would decide what I should do. So, I went out and got my brother. He came back, and after they had talked the matter over, he gave me the job. He highly appreciated the spirit in me relative to looking to my brother as my guide and counselor.

On the following morning, I took up my duties at the Bulkley Apartments. This was a family apartment, and at that time, there were six families living there. In those days, there were no furnaces or gas. I had to make the fires, take out the ashes, and clean up around the hearth or stove. I answered the doorbell, swept the halls and kept the stone steps scrubbed. After I had been there a short while, I kept the keys to the pantry and issued out the provisions for the cook. I had six pairs of shoes to polish every morning for which I received $1.00 a pair per month. I got along very nicely. I made an average of about $10.00 per week with my tips and saved nearly every cent of it. My landlady was very good to me. She gave me a great many things to wear which her husband had cast off, which were better than I was able to buy. She advised me in all things, just the same as I had been her own son. She had abiding faith in me, and I felt as dear to her as if she had been my mother.

The guests were very kind and generous to me and more so when they found out that I was trying to make money to go off to school. Mr. Bulkley, the proprietor, was one of those big-hearted men who believed in the brotherhood of man and the fatherhood of God. In fact, he knew no distinction. They had a daughter, Minnie, who resided in Carmel, California. At that time, she was attending night school at the Polytechnic School there. Every night, he would send me with her and give me money to pay our streetcar fare. He ordered me to sit with her in the car and help her off when she got off the car. Miss Minnie was much older than I was, but she always treated me courteously, because I always knew my place and kept it.

The help in the household consisted of five females and me. They were all white girls, and I must say that the relations existing among us were most cordial. And I have tried my best to keep in touch with every servant and especially, the employers.

On or about July 1, 1881, I was scrubbing the stone steps in front of the house when Miss Minnie opened the front door and with tears in her eyes said, "John! President Garfield has just been assassinated." I went into the house and shared their sorrows on account of their bereavement. It was a very sad affair. The city was draped in mourning. Bells were tolling all over the city. The flags on the boats on the river were hung at half mast, and the Post Office building was draped in mourning. The people of St. Louis were very deeply affected on account of the assassination of our beloved president.

Another incident which occurred while I was employed in the Bulkley home, that I think is worth mentioning. All through my life, I have been snake-like. They say if you step on a snake, it will bite you. I have always felt my importance to the extent that I should have the respect of others in all things, just the same as I respected others. For instance, I have seen men who were bosses on jobs who had no respect for the employees. They would say anything, and, in any way, they desired to say it to their help, regardless of the situation. They did not regard the employee any more than they would an animal.

My philosophy has been different, and that is that a man is a man, regardless of his condition and deserves the respect of a man. As I said before, one of my duties was to keep all the halls clean. On account of other duties, I was, on the morning, in question, late beginning to clean the halls. Mrs. Bulkley, the landlady, came downstairs and as I took it, in a very abrupt manner said, "You should have had this work completed long ago." I told her that she did not have to tell me how the work should be done and when it should be done. "I have worked for you for some months and have tried to please you. Now, you are finding fault of my work. If my work don't please you, pay me off, and I will go home." She went back upstairs without saying a word to me and told Mr. Bulkley that I had sassed her, and she felt very much chagrined over the matter.

That afternoon, he called me into his office and said, "Miss Mary told me you insulted her this morning, and I want you to go up and apologize to her for what you said." I knew Mr. Bulkley had implicit confidence in my integrity and honesty. And I knew that he did not want to lose me as a servant. I told him I was sorry for what I had said to Miss Mary, and I would go immediately to her and apologize. I went into her room. She was seated in her armchair, and when I approached her, she did not pay any attention to me. I walked right up to her and said, "Mrs. Bulkley, I came to apologize to you for what I said to you this morning. I am very sorry that I hurt your feelings, and I promise you that it will never happen again as long as I remain in your employment."

She accepted my apology in good faith and then gave me a friendly lecture, advising me of the best ways to get along through life and how to accomplish the things I wanted, the things I most earnestly desired. I never had an occasion after that incident to complain of any insult or domineering order she gave me concerning my work. I knew my duty and performed it, and whenever she wanted anything done, she told me, and I did it. I went back to the office and told Mr. Bulkley what I had done, and he said, "That was manly. Be careful in the future what you say, and you will not have to make any apologies."

I remained with the family for several months after this incident, and I have never in all my life had such parental teachings and advice as I received from this family. I was in the employment for one year. During that year, I had a bank account of $150.00, a lot of nice clothes and everything in readiness to go to Oberlin, Ohio to school. It was a sad day for me when I severed my connection as an employee of that family. I had never been shown such consideration before in all my life. In the first place, I did my work well, and it satisfied me. I had the good will of the household and all of them gave me something, mostly money, shook my hand, and bade me goodbye and wished me success in my undertaking.

After I had shaken hands with all the guests and members of the family except Mrs. Bulkley, I went into her room to bid her goodbye. I shall never forget how tenderly she caught my hand and with that mother smile on her face, said, "John, I know you have the ability to become a great man. Some day you will be a leader among your people. It takes hard work and untiring effort to succeed, and I know that you are equal to the occasion. Remember there is no excellence without great labor." And with this advice, she said, "Success to you. If you need me, I will help you. Goodbye."

I then went downstairs to say goodbye to all the help. All of them had learned to respect me and some of them to love me. The scene was very pathetic; they were so much affected on account of my leaving that they embraced me with kisses and tears in their eyes and wishes for my success in all of my endeavors in life. For my association with the servants, I have learned this lesson: "That kinky locks and dark complexion does not alter nature's claim. Skin may differ, but affections dwell in blacks and whites the same."

Within a few months after our arrival in St. Louis, my brother married, and I lost his companionship. On the night of his wedding, there were a few intimate friends and relatives of the family in attendance. Among them were several very good-looking and winsome girls. It appeared to me that they had been invited there expressly for my pleasure. One of them, as I have said before, was very attractive and so captivating that she completely mesmerized me. We played several different kinds of games which were customary at such affairs, and whenever it was my turn to choose a girl, I would invariably choose her and in turn, she would choose me, and the pleasure was ours. It was a case of love at first sight. Oh, how I enjoyed her company that evening. My soul seemed to have been an enchanted boat, floating on the sounds of her sweet voice, her size, eyes, color and her hair were my ideals.

When I thought of the happiness which was in store for me, my heart leaped for joy. She was everything to me; I was wholly enveloped with her charms. I escorted her home that night and while on the way, I felt as though I was in paradise. My whole being was entirely encompassed by her angelic demeanor. When we parted that night, I was at a loss to know how I could get along without her. I was blindly in love with her and insanely jealous. I had made an appointment to call on her the following Wednesday evening. I was at a loss to know how I could live so long without being near her side. At the appointed time, I was there. Her mother met me at the door and invited me to come in. She said, "Take a seat. Mary will be in in a few minutes." And she sat down on the sofa. We chatted on current events.

Suddenly, Mary came. I rose with a heart full of love and affection and greeted her most cordially and took my seat. She introduced me to her mother, and to my surprise, her mother was our guest the whole time I was there. I was hopeful that she and I would be alone, and I would have the opportunity of telling her how much I loved her and possibly a chance to feel the tender pressure of her lips to mine. But nothing doing. Her mother's presence, instead of cooling my love and affection for her, increased it. So, we all chatted pleasantly on different subjects, and when the time came for us to part, I prepared to go, and they bade me goodnight, after having made a date for the following Wednesday night.

I had now arrived at the point where I did not think I could get along without her much longer. The following Sunday night I met her at church and escorted her home. I had the opportunity to tell her how much I loved and adored her. By her admission, I found out that the feelings were mutual. I knew from our first meeting that she loved me, and I loved her, and someday she would be my wife. I had a very severe case of love. I could not sleep at night, nor do my work efficiently by day, nor could I think clearly on any subject. Having reached the climax of my feeling, I felt that I could not live without her being at all times in my presence and that she would have to go with me to and from my work. Then I stopped to consider. I asked myself was I crazy? And the answer came, quick and clear, "You are."

Then I decided that if I should marry a girl that I was so crazy about, the result would be disastrous, and the best thing for me to do, as I was so determined to acquire an education, was to sever my connection with her. On the following morning, I wrote her a note stating reasons for my failure for not filling the engagement, and on the following Sunday night, I met her at church services and escorted her home. We talked of our love and devotion for each other and what the future held in store for us. I failed to see her on the next meeting night. She came over to my brother's home to inquire about me, and my sister-in-law told her that I did not stay with them and that she had not seen me for several weeks. Although it gave me great pain to sever relations with her, I feel that it was the greatest feat which I have ever accomplished in all my life.

Chapter 5

After leaving Versailles and going to St. Louis, the opportunities for a young man to look on the higher side of life are much less than in a small, country town. Environments are conducive, as a rule, to lower standards of good citizenship, especially among the poorer classes of our group. In large cities, the housing conditions for our group are very poor. The poor class live in the ragged sections of the city where rent is cheapest, and others who are a little more successful will rent flats at a higher rate and do anything they are big enough to do to pay the rent. In a great many cases, the churches were not in close proximity, and the streetcar fare was quite an intrusion for that class. When country people go to the city to live, they generally choose the path of least resistance, and every avenue is open to lead one into paths of wickedness. Under these circumstances, we lose sight of our Sunday schools, our churches, our homes, our Christian training and become a prey for wicked and designing people. There is not very much employment for our group in large cities, and what they get, as a rule, are the most menial of all jobs.

I mention this to show that I know of a great many of the boys and girls who had good homes and were surrounded by good Christian influences, who left home and went to large cities to live, and very few of them have ever gotten their heads above the waves. Most of them have simply eked out a life of poverty and shame. In my case, it was different. My brother was a consistent Christian. He had lived in St. Louis before. He had established himself in the eyes of the people as a man worthy of respect and was admitted into the best society in the city, and being his brother, I followed the paths that he had made possible by his Christian integrity and industry.

Having accomplished the purpose for which I went to St. Louis, I packed my trunk, bought my railway ticket to Versailles, Kentucky, to visit my father and brother, and sisters before leaving for Oberlin College.

On August 1, 1881, I bade adieu to all my friends and relatives, and on the morning of August 2, I arrived in Versailles. I found my father and all the rest of the family well and very glad to see me. While there, I had an enjoyable time before leaving for Oberlin. I visited all of my old employers, and they were glad to see me and made many a gift to show their appreciation of my ambition to better my condition. Mr. Landsberg, for whom I worked in the store, told me when I needed his help, to let him know, and several times while I was in school, he sent me $25.00. I remained in Versailles for about one week. On the 8th of August 1881, I arrived in Oberlin to begin the schoolwork preparatory department of the college. I was a complete stranger, and the first thing I did was to find a boarding house which I thought was the most suitable. Board and room were $12.00 per month. I paid for one month in advance, deposited $110.00 in the bank and kept $6.00 in my pocket for current expenses.

I found that I had gotten to Oberlin about two weeks before school began. After I had arranged all the particular things, I thought I would take a walk around town. I passed a fruit stand where there were some very fine peaches. In those days, the people brought their fruit to town and would set their basket of fruit on a table in the street and put the price on it and leave a bowl or a cup to hold the money and go home or someplace else, as the case might be. The purchaser would go to the basket and select what he wanted and place the money in the receptacle and go his way. This was the first time I had seen such confidence placed in the public. I bought several nice, large peaches and dropped the money in the receptacle and continued my stroll through the campus and streets.

While walking on Professor Street, I passed under a tree which had a hornet's nest in it. I was eating one of my peaches. I never looked up to see what was in the tree. I was too busy eating. Suddenly, a swarm of hornets struck me on the head and knocked me down to the sidewalk. I rolled over and, in the scuffle, I tore my pants, jumped up, and ran away from the scene and left my hat under the tree. I was afraid to go back and get it. A man volunteered to get it for me, and I thanked him very much. And that was the initiation I received on the first day of my arrival at Oberlin.

After I had gone to my boarding house, changed my clothes, and doctored my big neck and head, I went down to a barbershop operated by a man named Sandy Tim. I told him my mission there and asked for a job in his barbershop on Saturdays. He said he was filled up at present, but he had a shop in Birmingham, Ohio, about 10 miles from Oberlin, and he would be glad to have me go out there and open that shop and stay there until school opened. I left the next day for Birmingham and stayed there until school opened.

On the day school opened, I matriculated. The fee for three months' term was $10.00. I was assigned to my classes and given a list of the books I had to buy. Then I was dismissed to return the following morning with the necessary equipment. The teachers were affable and kind to me. The students were also very agreeable. All of the teachers were white, and I saw only two Colored students besides myself. On account of my training, it was the most wonderful thing I had experienced in all my life, to be treated so civilly. There was no discrimination as far as I could see. The students, boys and girls, took pride in doing everything to make me feel that I was at home among them. In the classroom, we were seated indiscriminately, all over the room. No one objected to taking a seat beside a person because he was white or black. After school, we would walk down the streets with our classmates, and oftentimes we would escort the girls to their homes and no distinction whatever was made relative to our social affairs.

At the opening of each term, Tudor Peck, as we called him, one of the teachers in the preparatory department, would open his large and spacious house to all the students of the preparatory department to meet for the purpose of getting acquainted. In these meetings, a reception committee would be appointed to introduce each one to the other. Without fear or being embarrassed, we would chat freely with the white girls, and they with us, on any subject we desired to discuss.

The work assigned to me was in advance of what I had studied, and I had a very hard time trying to make even a passing grade. The teachers were very sympathetic and did all they could to help me to understand the work. I was the fun box for the class in any grammar class. I had no respect for the King's English. I wrote, "God" with a little "g" and the pronoun, "I" with a small "i." One incident which I remember, one of the white girls and I were sent to the blackboard to write sentences. I wrote "God" in one of the sentences with a little "g." Miss Dressler noticed the mistake in the sentence and pointed it out to me, and said, "Words referring to the Deity should begin with a capital letter." I have never forgotten that lesson.

Another lesson, I boarded with a lady by the name of Mrs. Wiley. She kept a large boarding house, and all of her boarders were men and boy students. A great many of the boys took pleasure in criticizing the mistakes of other students, one of them in particular, T. K. Bruce, who was very thorough in his English. This morning in question was very cold. I came into the sitting room, rushed right up to the stove and said to Bruce, "Let me get close to the fire, my feet is cold."

When I said that, Bruce exclaimed in a loud voice, "Oh! My feet is cold, my feet is cold." To the delight of all of them, he fell down on the floor and, clapping his hands, continued saying, "My feet is cold, my feet is cold."

I was very much embarrassed, but I can truthfully say that I've never made the same mistake since. Other common mistakes were in the use of prepositions, such as between you and I, and several others, which I used incorrectly. Those criticisms, though very harsh at the time, have been a great help to me in improving my English, and have caused me to be quite technical in my schoolwork, and have caused me at all times to be choosy in the selection of words to express my thoughts.

After the first month in Oberlin, having liquidated the money I paid for board, I rented two rooms, one for sleeping and cooking, and the other for a barbershop. During my spare time, I would do barber work. A great many of my classmates and some of the citizens would patronize me. This enabled me to make my current expenses. I bought a barber chair, table, mirror, cuspidor, bowl, pitcher, and a few other things which were needed in the shop. For my bedroom, I bought a cot, some blankets, a pillow, a tub, a stove and a few cooking utensils, etc. My work in school was very hard. I stayed up late at night studying my lessons and got up early every morning trying to prepare to meet my teacher the next morning. But the given work was too much for me to prepare. So, it happened that every time the teacher called on me to recite, she would invariably call for some part of the lesson which I did not know and, of course, I flunked. I was the poorest student in the class.

When I was called on to recite, there seemed to be a feeling of sympathy among the students and also the teachers for me. I was embarrassed to a superlative degree. I had stage fright, and that which I did know, I could not answer. Finally, the teacher quit calling on me to recite and gave me the privilege to volunteer to recite. She continued this method until I had gained self-confidence, but at the close of the term, I barely made a grade of 65%. Many a time, during that term, I was tempted to give up and go to work. Then again, I felt that if the other members of the class could succeed with the work, I could too. And also, I felt that it would be a disgrace to go back home and tell my people that I did not have the ability to master the work. All through my life, I had led in everything which I attempted. In playing marbles, I was the champion of the town. I was the best fighter, speller, best in arithmetic, and the best declaimer.

In the beginning of the term, our work was a review of *Harvey's English Grammar*, *White's Complete Arithmetic*, and *Elementary Geography*. We were assigned from five to 10 pages a day, and the fact is, that one page would have been enough for me in each subject in order to have good recitations. So, I doubled my efforts and resolutions and entered the second term determined to do the work which I was given. Not satisfied with my work in grammar and arithmetic, I asked my teacher to have me assigned to those same studies. He did so, and my grades were somewhat better than in the first term. My time was so taken up that I had no time to spare for anything outside of the requirements of the school.

The facts in the case are that my qualifications had not prepared me for the advanced grade in which I was entering, but by laborious and continued effort, I managed to get a better grade than in the first term, although I was far from being satisfied with my work. During my first two terms, I was a stranger and satisfied to observe all the rules of the college. I attended church each Sunday morning, was in my room at ten o'clock each night and remained there until morning. Report cards were furnished us, and we made our own reports. It was an honor system, and I can truthfully say that I never in that period of time made a false report. I remember a few other questions which we had to answer, namely, "Do you smoke? Do you chew tobacco? Do you drink? Are you in your room at 10:00 p.m. each evening?"

The first year in Oberlin, my report card was perfect every week. I had no time to do anything outside of studying my lessons, except baseball. The atmosphere which we breathed in Oberlin was pure and unadulterated. Everything was conducive to good morals. There were no sporting people, no gambling houses, no pool halls or speakeasies. The students went to the chapel for prayer service every afternoon and to the church of their choice every Sunday morning. The citizens were seemingly very devout in their devotion to the church.

In those days, women wore long dresses, and it was a curiosity to see a woman's leg above the ankle. One of the professor's wives was living in this 20th century, far ahead of that time. She was possessed with very beautiful legs, and when she came downtown, she made it a custom when crossing the streets, especially when it was raining, to gently raise her dress high enough to give the spectators a good view of her legs. The boys knew what days she would be out on the street, and they made it their business to pose themselves in places along the streets which she passed in order to get a good view of her legs. When she crossed the streets and gutters and began to gently raise her dress, oh, how our hearts would begin to flutter. But those thrilling experiences are passed forever. She wore the most fancy and attractive hose on the market, and the ones which attracted me most were those which were striped like a barber pole around the leg, not horizontal. The stockings were beautiful, and her legs more beautiful. I can't find words to express the symmetry or the fine curves which shape a perfect leg, but I am free to confess that it was the most beautiful calf that I have ever seen. It has been said that a thing of beauty is a joy forever. Years may come and go, but as long as I live, I shall always cherish with fond memory the beauty of those legs.

Having finished the second term without being satisfied with my work and feeling the work which had been assigned to me for the quarter was too much in advance of my early training, I decided that I would drop out of the college department, go to the union school, and start at the bottom and go up. I told Professor Peck of my intentions, and he advised me to continue in my work and said that by the end of this term, I would be more hopeful, and my work would be lighter. I took his advice and finished the term and felt better satisfied than I did at the close of each of the preceding terms. At the close of the term, I was three subjects behind my class, and in order to make them up, I decided to attend the summer term. I studied all summer, and at the close of the term, I was prepared to go on with my class.

In the fall term, I can't say that my first year at Oberlin was a success financially. I had spent about all the money I had when I landed there. I had not been able to build up a trade in my shop sufficient to defray expenses. I had denied myself a great many necessities of life, and the work which I had done in the school, although I had made the grade, was very unsatisfactory to me. I knew that the work which was assigned to me was several years ahead of me. And I felt that I should go back and start at the bottom. Socially, I made quite a few friends among my classmates, both boys and girls, whose companionship while in Oberlin I greatly appreciated and whose friendship since our association in school has been valuable to me.

Among my classmates were Dr. John E. Hunger, physician and surgeon, Lexington, Kentucky; the Honorable Philip Dabney, publisher, Cincinnati, Ohio; P.T. Hiller, principal of the Governor Street School, Evansville, Illinois, and quite a number of lesser lights. And also, a young lady, the daughter of the lady with whom

I boarded when I first arrived in Oberlin. She had been a student at Oberlin and was a great help to me in my work. Had it not been for her, I am sure I would have never made the grade. This girl finally became my wife. She was a great inspiration to me, and we shared life's pilgrimage together for many years.

During this year, one incident occurred which I shall mention. My barbershop was upstairs on Main Street, and every evening, I would come down and sit in front of the harness shop. Jumping three jumps was my principal sport. A great many boys would congregate there, and we would jump three jumps to decide who was the best jumper. My nearest competitor was a young white man named Sam Partridge. He was called the bully of the town. We jumped for the championship, and I beat him. He said, "I did not beat him, and that no nigger could beat him doing anything." I went over to where he stood and told him not to repeat that remark again. If he did, I would show him that I could not only beat him jumping, but I could whip him. He said that I couldn't do that. And we began to battle.

I knocked him down, and when he got up, I rushed him again, and shortly, he fell again. Nearly all of the spectators were white, and while I was getting the best of him, my friends would cheer me and say, "Sock it to him!" And when he would get the better of me, his friends would cheer for him. We fought for some time in this manner. Finally, he saw a rock on the ground and grabbed it. At the same time, I grabbed his hand, threw him to the ground, took the rock out of his hand, and began to pummel him over the head and the face until he said, "Take him off." Had I been in Kentucky, they would have attempted to mob me. The citizens there were delighted to see a good fight. It made no difference to them who won, and they saw to it that everyone would have fair play. But before we left the scene, the town marshal arrested both of us, and we had to pay a small fine.

Relative to my experience in school for the first year, it was very discouraging. There was nothing in the work to give self-expression, and at any rate, nothing to make me feel that there was any future for me. The same routine every day, with its monotony from which came no inspiration, no hope of ever accomplishing my chosen work. My early training had been neglected. I had never finished the elementary grammar nor the elementary arithmetic. I knew the fundamental principles of arithmetic and also the parts of speech and grammar but did not know their applications. Therefore, I entered into a work which I should have completed before I entered the preparatory department. I blame the teachers for my plight. Had they given me a fair and impartial examination, they would have told me that I was not prepared to enter upon the work.

At the time of entering the department, I was 21 years of age, and the teachers, no doubt, thought that I would be able, by hard study, to finish the course in three years, when, in fact, they should have told me that I was not prepared to enter that grade and sent me to the Union School. Then I would have been ready for the college preparatory work and would have been able to have made the grade. It was very embarrassing to me, indeed, to feel that I was the dunce of the class. I simply give this advice to those whose training is limited, that he be sure he is prepared for the work you are going to pursue before you enter upon it.

This brings us up to the beginning of my second year in Oberlin. My work was somewhat easier than in the first year. After paying my tuition, I resolved that I would make a better grade than I did in the previous year, and by hard work and untiring effort, I did. I was elected catcher of our baseball team during my first year, made such a good impression as a catcher that I was elected catcher for the second year. We had a very good team. In the beginning of this term, Algebra was one of my studies, which was very difficult to me. I did my best to have good lessons, but I could not understand it.

My teacher reported me to Principal White, and the following day, I received a card from the principal to appear at his office at 9:00 a.m. I called, and when I got into his office, he said, "Mr. Stradford, I understand that you are spending the most of your time in playing baseball and failed to get our Algebra lesson. Mr. Andres says that you are able to get your lesson, but you spend too much of your time on the baseball ground."

I told him that I did not spend any more time playing ball than I had to spend. He rose from his seat in a passion and opened the door leading into his rear office and told me to go into it.

Then he said, "For your pert answer, I am going to suspend you indefinitely. You don't need to think that you can go blindfold through the world without striking a snag. You must thoroughly understand that you can't have your way. You must be subject to the rules and be courteous and obliging to your teachers and principal."

It had been prophesied by some of the wiseacres in Versailles that I would not be in school a year before I would be expelled. I did not want that prophecy to come true, so I begged him not to suspend me. I promised that in the future, I would get my algebra lesson and would always be careful in the use of my words, and if he would not suspend me, I would never give by conduct another occasion to be called on the carpet for any violation of the rules. I told him I was sorry for what I had said and asked his forgiveness. He forgave me, and I kept up with my work. I continued in my Algebra class for several weeks but finally had to give it up. In my other studies, I passed with fairly good grades.

When I entered Oberlin College, President Fairchild was the chief executive. He was a man of Godly appearance and abolitionist of the Abraham Lincoln type. His sympathy for our group was most pronounced. He was generous, kind, tolerant, affable and very polite. One of his principles was that he would never let anyone be more polite to him than he was to them. He wore a silk, beaver hat and a Prince Albert coat. He was one of the most polite men I have ever seen. Many a time, we would line up on the street on which he passed, and the first one he passed would raise his hat to him. He would take off his hat and graciously bow, and for a full block, we would keep him with hat in hand, bowing and smiling. He was also very accommodating. I remember during my second year in school, after my finances had been exhausted, I went to him and told him of my circumstances, and he made me a loan of $25.00. In addition to the loan, he gave me the benefit of the Avery Fund which was $7.00 per term. The tuition per term was $10.00, a $3.00 bonus to be subtracted from the regular fee. He was less void of prejudice than any I have ever been associated with. He was idolized by all the teachers and students. There are few men of this type living today.

When I went to him to borrow the $25.00, he was very much interested in my general welfare. He asked me from what source I got my support and how much it cost me to live per week. I told him from $0.60 to $0.75 per week. Doubting the accuracy of my statement, he took his scratch pad and had me to give a list of each article I used and the price I paid for it. He also had me to show him the receipts of my barber business and amount of rent I paid per month. After I had given him the information he asked for, he found that my statement was true.

He said, "Relative to your board, I can't see how you can live so cheaply. Relative to the other items you are using, the strictest economy." And he was satisfied that I would be able to meet my expenses, and if I should need him anymore, not to fail to call on him.

During this year, I had developed into a great baseball catcher and played first base on our club, which was the best in the preparatory department. At the close of the year, by hard work and untiring efforts, I had made quite an improvement in my work and was ready to enter the senior year with two studies short. My finances had fallen below par, and I was in a quandary to know how I could secure funds to enter into the work of the next year. I was advised by a friend of mine that Saratoga Springs, New York was a health resort and a great many people went there each year for health and pleasure and that as many as 40,000 or 50,000 people were there during the season and that I could make enough money there during the season to defray all of my expenses for the incoming year.

On his advice, I decided to go. I consulted the principal of the department, and he gave me permission to leave my classwork three weeks before commencement. I immediately sought work in Saratoga as a barber. I went into a shop near the town hall run by a man named John Woods. He was a very fine man, kind-hearted, sympathetic, and always ready to lend a hand. I told him my purpose and how hard I had labored to keep in school, and that

I had come to Saratoga to make money to pay my expenses for the coming year. I showed him a letter of recommendation from President Fairchild. I told him I was not a first-class barber but was willing to do anything that was necessary if he would help me to accomplish that end. He gave me a job in his shop. His shop consisted of four barber chairs and bathrooms complete, a very cozy shop, indeed. His head barber, Mr. Josh Boone, was a very fine barber and had a very good trade. I was placed under his direction.

The custom in the shop was that each barber kept the money he made, made his own change, and turned into the proprietor each night his receipts for the day. They were very kind to me, and whenever I got a hard job, they would always come to my assistance and show me just how to do the work, and many a time would take the razor or shears, as the case might be, out of my hand and finish the job for me. This was continued for several months, and I was glad to get the instructions. Things went along all right for a season. I had become a passable barber and gave a strict account of every cent I made on my chair. Mr. Boone did one-third more work on his chair every day than I did, but my receipts were more daily than his. He was a man who drank whiskey, and there was a saloon next door to the shop. He would go into the saloon a dozen times a day after each shave and take a drink whenever someone was not waiting for him to shave them.

Mr. Woods called his attention to that fact and seemed very dissatisfied about it. Boone became enraged at me and determined to make it so unpleasant for me that I would either quit the job or he would have fired me. So, he began to boss me, telling me what to do and how to do it. He would scrutinize my work very critically. He would come over to my chair when I was working on a customer, take the scissors or razor out of my hands very abruptly, and say, "You should do it this way or that way," as the case might be. Mr. Woods, the boss, had noticed his discourteous way of treating me and told him to treat me more humanly.

Disregarding the orders of the boss, he continued humiliating and insulting me. The boss did not stop him from interfering with me altogether because he had been in his employ for several years and controlled a greater part of the substantial trade of the shop. I was making good on my chair, was saving my money, and so I submitted to his insults and mistreatment because I was there for a purpose. When I went to work in the shop, I told them that I was not a first-rate barber and asked them to instruct me in what I was deficient in. They were very nice to me and were of great help to me. Mr. Woods had okayed my work and placed me on equality with the other barbers.

After I had been there for about three months and, knowing that I could do good work, I decided that I would not submit to insults and mistreatment any longer. One day, a customer came in and took my chair. While I was cutting his hair, Mr. Boone came over to my chair and attempted to take the scissors out of my hand to show me that I was not doing the job right. I objected to his doing so and told him that I did not need his assistance, and that I was tired of him making me feel so humiliated before the customers, and that if he ever repeated it again, I would give him a sound beating.

In the heat of the argument, Mr. Woods said, "Men, let peace and harmony prevail among you. We can't afford any fighting in this shop."

From that day until the season closed, I never had any more trouble with Boone.

In my quest for making money to defray my expenses in school for the next scholastic year, I denied myself all the pleasures afforded for the enjoyment of the visitors to the city. I shall mention some of the places of interest and also some things that happened while I was there. Saratoga is a beautiful little city in New York, about 40 miles north of Albany, the capital, and about 20 miles west of the Hudson River. It is noted as one of the greatest health resorts and also pleasure resorts in the United States. It is also noted for its mineral springs, the waters of which are shipped all over the United States for their medicinal purposes. The names of the leading waters are Congress, Hawthorne, High Hook and Vicky. At each of these springs, there were cups furnished to the public to drink as much as they wished of the different kinds of mineral water.

The principal public building was the town hall. Lake George was about seven miles east of the city, a very beautiful lake. The racetrack was at that time about the same distance from the city, and there was a most wonderful boulevard running out past the lake and also the racetrack. Mr. Vanderbilt, the owner of Maud S. and Aldine (horses) was there that season. And I had the pleasure of seeing him drive his famous team down that boulevard so fast that it made the hair stand on end. I had the pleasure of hearing a story told by a man who drove Dexter, the famous stallion, on that road when Vanderbilt drove past him with his famous pair. He said that he was going so fast that he would only see the dust that his team made when they passed him.

Another place of interest near Saratoga is Mount McGregor, a most beautiful place. There are a great many places of amusement and comfort on the summit of the mountain, hotel, dance pavilions, and a great many refreshment stands. General Grant died upon that mountain. I remember while standing at one of the stands, a little white boy with his parents approached me and asked me to whistle for him. When I told him I could not whistle, he was very much disappointed and told me he thought all Colored people could whistle.

During that summer, the Democratic State Convention which nominated Grover Cleveland for the presidency of the United States, met in Saratoga. I have never seen so fine a delegation of men in all my life. I don't think any of them were less than six feet and weighed less than 200 pounds.

This convention was held in the summer of 1884. Saratoga Springs had some of the largest hotels; in fact, at that time, the largest hotel in the United States, the Grand Union Hotel, and a score or more of other large hotels. The leading park was the Congress, in which nearly every night there would be a great display of fireworks. I have never seen such a gorgeous and magnificent display of fireworks in all my life. The illumination was grand and very attractive. Saratoga Springs was also a convention city. There was an average of three or four conventions each week. The city was thronged with visitors every day from all parts of the world. The first time I had ever met any Swedes; I shaved several of them who were from Christiana. They explained to me the difference between barbershops in Sweden and ours. In Sweden, the barber shaves the customer. Then the customer gets out of the chair and goes to the lavatory, washes his face and combs his hair, and then goes to the cashier and pays his bill. There were no porters or bootblacks in the shop.

At the close of the season, I had saved enough money to defray my expenses for the greater part of the ensuing year. I prepared to leave for Oberlin. On the morning of my departure, I went to the shop to bid all the barbers goodbye. Mr. Woods came up to me and said, "I hope you will be successful in all of your undertakings in life. I am almost certain that you will be. You are frugal, industrious, and honest, and have the ability to accomplish anything you undertake. You have my best wishes, and I really hope that you will have success through life." With this benediction, I bade them all farewell and boarded a train for Oberlin College.

The time I spent in Saratoga Springs was a school of experience for me. I found a few people who were in sympathy with a struggling student but were willing to give me all the necessary moral support in their power. But only a few were willing to give any financial support, and those who were able always had some excuse for not helping. I also learned in my struggles to prepare myself for future usefulness that it not only took untiring efforts and self-sacrifice, but a devotion to the work which equals the devotion which Ruth had for Naomi. I also found that true friends were few, and that temptations to depart from the path of rectitude were so numerous that it took a person with almost an iron will to resist. I also found that there are very few honest-to-God men, especially in dealing with their pocketbooks. The people of today are so materialistic, so greedy for gain, that they have lost sight of the spiritual side of life. The Golden Rule has been laid upon the shelf, and they have substituted, "Do others or they will do you."

As soon as I arrived in Oberlin, I paid my tuition and entered upon the work which was prepared for that term. It was not so difficult as it had been prior to this time. I had begun to feel at ease in the classrooms and was able to recite when called on. During this term, James G. Blaine, the plumed knight of Maine, was the Republican nominee for president of the United States. He came to Oberlin during his campaign and made a most wonderful speech advocating his candidacy. He knew and told us more about Oberlin than we knew. During this term, John B. Gough, of national fame as an orator, lectured to the citizens in the Second Congregational Church. He was indeed a master of the art of speech-making. He could sway his audience at his will. Sometimes they would laugh and then they would cry, and when he would go off on excursions of fancy and flight in oratory, our hair would stand on end, and we were wholly under his mesmeric spell.

I have listened to a great many of our noted speakers, among them J.G. Blaine, Benjamin Harrison, Mark Hanna, William McKinley, Albert J. Beveridge, and Robert J. Ingersoll, the agnostic. Not one of them ever approached him in the art. He was sublime, grand, forceful, and attractive. After two months of the term had elapsed, I received information from my father that he had secured a school for me to teach, and he wanted me to come at once to take charge of it. Knowing that I could not care for my father, who was declining, and continue in school, I decided to sever my connection with the school and go back to Kentucky and engage in the business of school teaching.

I left Oberlin on the evening of the 3rd of November 1884 and arrived in Versailles on the morning of the 4th of November 1884. My father and all the family were glad to see me and gave me a hearty welcome. On the following Friday, I took the teacher's examination and got a second-grade certificate to teach school.

The school in which I was employed to teach was one in which the children were so bad that they had run all of the teachers away from it. Most of them were large boys and girls who had curtailed their schooling on account of fighting their teachers. I was apprised of that fact, and I intended to meet the emergency. I opened the school on the following Monday morning. In the outset, I talked to the children, told them what I expected of them and that any violations of any of the rules would be met with severe punishment.

Our school opened at 9:00 a.m. and that meant 9:00 a.m., and not one minute after. If a pupil had a written excuse for not being there on time from his parents, I would excuse him. Several had come late intentionally and had been punished. The Trustee Board consisted of three trustees. One of them was the Chairman. His duty was to attend to the employment of the teacher, to prepare a place to teach the school, and to furnish fuel for said school. I boarded with the Chairman of the Board and his family, who were very courteous and kind to me. Two of his children had been the cause of several teachers leaving the school before their time expired. The boy was 17, weighed about 170 pounds, and was more than six feet in height. Our school was about one mile from his residence. The Chairman sent coal by his son to the schoolhouse to make a fire and clean up the schoolroom each morning.

The boy took the coal about halfway to the schoolhouse and placed it on a stone fence where I would have to pass in going to school. I never paid any particular attention to the sack when I got over the fence. When I got to the school, I found the children all around the stove shivering with cold. I then asked Jim where the coal was that his father had sent by him to the schoolhouse. He replied that he had carried it halfway and left it on the fence where we climbed over so that I could see it and that I could bring it the remainder of the distance. I told him to go immediately and get the coal. He said that he had carried it halfway and if I wanted the coal, to go after it myself.

    I told him it was his duty to obey the orders of his teacher and further said that he was too large for me to whip, and by his disobedience, he would ruin the decorum of the school. I didn't want to make an example of him and so I told him to either go and bring that coal or go home. He said he would neither go home nor get the coal. I advanced toward him. There was a piece of walnut fence panel which was used for a poker, laying on the floor. I intended to pick it up to use in making him leave the room. He was standing near the heating stove. The stove was about six feet high and had a very large base. Just as I attempted to pick up this poker, he started to reach for the large iron door laying on the floor. Seeing that I did not have time to get the poker before he got the door, just as he stooped over, I struck him in the temple with my fist and knocked him over one of the benches, jumped on him and beat his eyes and face into a jelly. When I finished beating him. I got up off of him, pulled him upon his feet and told him to turn on the fan. He was a little slow, and I kicked him as long as I could keep up with him. I succeeded in closing both of his eyes and his nose was bleeding profusely.

Chapter 6

The fact is that he was beaten very severely, so severely that he could scarcely find his way home. When he reached home, he found his mother and father there. When they saw his condition, they flew into a rage and said they were going over to the schoolhouse and kill me without asking the lad what it was all about. So, the father armed himself with an ax and the mother with a hoe, and they started for the schoolhouse. I was expecting them at any moment. Our school door was fastened with a latch, and the latch string hung on the outside. I pulled the string on the inside of the door and told the children if anyone came to the door, not to open it.

In a short time, they came and banged on the door and cried, "Stradford! Stradford! Open the door!"

I asked, "What do you want?"

And he repeated, "Open the door! Oh! Open the door! Oh, how you have beaten my boy."

I said to him, "If you want to reason about the matter, I will open the door. If not, my advice to you is to leave that door at once."

He said he wanted to know just what caused the trouble and was willing to reason over the matter. I then opened the door, and as soon as the door flew open, his wife cried in a loud, excited voice, "Kill him, Jim!"

I said to her in a low, firm voice, "Don't be excited, madam. If any killing is to be done, I will have a hand in it."

Mr. Johnson told his wife to keep quiet and then asked me to state the facts in the case. I told him just what happened, and he asked the boy was that statement true, and he said it was.

"Well," he said, "There was nothing else for you to do."

Then he took that piece of fence railing, made the boy get down on his knees and put his head between his legs and gave him an unmerciful beating. His mother cried and begged for him, but to no avail. His father whipped him until he thought he had punished him sufficiently. They left for home and took the boy with them. He never attended school after, and I never had any trouble after that. All of the pupils who had been fighting their teachers became as lambs, and my orders were obeyed by all of them. At the time of this incident, I was boarding with this family, and the mother was the cook. She treated me so differently that on the following day, I changed my boarding place against the wishes of the father.

During this term, one of the saddest incidents of my life occurred to me. My father, who had arrived at the age of 71 years, became ill and after lingering a few weeks, died of paralysis of the throat. One Friday afternoon, when I came in from school, he called me to his bedside and said, "I am going to die, and I want to tell you something I want you to do for me."

I ignored the statement and said, "You're not going to die soon. You will live for five years yet, and I don't wanna talk to you on that subject. I know you will be better by next Friday, and then you may tell me what you want me to do."

On the following morning, I left for my school, and when I returned on the following Friday afternoon, his tongue was paralyzed.

I said, "Oh! Father, speak to me and tell me what you want me to do," but there came no response. And with a wistful look, he turned his head. I shall never forget the expression on his face when he turned his head away from me. And from that day until this, I have regretted in the greatest degree that I did not permit him to tell me what he had in mind to tell me. Oh, if I could have called back time in its flight and let him tell me what he wanted me to do, of all men, I would have been the most happy. On the following evening, January 1, he gave up the ghost and died [he passed onto the world beyond].

At that time, the State of Kentucky provided five months of school for the pupils, and when the time expired, we had to find something else to do. My father had taught me how to garden, so as soon as my school closed, I secured several gardens to cultivate on shares, and I worked faithfully to make a good crop. The principal products of my gardens were corn, beans, tomatoes, potatoes, and onions. It was a very favorable crop year, and I made enough out of my half to supply the household and sold quite a quantity of the vegetables to neighbors. I remember I sold Irish potatoes at $.25 per bushel. These are articles I peddled from house to house.

During my vacation, I made many inquiries relative to getting employment for the ensuing scholastic year. Having had several propositions, I selected the one which was the most lucrative. I had gone to Lawrenceburg, Anderson County, Kentucky, and found that the number of children of school age in that district was 325, and the pro rata for each child was $2.45. The Trustees made a contract with me to teach the school for nine months and furnish the house, or in other words, to pay the rent for the house in which I taught. After having secured this contract, I returned home, very much satisfied and prepared to take up my work on the 15th of September 1885. One of the considerations of the contract was that I should make a first-grade certificate.

On a later date, I went back to Lawrenceburg on the day of the examination and secured a first-class certificate. At the appointed time, I took up my work as principal of said school. My salary was $70.00 per month, which was a great deal more than the average teacher. And I was delighted indeed, above measure, to know that I had secured such a lucrative job. I felt that I would soon be able to marry my future wife, whom I had met at Oberlin. I felt that I was on the road to wealth and happiness. Lawrenceburg, the County seat of Anderson County, was not only noted for its bad men—it was the home of the Witherspoon's, Portwood's and the Bond's—but it was also noted for its many distilleries and the celebrated whiskey which was made in that county, namely, McBrayer, Bond and Lillar, T.B. Ripy, Dowling and Old Frazier and many other brands of good whiskey. The chief industry of the county was distilling whiskey. Most every family kept a jug of whiskey for their own consumption and would give their children toddies every Sunday morning. I never saw a drunken child, and very seldom ever saw a drunken woman.

In addition to my school, I had a barbershop which I operated. Each evening after school, I would go to the barbershop and look after the business. I not only became acquainted with the leading citizens of the city but had business dealings with quite a few of them. During my dealings with them, I found out the real feeling which they had for our group. They say that a Negro has no rights they are bound to respect and act in all their dealings with him. So long as a member of our group keeps his place, they say, he is a good nigger. Whenever he asserts his manhood and demands the treatment of a man, they say that he is a bad nigger. From my earliest existence up until the present, I have always known that I had rights that everyone had to respect. And during my boyhood, I fought any boy in the town who violated any of my rights, regardless of color or race.

Not only in my boyhood did I fight for my rights, but all through my life I have demanded my rights at all times, under great disadvantages at times. I have often wondered how I have escaped the assassin's bullet. But the man who fights in the right is not as liable to be hurt as a man who fails to take his part. No man will deliberately put his hand into the lion's mouth. My first year in Lawrenceburg, I operated a barbershop in Tyrone, a small town on the Kentucky River, 4-1/2 miles from Lawrenceburg. My brother operated it through the week, and on Saturday morning, I would go down and assist him. There were several saloons there. The citizens were mostly roughnecks and very oppressive to our group.

After closing the shop at noon on Sunday, my brother and I stopped in Gus's Saloon to get good and warm before starting for home in Lawrenceburg. It was a very cold day. In the rear of the room, there was a large coal stove, at least six feet high, and the diameter was at least two feet. There was a frame built around it, four inches high and five feet square, filled with sawdust in which to expectorate. I was standing within this frame.

A very tall white man came into the saloon about half drunk and walked over to where I was standing and deliberately stepped on my foot and said, "How do you like that, Mr. Nigger?"

I immediately, in return, stepped on his foot. He pulled out his large hog-bill pocketknife, and I reached for my razor. I had wrapped all of my razors up and put them in my suitcase and did not have one in my pocket as I thought. When I found that he had me, I threw up both hands and said, "Don't do anything rash. I was just playing with you. You white folks always start something and the first to get mad."

He kicked me several times and said, "You black impotent S.B., I ought to kill you," and made me leave the room.

My brother and I left for home. Sometime after that occurrence, I had moved my barbershop to Lawrenceburg. One Saturday night, that same white man came up to Lawrenceburg to have a good time. He met some boys there who knew me, and he told them that he knew me and brought them in to see me, saying that I knew him.

I said, "Yes, I know you, but I don't know any good of you," and immediately, I drew my razor from my vest pocket, drew on him and began to beat him up. I reminded him of what he had done to me and dared him to raise his hand. I beat him until I got tired and made him run up the street. The boys of our group, who saw me beat him, became very much affrighted and said that I would surely be lynched. But he never came back, although he told me he would get even with me.

A few months after this occurrence, I received a telegram notifying me of the death of my grandfather, whose residence was in Versailles, Kentucky, about 11-1/2 miles from Lynchburg. In going to Versailles, I had to go through Tyrone. Tyrone was the home of the man, James, whom I had beaten. There was only one straight road that I could take to go to Versailles. I hesitated for a while as to whether I would go to the funeral on account of fearing that I would meet the man. Finally, I decided that I would go. I hired a horse and buggy, drove it back and got my wife. Before starting, I laid my six-shooter on the seat by my side so that if I should meet him, I would have some protection. Tyrone was situated in the river bottom, and the main road ran alongside the cliff.

The night before, there had been a storm, and a large tree had been blown down across the road. When I arrived at this place, I had to get out of the buggy and lead the horse by the bridle. The ground was so inclined that I had to be very careful, or the buggy would turn over. Just as I got out of the buggy and led the horse by the stump of the tree, to my amazement there stood this man, James, with an ax in his hand. I jumped around on the other side of the horse, but to my utter surprise, he did not say a word to me. A few months after that, he got into some serious trouble and absconded, and that ended all fear from that source.

When I took charge of that school in 1885, the people of our group in Lawrenceburg were very backward. You seldom ever saw a Colored man escorting his wife on the street. And they seldom ever sat with their wives in church. It was an unheard-of thing for them to have baby buggies and take their children out for a ride in them. I remember one incident which occurred in connection with taking my children for a buggy ride. It was our custom to take our children out every morning and evening for a ride in their buggy.

I was met in a grocery store by a white man named Hanks, who cursed me because I had my children out for a ride in their buggy and said, "You black son-of-a-B. You must think you are as good as white people."

I did not answer him, but said to the grocer, "Mr. Ottenheimer, who is this man?"

He said, "Pay no attention to him. He's drunk. He is drunk."

I told him that I did not feel that his condition would justify him in speaking as he had to me, but he still insisted that I should pay no attention to what he said. I took his advice and left the store, but not before I told Hanks not to repeat the same thing again.

A few days after that, I was out early one morning with my children in their buggy. I met this same man in front of the Arthur Hotel. He cursed me again and called me all the vile names he could think of. Mr. Arthur came out of the hotel and told him he ought not to treat me in such a way.

He said, "That nigger thinks he is as good as white people and should be run out of town."

Then I said to him, "If you think you can run me out of town, you had better try it."

At that time, he started for me. Just as he got within arm's reach of me, I struck him on the chin as hard as I ever struck a man in my life, and he fell to the ground like a rock. The blood gushed from his nose, almost as profusely as pouring coffee out of a coffee pot. He failed to get up. I immediately took my children and went into my house, which was across the street from the hotel. I closed the front door, expecting every minute to be assaulted by a mob. Mr. Arthur helped him up and took him in the office and washed the blood from his face and clothes. He said that he was going over to my house and kill me. Mr. Arthur told him not to go over there, for I was a bad nigger and would surely kill him if he did so. He took Mr. Arthur's advice, and I was never interfered with by him since that time.

    I will record an incident which will show how little respect the average white man in the South has for our group. At that time, there were no respectable houses which Negroes could secure for homes. And so, I decided to buy a lot and build a residence. A white man, McGinnis, had a lot for sale that was just the lot I wanted. It was beautifully located, the size or dimensions of it 75 x 200 feet. I consulted him about the price of it, and he agreed to sell it to me for $300.00—$150.00 cash and payments of $25.00 each, with interest until paid. After I had made several payments, he came to me and asked me to pay him $25.00 before the next note was due. I told him if he would give me a receipt for the money so that I could apply it on the next note, I would let him have it. He said I did not need a receipt for the money, that he would credit the note for $25.00.

    But I contended for a receipt. He asked me if I doubted his word, and I told him that I would not give him the money unless he gave me a receipt showing that it was to be applied on the next note due in the bank. And I also said, "If you wanted to do the right thing, you would not ask me to advance you $25.00 unless you were giving me assurance that it would be returned. I see you are trying to beat me out of the money, but I will never let you do it." He replied that no nigger should doubt a white man's word. I warned him not to call me a nigger. He said I ought to be strung up and that any nigger that would talk to a white man that way—

I did not give him time to finish his sentence before I had knocked him down and stamped him under my feet. I left him lying on the ground.

It was some time before I saw him after that incident. I was not arrested for the assault, and before I finished paying him for the lot, we were on friendly terms. He never mentioned anything about that occurrence, although I carried my pistol every day to protect myself from any injury which he might attempt to inflict upon me.

My first year in Lawrenceburg was a very agreeable one. The schoolwork was very delightful. My association with the children in the schoolroom and on the playground was very congenial. I loved all of my pupils, and they loved me. On the playground, I played every game they played and beat them at each of them—marbles, tops, running, jumping, and baseball. And when the bell rang to take up school, perfect order prevailed in the room. We taught that punctuality was the key to success and that cleanliness was next to Godliness. In those days, the parents seemed to be glad to get rid of their children by sending them to school, and very seldom prepared them to meet their teacher in a tidy manner. They would send them to school without combing their hair, some ragged and dirty.

I made it my duty to remedy this condition. When a child came to school ragged or dirty, I would send him home and tell him to tell his parents or guardian to patch his clothes or put on a clean waist and wash his hands and face. I bought a comb and brush, and when any of the pupils came to school without combing their hair, I would comb it for them, and I would comb it so hard that in a great many instances, they would cry bitterly. And I soon had all of the pupils coming to school with their hair combed and their clothes cleaned and patched. And those who were able had their shoes shined. The appearance of the pupils was improved 100 percent. They were not only improved in their appearance but also in their intellectual qualifications.

My first object was to teach the child how to think, and I would use the methods which would bring about that condition regardless of his book lessons. We had a very few dumbbells in our school. The relationship which existed between me and the children was most cordial, but I could not get along with the parents very well, especially those who wanted to boss the teacher. I made them know I was the boss of my school and allowed no one to dictate the manner in which I governed the school. But on account of my instruction to the children, I was considered a very proficient teacher and was very popular as a teacher.

I was strict in having all the rules of the school obeyed, and the examples which I placed before the children by my right way of living were worthy of emulation, not only by the pupils, but also by the community at large.

Corporal punishment was a part of the curriculum of the school, and the teacher was at liberty to use any method he saw fit to employ. In a great many cases, the method used depended upon the size and sex of the pupil. On one occasion, I had a large girl pupil who was very obstreperous and thought nothing of disobeying the rules of the school. I tried in every conceivable way to get her to obey the rules without inflicting or whipping her, but to no avail. One morning, I called her to me and told her that when school dismissed at noon to remain in her seat and not go out for recess. After all the children had gone out, I called her to me and told her I was going to punish her for what she had done. She said she did not care how much I whipped her, if I did not whip her on the palm of her hand, in other words, in her hand. I told her that was just the place I was going to whip her.

So, I took my strap from my pocket and gave her several pretty hard licks on the palm of her hand, which proved very injurious. Her hand swelled considerably from the effect of the licks. She failed to come to school in the afternoon. When her father came from work that night, she told him of what had happened and showed him her swollen hands. He became very indignant about the matter and said that he was going to kill me at first sight. And for that purpose, he did not go to work the following morning. The Chairman of the Board of Trustees, Matt Ellison, heard of his threats. He went to see him and tried to persuade him not to carry out his threats, but he was firm in his determination to do so. Finding that he could not change him in his determination to kill me, he came down to my house and apprised me of the facts. He advised me to leave town as soon as I could get away. He further said that Charlie Ambrose was a bad man and told me of several men he had killed and that he would surely carry out his threat.

I said to him, "As Chairman of the Trustee Board, I think you ought to report this matter to the city authorities and have this man arrested. If I have him arrested, he will think I am afraid of him and would cause me a great deal of trouble in the management of my school." He further told me that the irate man was leaning on the gatepost in front of his house with his double-barreled shotgun by his side and said that as soon as I pass by, he was going to kill me. I remonstrated with the Chairman to go report it at once to the proper authorities so that I could go to take up school on time, but to no avail. He said he did not want to see me killed and advised me to leave town. Finding that my pleading fell on deaf ears, I said to him, "Wherever duty calls me, I had never failed to obey its call. Charlie Ambrose, you say, is standing between me and my duty with a shotgun to take my life when I get within shooting distance. No man, by threat or coercion, can swerve me from my duty."

It was now time for me to start for school, and regardless of consequences, I was going to my post. My wife begged me not to go, but it had no effect on me. I went to the dresser drawer, took out my 39 Smith & Wesson Revolver, put it in my pocket, and started to go to school. The man's, Charlie Ambrose's, residence was between my home and the schoolhouse, and I had to pass his house which was across the street from me. When I approached his house, I saw him standing at the gate in front of his house with his shotgun by his side. I reached for my gun and was ready for the fray. He never attempted to move an inch from the position which he occupied when I passed by him. He did not say anything to me, nor did I say anything to him. This matter passed without further interruption, and the girl in a few days came back to school and was much more dutiful in her work and also in obeying the rules.

I also had at my school a boy by the name of Dick Harris, who was the most disobedient pupil I had ever come in contact with. He was never in harmony with any of the rules. He was not only disobedient, but he would fight the other pupils and keep up a continual disturbance among them. I considered the matter of expelling him, but his parents were so anxious for him to continue in school that I dismissed it from my mind and decided to retain him in school and use every drop of energy to make a good boy of him.

Prior to this time, I had punished him several times, very severely, but it seemed not to make any change in him. He played truant several times, and it was my duty to round up the truants. One afternoon, I called his home to find out from his parents why he had not been to school. They said he had taken his books every morning and started for school, and at noon would come in to lunch and would immediately start for school after school was over. They regretted it very much and turned him over to me to whip him for his conduct. On the following morning, he came to school, and that day he was a model pupil. At the close of the school, I kept him, and, to his surprise, I lectured him, and he promised that he would never play truant again, and if he did, he said that I could whip him as much as I liked.

In the following week, he played truant again, and I decided to give him a second whipping. When I began to whip him, he showed fight, but I soon convinced him that I was the better man. He told me during the time I was whipping him that if he ever lived to be a man, he was going to whip me. Years afterwards, I went back to Lawrenceburg on a visit. This young man had reached the years of maturity and was a fine-looking fellow. He was about the first one I met after landing there. He was so very glad to see me that he seemed to go mad with joy on account of my presence in Lawrenceburg.

After we had finished shaking hands and sharing other formalities, I said to him, "Dick, you are a man now. Do you remember you said that if you ever got to be a man, you were going to whip me? Are you ready now?" He walked all around me and looked me over carefully and said he was not quite ready to undertake it. He had grown to be a very useful man in the community and said to me, "If it had not been for teachings by precepts and by example, I would have gone to the penitentiary years ago." He praised me and extolled me to the highest and said that I had been his salvation.

The relationship which existed between me and the superintendent of the schools was of the most friendly nature. I did his barbering, and my work pleased him very much. He recommended my work to his friends, and it was quite a financial help to me, and I appreciated it very much. This day in question, he brought one of his friends in for me to shave. The man wore a silk half-stove-pipe hat, a Prince Albert coat, and patent leather shoes; he was dressed in the height of fashion. He was about five feet six inches tall, weighed about 180 pounds, and his hair was red. The superintendent left the shop and told him he would be back by the time I had finished him. I took his hat and coat and hung them on the rack. He got in my chair, and I prepared to shave him.

Just as I had finished lathering him, my wife came into the shop and asked me for $5.00. I gave it to her. After she had gone, my customer said to me, "Barber, who is that woman?"

And I said, "My wife."

He said, "Don't kid me. Who is that woman?"

I emphasized my answer, "She is my wife."

He said, "Can I see her tonight?"

I told him that I was in the trading business and that if he had a wife or a mother or a daughter he wanted to trade, I would trade with him.

He answered in a very indignant manner, "Nigger, to whom are you talking?"

I snatched the breast cloth and towel off his breast, took his hat and coat, and threw them out on the sidewalk, and he went with them. He asked me to let him come back and wash the lather from his face. I refused to let him come in and told him if he came back in, I would kill him. He took his hat and coat and left the scene.

The superintendent came back in due time. I told him what had transpired. He said that he was very surprised. He had no thought that his friend would be guilty of such unbecoming conduct for a man of his ability and standing. Openly, he took no sides with me while in my presence, but that occurrence caused his friendship for me to wane. The interesting meetings and friendly conversations which we used to have were at an end, and the kindly favors which he had bestowed upon me were of the past. I mention this incident to prove that blood is thicker than water. Had I been a white man, he would have complimented me for my action, and no doubt would have said that I should have killed him.

Caste, the bane of American civilization, has placed a wall of prejudice in the hearts of the white man against the black man which seemingly is insurmountable. The brotherhood of man and the fatherhood of God is in his estimation only for white people.

Finding myself at the head of a family and the principal of a school, I was very desirous of bringing up my family in the fear and admonition of the Lord. I was not sure on what denomination in which to cast my lot. All my people were connected with the Baptist denomination, and my father was very anxious for me to join his church. By the way, he named me for a Baptist preacher, the one who came preaching in the wilderness of Judea, saying, "Repent ye, for the kingdom of Heaven is at hand." To do justice to myself and to the cause, I desired to repent. I felt that I should give the matter a thorough investigation. In pursuance of this purpose, I read studiously the creeds, disciplines, and foundations of quite a few denominations. I found only one in my judgment that I could consciously subscribe to on the terms of the New Testament structure, and that was the Christian Church. In other words, the Church of Christ.

After having decided to live a life for Christ, I began to attend the Christian Church. Each Sunday morning and evening, I attended church for several months for the purpose of learning what was required of me in order that I might be saved. My teachers had been saying that it was necessary for one to become a Christian to go to the mourner's bench and pray to God that He might forgive your sins in order that I might become a Christian.

In all my investigations, I could not find that teaching in the Bible, but I did find four places where the question was asked, "What shall I do to be saved?" And in each instance, the answer came quick and plain. Paul, on his way to Damascus to persecute the Christians, asked that question. The answer was, "Go down to Damascus and see Ananias, and he will tell you what to do." Ananias said to him, "Be baptized," and he was baptized.

Another time, the question was asked on the day of Pentecost. After hearing the story of Jesus, they had faith in it. They repented of their sins and were baptized in the Name of Jesus Christ and received the gift of the Holy Ghost, and 3,000 were added to the church the same day. Another instance was Phillip and the Eunuch. In the case of the Eunuch, his faith in Christ came by hearing the story of Christ. He repented and was baptized. The fourth was the conversion of the jailer. After he attempted to take his life by falling upon his sword, Paul cried with a loud voice saying, "Do thyself no harm, for we all are here." Finding the prisoners all there, he came in trembling and fell down before Paul and Silas and, after bringing them out, said, "Sirs, what must I do to be saved?" And they said, "Believe in the Lord Jesus Christ and thou shalt be saved, and thy house." And, washing their stripes, he took them into his house the same hour of the night, and spoke unto him, and the words of the Lord, and all that were in his house were baptized.

In support of my finding, I found the plan of salvation which I feel is the only true way by which sinners may come to Christ, and that is, faith, repentance, confession, and baptism. After my investigation, I still continued to attend church, but it was a hard matter for me to make a final stand to accept Christ. One Sunday evening, the pastor preached a most eloquent sermon, one which clearly convinced me that Jesus had died for me and that I was a sinner and in need of his loving kindness to redeem me from under the curse of the broken law. Soon the choir began to sing the invitation song: "Why do you wait, dear Brother, why do you tarry so long? Your Savior is waiting to give you a place in His sanctified throng. Why not come to Him now?"

I arose from my seat and said, "I will go." I tottered up the aisle to the front seat. I gave the preacher my right hand and

God my heart and made the good confession and was baptized into Christ. I turned about face, ceased to work for the devil, and began to work for Christ, and continued steadfast for a season. My wife also accepted Christ and became a leading worker for the cause. She was elected president of the Christian CWBM and the leader of the church choir. I was chosen as a deacon for the interest we took in the church work. We were called the pillars of the church, and we reared our children under Christian influences.

The life we lived in the community had its effect for good, not only upon the sinners, but also on all whom we came in contact with, and we made the community better on account of our living there in it.

Another incident which I feel is worthy of mention. At the outset, I said Lawrenceburg was noted for its bad men. My barbershop was located on Main Street in the business section of the town. There was no exit in the rear. On the night before this incident, the town marshal and Wick Bond, a saloon keeper, had engaged in a heated argument on account of an arrest made by the marshal of Wick Bond. In the course of the argument, Bond abused the marshal and told him to prepare for the fray because he was going to kill him. The marshal told him he was not armed. Bond told him to go and get ready, for the furor was going to fly before that time tomorrow night. The marshal left the scene, went home, and stayed there the balance of the night. On the following morning, about ten o'clock, Dr. Witherspoon and the marshal were having quite a heated conversation across the street in front of Bond's saloon.

Bond came out of Dr. Witherspoon's office, adjoining my shop, and said, "Give it to him, Doctor! Give it to him! G-damn him!"

The marshal said, "You can't give it to me," and when he spoke, he drew his .45-caliber revolver and emptied its six bullets into the body of Wick Bond.

His brother, Jeff, who was tending bar at that time, heard the shots and came to the door. He saw the marshal leaving the scene, and he rushed back into the saloon to get his Winchester rifle, but just as he got back, the marshal went into his house. During the shooting, I was in my barbershop. There was no back door for me to get out, and I was so excited that I tried to break a hole in the back wall to get out.

After the sound of the shooting died away, I rushed to the door. I met Wick Bond at the door. He leaned against the side of the door, eased himself down on the pavement, and said, "Take my boots off. I don't want to die with them on."

They took him into the doctor's office, but in a few minutes, he was dead. There was no prosecution, not even an arrest. This ended the life of one of the most dangerous men in Lawrenceburg, Kentucky, a man who had no respect for our group. Many a picnic our group had given, which he had attended and caused consternation to rule supreme by shooting out the lights at night, or by day, shooting among them and running them and scattering them like birds and breaking up the gatherings. We were all glad to hear of his death; not a word of sympathy or a feeling of sorrow was expressed for his passing, not even members of his own race regretted his passing.

There lived in Versailles, Kentucky, a family of people identified with our group. No one who did not know them could tell that they were Colored people. I had known them all of my life. Our family and theirs were on very friendly terms. When I went to Lawrenceburg to live, there were no railroads between Versailles and Lawrenceburg, and every Monday morning, I would walk from Versailles to Lawrenceburg, a distance of 11 miles, to open school by nine o'clock. At the close of school on Friday evening at four o'clock, I would have to walk back to Versailles until I moved my family to Lawrenceburg to live. The Louisville Southerner, a corporation under the promotion of Bennett Young, built a railroad running from Louisville to Lexington, by way of Lawrenceburg, a distance of 80 miles. When that road was completed, there was no separate coach law in the State of Kentucky.

I was elected a delegate to the Republican State Convention at Louisville, Kentucky. On the morning of the opening convention, I boarded the train for Louisville. I went into the lady's coach and saw a member of the Craig family. When she saw me, she beckoned for me to come and sit with her, and so I did. Dr. Owen Witherspoon was on the same train going to Louisville. He saw me when I sat in the seat with this supposedly white woman and chatted with her all the way to Louisville. Little did I think that I was offending anyone because this woman was one of our group. Dr. Witherspoon thought she was a white woman and became very indignant at me.

The following Saturday, after returning home, he came to my shop after tanking up whiskey. With his six-shooter in his hand, he abused me in the most violent manner. He said, "You must think you are as good as white folks. I saw you sit yourself in a seat with a white woman on the train."

Chapter 7

"You black S.O.B. If she was anything to me, I would kill you."

I tried to explain to him that the woman was classed with our group. He would not let me talk and told me if I uttered another word, he would kill me. After he had finished abusing me and had gone out of the shop, I explained to the other customers, but on account of his attitude toward me, feelings ran very high against me. And there were rumors of a necktie party, but, happily, they passed away. He was so bitterly against me that he circulated a petition asking for a separate coach law in the state, and during the next session of the legislature, the measure was made law by an act of the legislature.

Another incident I shall recall which shows the status of our group in the South: there was a white farmer in Shelby County, adjoining our county, who had in his employment a Colored man who had worked for him for many a year. He helped his wife to do her household work, such as cooking and all other things around the house. On account of their constant association for a number of years, an affinity grew up between them that caused the husband some uneasiness. Whenever he left home, he would leave his wife and everything in charge of his hired man. One day after he had gone from home, he returned unexpectedly and found his wife in the embrace of her servant. She cried rape when she saw him, and the Colored man ran for his life.

The alarm was given, and a posse was formed to lynch him. They scoured the country in every direction, hunting for him. By dusk, he had made his way about 25 miles from the scene. They caught him near Lawrenceburg, put him in jail, and it was rumored that they were going to lynch him that night. Our group was very much excited over the affair. Some of them left home that night and went out in the woods for safety. I did not get excited but was determined to see the lynching. I lived about 100 yards from the jail and could see the jail very plainly, and anyone who was there. I concealed myself about 100 feet from the jail in order to see those who took part in the lynching.

About 12:00 a.m., the crowd began to gather. There were no more than a dozen men. They went to the jail, unlocked the door, and quietly took their prisoner out. They went north on Main Street, and I followed. I knew nearly every man in the mob. On account of the threats they had made against me, I decided it was best for me to go back home. They took him about one mile from Lawrenceburg and hung him to a tree, and posted the inscription, "Nigger, beware of insulting white women."

The following morning, he was cut down and brought to the undertaker's office. His neck was not broken. He had died from strangulation. I have never seen a tongue as large as his was in all of my life, nor did I think it possible for a man's tongue to be so large. It protruded out of his mouth for at least eight inches, and it looked as large as a beef tongue. The verdict of the coroner's jury was that he came to his death by unknown hands. And I knew nearly every man who was a party to the crime. They had buried him in the Potter's Field. Not a soul was there to shed a tear, no loving relative or friend to put a wreath of flowers on his grave. Consternation reigned supreme in the hearts of our group, fearing that at any time a like fate would befall some other innocent party of our group. No investigation was made, no warrant issued for the guilty parties, and no arrests made. Why? The inescapable verdict, "He was nothing but a nigger."

In this wonderful country of ours, where they teach us to sing, "My country 'tis of thee, sweet land of liberty, of thee I sing," and whichever way I look, I can see members of our group hanging on trees, hunted like wild beasts, and shot down like dogs for trivial offenses. In most cases, the officers of the law are leading the mob or condoning, intimidating, coercing, debauching, and raping our women, murdering men of our group about our own women, burning men and women at the stake, suspending business and declaring a holiday when the governor of a state grants extradition papers for the return of one who they claim is guilty of a crime, to mob, burn or crucify him! This sweet land of ours, where the Constitution declares that every man, regardless of color or previous condition of servitude, is entitled to certain inalienable rights. The rights of life, liberty, and the pursuit of happiness. Every man who is elected to any public office takes a solemn oath, an appeal to God that he will enforce the laws of the land.

President Hoover took that oath, and is he enforcing the law? I say, "No!" If he says he is, he is a liar, and the truth is not in him.

If the Fourteenth and Fifteenth Amendments to the Constitution are bad laws, why does he not say to Congress, they are bad laws and should be repealed, and see to it that they are enforced until they are repealed? The fact is, he is not big enough. He is guilty of perjury and should be tried for the crime of perjury. He is a party to every crime in which life is taken by mob violence in the United States. The governor of each state is equally guilty with Hoover. The sheriff of each county and the chief of police of each city are equally guilty. If every officer of the law would do his sworn duty in the execution of the law, mob law and violence from now on would be of no effect in this country. No man or group of men who know that they are in danger of their lives being taken from them, will attempt to take the law into their own hands to redress some private injury or public wrong.

In 1895, when William McKinley was governor of the State of Ohio, a mob was formed in Washington Courthouse for the purpose of mobbing a man of our group. On the day in question, McKinley was billed to address the Republican State Convention, held in Liederkranz Hall, Louisville, Kentucky. He cancelled that date and said that the fair name of the state of Ohio would never be tarnished by mob law while he was governor of the state. He forthwith ordered out the Militia and went in person with it to the scene of the disorder. When he arrived there, he found the mob attempting to storm the jail. He ordered them to halt, but they did not pay any attention to the command. He ordered the Militia to shoot over their heads and still the mob continued to advance. Then he said, "Shoot to kill," and they did. A great many were killed and wounded, and the remainder of them who could, scampered away to places of safety.

The following year, William McKinley was elected President of the United States. If the law enforcement officers would follow his example, this would be one of the greatest countries on earth. But here is the great enigma. Why do they say of our group, "You are the law violators, you are bad, per se?" Why do they tell us to be good citizens, stop lying, stealing chickens, watermelons, etc., when they are committing greater crimes every day? They unlock the cells of the prisons for fees and turn the most dangerous criminals scot-free to continue their nefarious practices and care nothing for sin or crime in their greed for filthy lucre.

This country is paving the way to its downfall. It may not come from without, but it is sure to come from within unless a miracle changes its course. Instead of teaching equality and goodwill to all men in order that we shall all be united in peace and harmony, and should danger come from without, we would, without a dissenter, march boldly to the fray as one man and eject the invader from our gates. But the house is divided against itself and can't stand. Our God-given rights have been taken away, the rights of life, liberty, and the pursuit of happiness.

Our political rights are abridged, and we feel the effects of it to such an extent that we would welcome the enemy from without and would turn traitor at the first opportunity to avenge our oppressors. We fought in World War I for universal democracy, and when we returned, many of our boys were killed in cold blood because they wore the suit which Uncle Sam gave them to wear to fight for the benefit of democracy. Uncle Sam sits passively by and condones it. The Ku Klux Klan and the Black Shirts, outlaw organizations, organized for the purpose of regulating the affairs of government by inflicting summary punishment upon those whom they will or may, without due process of law, deny the citizens the enjoyment of their civil and political rights. And Uncle Sam places his okay on what they do by not seeing to it that the majesty of the law is obeyed.

The 18th Amendment to the Constitution has divided the people of this country to the extent that they are at daggers point against each other. Agitation is great, and feelings are as intense between the opposing factions as it was before and during the Civil War. If this animus continues, no doubt, it will precipitate a greater war than that of the rebellion.

Another danger which lurks at our door is the doctrine of communism. Red Russia is circulating its propaganda, not only in this country, but in nearly every country of any importance on the globe, and to great effect. It sounds good to me, and I am welcoming the time when this country shall be subdued, and a new regime shall take over the reins of government and give to every man his equal rights before the law. And one would be just as secure in the enjoyment of those rights on the Southern banks of the Mississippi as he would be on the Merrimac River. Caesar had his Brutus, Napoleon, his Cromwell, George III, his colonies, and Uncle Sam will have his Reds. And our group will have its rights as other citizens.

During my stay in Lawrenceburg, I was engaged in several sidelines. My residence lot was about 200 feet long and 60 feet wide. I had a fine garden in which I raised more than enough vegetables to feed my family. I also raised hogs on the back end of my lot and every year, I would kill several hogs which furnished enough meat and lard for my family for the ensuing year. In addition to those enterprises, I had a barbershop which was a paying venture. Financially, I was very successful. I paid for my house and lot and also the furniture which adorned the house, which was first class. And above all, my wife was the best-dressed woman of our group in Lawrenceburg, and I was very proud of that fact.

At the end of my fifth year of teaching in Lawrenceburg, I had a call to a better-paying position in Shelbyville, Kentucky. I resigned my position in Lawrenceburg and took up the work in Shelbyville as principal of the school. Things were not so rosy in Shelbyville. The man who preceded me, M. H. Vaughan, was a very able teacher, but for some reason I can't recall, had become unpopular among the patrons and several complaints had been preferred against him. When the time came to make the appointments, two of the trustees voted against him, and that relieved him of his position. The superintendent was his friend and used his influence to retain him in his position, but to no avail. I was elected in his place. I found the fight had extended to the children. Those who favored Vaughan, especially those in the eighth grade, were very unruly, insulting, and obstreperous.

On account of the discord and animus which the superintendent and the former teacher had against me for having accepted the position, they plotted to revoke my certificate on the grounds of incompetency and reinstate the former teacher. In furtherance of this plot, the superintendent employed the former teacher to conduct the Teachers Institute, which lasted five days. The conductor of the Institute arranged the program for the meeting and assigned me the subject of higher mathematics. When my subject was called for discussion, before entering upon it proper, I spoke briefly on the subject of primary arithmetic, which had been presented by one of the other teachers. I criticized the way she had presented it in failing to observe the variation of the signs. For example, (3 + 4 + 7), (3 - 4 + 2 = 7), (5 + 4 + 6 = 15), (10 + 6 (divided by 2 =30), but not (10 + divided by 2 = 32). Also (6 + 4 divided by 2 + 8), not (8 - 4 x 3 = 12).

The rule points out plainly that addition signs and subtraction are taken in the order in which they come, but multiplication and division take precedence. After making this criticism, a storm of protests arose against me. At first the superintendent pounced upon me and made it very plain that I was not qualified to teach that school and my certificate should be revoked on account of my ignorance. The conductor agreed with him in his criticism of the method I taught. I defended myself as best I could under the circumstances, but the conductor and the superintendent had convinced the audience that I was not qualified for the position I was holding.

After they had finished their tirade against me, a Professor Sampson, who was in the room and had listened to the arguments, arose from his seat and asked permission to speak on the subject discussed. He had a private school there and was held in the highest esteem by the leading educators of the state, and also by the citizens of Shelbyville. His word was considered authority. He was tall, graceful, and had red hair and a beard. He said he could not understand why the conductor and the superintendent had criticized me so severely for presenting my subject so correctly. He substantiated everything I had said, relative to that subject, and told them that they were wrong and should apologize to me for the injustice which they had done to me. The argument was focused upon Professor Sampson, and the professor was master of the situation. He told them that they ought to help the young man instead of trying to lower him in the estimation of the citizens. In that crucial hour, Professor Sampson came forward as my savior and delivered me from the hands of my enemies. And this gave me a reputation of knowing more than the county superintendent and the conductor of the Institute. From that day until the close of school, the attitude of the pupils and also the parents changed toward me, and my stay in Shelbyville was of the most cordial nature.

On the last day of the Institute, the superintendent was on the program for an address. The address was more of an advisory nature, telling us what to teach and how to teach loyalty to our country and to our flag, which meant liberty and union, now and forever, one and inseparable. He said that we should teach the children such songs as "America" and "The Star-Spangled Banner." After he had closed his address, he received a tremendous applause and cheering from the audience. And quite a few of the teachers lauded him in the greatest degree on what he had said. The conductor called on me to express my sentiment relative to his address.

I arose from my seat and addressed the president and said, "I have listened with pleasure to the address of the superintendent, but not with that pleasure which results from a sound course of argument. The statement is delightful to the ears of those who are thinking only on the surface. But to those of us who know what our Constitutional rights are and are clamoring for them to be in force, such high-sounding words and patriotic advice is farcical, repulsive and damnable. I would indeed be glad to teach my pupils to sing such songs as have been recommended by the superintendent if conditions warranted it. But I will never teach my pupils such songs as long as I can see members of our group mobbed, lynched, burned at stakes and hunted like wild beasts and riddled with bullets."

For a few moments after taking my seat, there was a lull; not a sound could be heard, but as soon as the teachers awoke from their slumber, pandemonium reigned supreme. The superintendent resented what I had said. Since he was a white man invested with the power to hire and fire the teachers, most all of them took sides with him and demanded that I leave the room. Some said I ought to be lynched, and a great many opprobrious threats were made toward me, but no one would attempt to assault me. They all knew that I could fight better than I could do anything else and welcomed a fight at any time. During the remainder of my stay in Shelbyville, things went along very smoothly. Professor Sampson, by his stand for me, had put the stamp of approval on my ability to fill the position which I occupied. The trustees were drawn closer to me by the contact which I had with the superintendent and the conductor of the Institute. The parents, especially those who opposed me, laid down the hatchet. The pupils were more courteous and obedient.

At the close of school, six young ladies were awarded diplomas for having successfully completed the work prescribed in the curriculum. On account of dissensions and strife among the people and for the good of all, I resigned my position and sought work elsewhere. I found in Shelbyville a most orderly group, honest, trustworthy and dependable. Quite a few of its citizens have become nationally known. The Reverend John W. Robinson of New York City, who has been connected with many a project for the betterment of our group, notably, one of the promoters of the Douglas National Bank, Chicago, Illinois. Also, one of my pupils, Lucretia Lawson Knox, who has arrived at prominence as a Prima Donna and is nationally known and is now residing in Indianapolis, Indiana.

During the summer of 1891, I secured the principalship of the Harrodsburg, Kentucky City School. It was a fair job financially, much better than the one in Shelbyville. I held that position for four years. In the following fall, after having sold my real property, I moved my barbershop and the household effects to Harrodsburg, Kentucky. I had a barber in my employment who ran the shop for me. I had a three-chair barbershop. Two barbers worked each day, and on Saturday, I would work. The shop was doing a very good business. It paid much better than my salary for teaching. On the solicitation of my foreman, I sold him one-half interest in the shop for $250.00, $100.00 to be paid in cash at the signing of the contract and balance to be paid in installments of $25.00 per month.

He paid two installments and refused to make any more on the ground that he put in full time in the shop and unless I gave him one-half of my salary for teaching, he would not pay me the balance of the debt. I told him his demand was preposterous. Our agreement was that each one of us gets 60 percent of what we took in on our chairs, and the other 40 percent was to be used to defray expenses. Anything left from expenses was to be equally divided between us. But he still insisted that my salary should go into the pool and be divided among us and would not pay any more on the contract. I knew that he had more trade than I had, and the other barbers in the shop were inclined to his view of the subject, and should we dissolve the partnership, I knew they would follow him to his new location, and I would have no business. I decided to consult a lawyer. I went to see Ed Gaither, one of my customers and one of the most prominent lawyers in Harrodsburg. He said that our business was a partnership, and he had the same rights and privileges that I had. The only way that I could collect the balance on that note was to dissolve the partnership. I told him that everything in the shop was mine except the barber chair he was using. I told him that I had offered to sell my interests in the partnership to him or buy his interest. And he had refused both offers.

Then the lawyer said, "Forcibly put him out and let him sue you."

The following afternoon, after closing the school for the day, I went home, armed myself with my revolver, and went down to the barbershop. I called Francis to one side and asked him what he intended to do, and he remarked that he had told me what he intended to do, whereupon I took his chair and threw it out on the sidewalk. I came back into the shop, got his hat and coat, gave them to him, and then drew my revolver and punched him in the side with it full cocked and said, "Move out or I will kill you." He obeyed orders, and I was in possession once more. But that act proved to be my undoing as far as the barber business was concerned in Harrodsburg. Before we moved in the spacious room across the street, opposite our old location, we had only a three-chair shop. We enlarged the shop by putting in three bathtubs and a center laboratory with hot and cold water. We had a very modern shop. The plumbing and fixtures cost $600.00, not including the furniture.

I had a sign placed on the large, plate-glass window: Mammoth Barbershop. I gave one of the barbers the foremanship of the shop. Things moved along nicely for several weeks. The room which we had formerly occupied for our shop across the street was vacant, and my former partner rented it and opened a very nice shop and succeeded in employing my leading barber to work for him. In those days, nearly all of our customers had their private mugs. I had a large mug case which held about 200 mugs, and in a short time, more than half of them were taken over to the other shop. The trade was cut to less than one-half in one month, and in less than four months, I was forced to close and store my barber outfit.

After the legislature had passed the Jim Crow car law in Kentucky, I decided never to pay to ride on any common carrier which discriminated against me on account of my race or color. So, I bought a bicycle and rode to every place in the state that I desired to go. On one occasion, I rode from Harrodsburg to Versailles, a very tedious ride indeed. The hills were very long and steep, and I would have to walk up a great many of them and push my wheel. In those days, there were no coaster brakes on the wheel, so that you could regulate the speed of the wheel going downhill. But on each side of the fork of the wheel, there were footrests so that in going downhill, you could put your feet on them and coast down the hill.

I remember after climbing one of those steep hills between Harrodsburg and Versailles, I was very much fatigued. When I started down on the other side, I put my feet on those rests on either side of the fork over the front wheel and let the wheel go at breakneck speed down the hill. I was holding the wheel firmly by the handlebars, and my feet were pressing firmly against the rests on the sides of the wheel. All of a sudden, the fork broke, and I was thrown violently to the ground. I lay there for some time unconscious with my shoulder broken. Finally, I was carried to Versailles in a spring wagon, and my wounds were dressed. I was disabled for several weeks.

Another incident in my wheel-riding career. In Kentucky, I was coming home from Cincinnati to Harrodsburg—I passed through a small town, Williamstown, I think. Just as I was approaching a crowd standing in the road, I heard one of the boys cry out, "Oh, there comes a nigger." I was riding at a very fast clip and just as I passed them, they began to throw stones at me. I turned on the speed sure enough. For at least 100 yards, they pelted me with stones. I was struck several times, and the wheel also, but in a short time, I outdistanced them and went on my way, rejoicing, thanking God Almighty that things were no worse than what they were.

All over the Southland, that is the attitude of the white man towards our group. They assault, beat, maim, and kill us with impunity, without fear of punishment. And that same feeling is harbored in the attitudes of those who have immigrated from the south and have sown the seed of race hatred in the hearts of those with whom they have come in contact. The foreigners are taught to show the same disrespect for us. Abe Lincoln said that this government could not exist, half free and half slave. And I say, this government can't endure unless equal rights and equal opportunities are guaranteed to every citizen. The motto of our flag is, "Liberty and union—now and forever—one and inseparable."

During our partnership, men who had mugs in the shop were extended credit, and when the dissolution came, most of them took their mugs or would send an order for them. Quite a few of the mug customers would send for their mugs and did not send the money to pay for their accounts. I refused to let them have their mugs until the accounts were paid. Bud James, a liveryman, sent over for his mug. I told the bearer that he would have to pay his barber account before he could get his mug. When he was informed of what I had said, he became very indignant and came over to my shop in great haste and went directly to the mug case to take his mug. I told him that he could not take it until he had paid his bill. He then attempted to take it by force, and I threw him out of the shop into the street. He called me vile names and said that he would be back in a few minutes and kill me. Feeling that he would come back and execute his threats, I closed the shop and walked two blocks from my shop and hid myself from plain view of the shop.

In a short while, I saw him and the city marshal with a gun in his hand, approaching the shop in great haste. They tried to get in but could not, and after they had stayed there for some time, they left. That evening after I had gone back to the shop, the marshal came back to the shop and demanded the mug. I refused to give it up and told him the circumstances relative to my holding the cup, and the matter dropped. But the owner of the cup swore that he was going to kill me for throwing him out of the shop. I knew that he was rated a bad man, and should he kill me, I would be paid for. Should I kill him, I would surely be hanged. So, I decided to leave Harrodsburg and left as soon as I could arrange matters.

My partner, having been forcibly ejected from the business, sought redress through the court and secured a judgment against me for $188.00 and all proper relief. Sixteen years after this was rendered by the court in Harrodsburg, Kentucky, he sent it to Tulsa, Oklahoma for collection. At that time, I had a good business and owned a lot of very valuable real estate, but in Kentucky, the life of a judgment was 15 years, so on account of the statute of limitations running against the judgment, it could not be collected.

Relative to my schoolwork during my three years' stay in Harrodsburg, it was a success. I had one assistant teacher who was very proficient. She was loved and respected by all, and she contributed in a large measure to the wonderful success of the school. We abolished corporal punishment the last year I was there. The parents were helpful to us in the management of the school. They trained their children at home, and I don't think there was any disturbance of any kind during my last year there. The pupils were polite, kindhearted and obedient, and some of them were very brilliant in their work. Among them was W. C. Hueston, who is now an assistant Postmaster General in the Post Office Department in Washington, D.C.

The difficulties through which our group had to pass, the segregation and discrimination of all kinds of persecution, was so unbearable and so repulsive to me that I decided to leave the South, never to return, looking for all the liberty and freedom that I could find. I wound up all business relations in Harrodsburg and resigned my position as school principal and left for Youngstown, Ohio. I was there several days looking for a location but was not pleased with the town. So, I decided to go to Indianapolis,

Indiana. I found conditions more hopeful there, both financially and socially, although the housing conditions for our group were poor and unsanitary.

Our group lived mostly in alleys, on side streets, and wherever they could find a place. At that time, there was very little work for men of our group, but women could find plenty to do. The support of a family depended largely upon the work of a woman. After making a thorough investigation as to the conditions, etc., I decided to locate there. I secured a location for a barbershop and bathhouse on the corner of Illinois and Maryland Streets. The rent was $75.00 per month, payable in advance. After securing the lease from month to month, I returned to Harrodsburg to take my household effects and barber outfit to Indianapolis, Indiana. I had also secured a dwelling house at 419 North West Street, which consisted of eight rooms. I chartered a freight car and put all of my effects therein and shipped them to Indianapolis. After weeks delay, they arrived. My first duty was to my family. I furnished and arranged all the details of the home, then equipped my barbershop, which consisted of five chairs, three bathtubs and a bootblack stand. I secured a quota of educated barbers and opened the shop for business.

I selected several of the barbers who were working in some of the larger shops who had reputations of being expert barbers. I had a very nice shop, and it was equipped with a fine-looking set of barbers. Everything bade fair to a successful undertaking. Unfortunately, business was not so good as I expected. I remained there for six months with the income not sufficient to pay the expenses, and at the expiration of that time, I was forced to close up.

When I left Harrodsburg, I had $1,500.00 in cash, and after I had been in Indianapolis one year, giving all of my time to my business and my wife doing everything to help in a legitimate way, we had only $500.00 left of the $1,500.00. Since I was unable to sell my barber outfit, I had to place it to the very best possible advantage. I set up a two-chair shop for one of my barbers and sold it to him on payments. I used two of the chairs myself in another location and set up another shop with the two remaining chairs for a barber by the name of Waring. The bath outfit, I sold to the junk man.

During my schooldays, I had a classmate, Louis Williams, who was a rival of mine in my classroom work, and also in the debating society. I stood ahead of him in our classwork and had won several debates against him. When we left school, he became a successful businessman and accumulated some valuable real estate and had also become one of the most successful undertakers in the community. I took up the profession of teaching school, doing everything that I could find to do for the upliftment of our group. For 11 years, I taught, and at the expiration of that time, I did not have a hundred dollars to show for my labor and time. I felt that if my classmate could make a fortune in business with inferior knowledge, I could do as well as he could.

With this determination, I landed in Indianapolis to begin a business career. I did not find things as prosperous as I had expected. I had opened a first-class barbershop and bathhouse and failed. The greatest part of my money which I brought to Indianapolis had been lost in my business venture, and I was forced to get a location which I could barely make my expenses. In order to make a living, I continued in the shop looking every day to find something else which I might engage in which would put me on the way to prosperity.

At that time, the bicycle craze was on in Indianapolis. I knew a man who induced me to engage in that business. I equipped a store for him and furnished it with the new wheels and a great many second-hand wheels for hire.

Chapter 8

We had a complete repair shop, and the business was very successful for a while, but then the wheel-renting business proved dubious in those days, and a great many of our wheels were rented to many of the customers who would ride them out of the city, and we would never see them again. Otherwise, those others we encountered that did not steal them or ride them out of the city would return them in need of repairs. I became disgusted with the business and decided to sell it to my partner for less than one-third of its cost. He kept it for several years without making a success of it. Another one of my business ventures was a grooming house, which we did not find very lucrative. I continued in my barbershop, barely eking out an existence and still looking for an opportunity to better my condition.

As a rule, the people who go to the city from the country forget Christianity. The glare and glamour of city life cause them to see things differently from what they are in reality, and they have very little time to practice Christianity. Not so in our case. As soon as we arrived in Indianapolis, we connected ourselves to the church of our persuasion and in a short time became valuable members in the church. My wife was made leader of the choir and elected president of the CWBM. I was ordained as a deacon in the church. We worked in season and out of season, disseminating the gospel of Jesus Christ among the people with whom we came in contact. We were not only helping in a spiritual way but also in a financial way. We gave many entertainments for the purpose of raising funds to defray current expenses of the church.

First, we had a spelling bee. Prizes were given away for the best speller. I can only remember the first prize. It was a book, the title of which was "In His Steps." I took pleasure in recommending that book to all Christians who desired to know when temptations present themselves. When grave problems confront you, before deciding, ask the question, "What would Jesus do?"

This entertainment proved a great financial success. We also gave a checker tournament in the Odd Fellows Hall. All of our best checker players and a few of the whites engaged in the contest. There were three grades of players: Class A—first prize, a fine inlaid checkerboard, which was won by Marcelus Neal, principal of one of the schools; Class B—second prize, a gold-headed umbrella, won by J. B. Stradford; second prize in Class B—a beautiful chafing dish, won by Andy Lockyear. This was a wonderful entertainment. We served refreshments and employed an orchestra, and the people danced until the wee hours of the morning. Financially, it was a great success, and we received the plaudits of our group.

I was still looking for an opportunity to improve my financial standing. I learned of a barbershop which was for sale that was doing a profitable business. It was owned and operated by a man named Willis Kersey, one of the leading citizens of the city. I visited the shop several times to ascertain the volume of business it was doing as nearly as possible. From my observation, I found the shop was doing a good business and felt that it would be a good buy. He wanted $700.00 for the shop and his lease on the building. I refused to pay his price, and so the deal was called off. In about a fortnight, he came to me and said that he would take $600.00 for the shop. I refused his offer and told him that I would pay him $500.00 cash for the shop. He accepted my offer.

The shop consisted of three barber chairs, two bathtubs, a three-chair combination, mirrors, a case, and everything that was necessary to make a complete barbershop. I paid him the cash for the shop and took possession of it. It was a neighborhood shop and was patronized by all the aristocracy of the neighborhood: bankers, lawyers, doctors, oilmen, presidents of insurance companies, clerks, and businessmen. The barbers were a fine-looking set of fellows and were tonsorial artists. Each one of them had their personal trade and very seldom would any customer of one barber let another barber wait on him. There was very little transient trade that came to the shop. And I had to build a trade for my support.

When the proprietor left the shop, all of his trade followed him, and I had very little to do. My barbers were very loyal to me, and I found it quite an easy matter to pay the expense of the shop with the 40 percent I retained from what they made on their chairs. I had plenty of leisure and the most I did was to act as cashier and be polite and obliging to the customers. Every now and then I would get a customer and in the process of time, I had a very good trade, most of which was at night.

In my boyhood days, I selected law for my profession, and while teaching school in Lawrenceburg, Kentucky, I took a correspondence law course from a Professor Simms, who conducted a correspondence school in Indianapolis.

One of my customers was the son of a railroad president by the name of Mansfield. He had finished his first year at the Indiana Law School. Knowing that I was anxious to finish my courses from a law school, he suggested to me going down to the school and giving my name to the president about entering the school. I was able to enter the school, and several of the professors were customers in the shop, namely Judge Fishback, Judge Elliott, Mr. Kappies, and others. I had plenty of time throughout the day to attend class and study. So, I went and matriculated and was assigned lessons with the class without paying any tuition.

During my first year in law school, I made several lasting friends who were able to assist me in my struggle financially. The most important was Mr. A. H. Sweeney, president of the State Life Insurance Company and also commissioner of the city schools. I found him to be affable, generous, kindhearted, a believer in equal opportunities for all men, and at all times willing to lend a hand to the needy and oppressed. He was also a good entertainer and was never at a loss for words to express his sentiments. He was very inquisitive about what I was doing in a business way outside of my shop. He said, "Stradford, any man who is endeavoring to secure something financially for himself and family for future use should be helped in his struggles." He said, "You have a rooming house, a bicycle store where you sell cigars and tobacco. You have this shop, and you are studying law. You are giving employment to six or eight people, which I think is worthy of the most hearty approval. When you graduate from law school, I am going to do something of a substantial nature for you." I thanked him very much for the interest which he had manifested in me and told him that if I never graduated from law school, I would not ask anything from him.

Relative to buying a barbershop, I want to say by way of advice to those who have money to invest, it is far better, as a rule, to establish a new shop and build your own business rather than to buy some established shop. Each barber has his own personal trade, and wherever he goes, his trade will follow him. When Kersey left the shop, he went down on the circle and opened another shop, and all of his trade followed him. One of the other barbers left in a few months, and his trade followed him. The weekly receipts of the shop were cut in half and were not sufficient to pay me a decent living wage.

Not being able to pay my tuition in the Indiana Law School, I went to the Indianapolis School of Law, took the examination and entered the senior class. During my first year in the Indiana Law School, I succeeded in the work very nicely and got a passing grade which was very remarkable considering the many handicaps under which I labored. I made a great many friends among my classmates who have shown their friendship to me since our association in school. Notable among them Walter Van Nuys, one of the leading Democrats in the state of Indiana and a great lawyer. Our lecturer in International Law was ex-President Benjamin Harrison. Our lecturer on Constitutional Law was the Honorable Addison C. Harris, who was appointed Ambassador to Turkey. Before leaving for his post, he came to the class one morning and made his farewell address to us. Besides giving us advice as to how to use our clients professionally, he said, "Look upward and not downward. Look forward and not backward. Lend a hand." I have made that command my model all through my life, and I feel that if I had not learned anything more than that command, I would have been amply rewarded for the time and hardships I had while attending that school.

Also, during that year, our class was given tickets to attend a lecture by Robert G. Ingersoll in the English Theater. His subject was, "Fear is the Dungeon of the Heart and Superstition is the Dagger with which Hypocrisy assassinates the soul." He further said that if we did not fear that God would send us to hell when we died, there would be no churches. Mr. Ingersoll was a tall, graceful, handsome, entertaining, and convincing speaker. His diction was forensic and made one feel like he was listening to Cicero in his prosecution of Verres for taking the life of a Roman citizen, or Demosthenes, or Abraham Lincoln. His speech made a lasting impression on me. It convinced me that there were two sides to all questions. I have always believed in the existence of a personal God, and he failed to change my belief.

When I arrived in Indianapolis, Thomas Taggart was the mayor of that city. He was the idol of not only the white people but also of the Colored people like Absalom of old. He had stolen the hearts of the people. He was the most polite, courteous, liberal, obliging and friendly person that I ever met on the street. He greeted everyone with a smile and was ever ready to help those who needed assistance. When the churches of our group had rallies for the purpose of raising money, regardless of denomination, he and his wife would attend the services that night and when the collection was passed, he would always give his check for from $50.00 to $500.00 to be added to the collection.

Taggart was a Democrat and our group at that time were blind Republicans. Indianapolis was a Republican city, but our group elected him mayor. I became personally acquainted with him. He was a patron of my barbershop occasionally, and in each campaign, he solicited my support. I refused to support him on the ground that I was a Republican and fought him with every bit of energy I had, but it was to no effect. Many people loved and adored him, and he showed his appreciation for their support by giving them clerical positions in the City Hall, in his home and on public works. The critics called the City Hall, "Uncle Tom's Cabin." He was also owner of French Lick Springs in Indiana where nearly all the help was of our people's group. Before closing this memoir, I will say more about him and the respect he had for our group.

I continued law school until I had finished the prescribed course and graduated. A few days before the night of the graduation exercise, Mr. Sweeney asked me what I intended to wear on the night of graduation. I told him I had only one suit of clothing, but it was not suitable for the occasion. He suggested that I wear his full-dress suit, patent leather shoes, pleated-bosom white shirt, and his diamond stud, which was one carat. I accepted his offer with pleasure and on the night of the graduation, I was dressed entirely in his clothes. I was the finest-dressed man in the class, and it was said by one of my friends that the diamond lit up the class.

On the following morning, I returned the outfit and thanked him for his kindness and generosity. In a few weeks after I graduated, I called his attention to his promise to me. He then asked me what I wanted, and I told him I wanted him to build me a hotel. He instructed me to get an architect to draw the plans and specifications and submit them to him for his consideration. I immediately secured an architect who drew up the plans and specifications, and I also secured a site for the building and presented them to him. The cost of the building to be completed was $50,000. After making a thorough investigation of the project, he came to the shop and told me that he did not want to invest that much money at that time in the project for me, but he gave me $1,000.00 in cash and told me to go to where there were a great many of my people who had good jobs, and where there was plenty of work.

There were more than 50 factories which were located there on account of cheap fuel. Natural gas was plentiful. Some of the factories were the Kelley's Ax Factory, Plate Glass Company, the Republic Iron and Steel Mill, and the Lamp Chimney Factory. The city was installing its sewer system, and the contract was given to a member of our group, Bob King. He had a large number of our men employed on it. Kelley's Ax Factory employed 500 of our group. The Republic Iron and Steel Mill employed three hundred or four hundred. The town was full of our group. All of them had good jobs and were doing fine.

That is why he advised me to go there and make the money to build a hotel. I refused to take the money on the grounds that I was a deacon in the church. And I did not want to be a party to making widows and orphans and having me filling drunkards' graves. I also told him my wife was the choir leader and the president of the CWBM and that our work was to build up, and not to tear down, and that we were bitterly opposed to any business which lowered the standard of the people. He pushed the money back to me and said, "Take it. Study over the matter carefully and after you have made a thorough study of it, if you feel you can't use it, return it to me." He further said that my association with that class of people for a few years would not destroy nor debase my manhood, that after I had accomplished the purpose for which I engaged in the business, I would be able to be of great service to my group.

I took the money with no intention of using it for the purpose he wanted me to use it for. I took it down and showed it to my wife and told her how I had come into possession of it, and also the purpose for which it was to be used.

She said, "Give it back to him, unless you can use it for some other legitimate business. I would rather be poor all of my life than to be the cause of dragging people down to degradation and to ruin. And besides, Jesus would not approve of our engaging in such a business."

We were fully in accord on the proposition. I kept the money in my pocket for two weeks. During that time, I consulted a great many of my friends and also the pastor of our church and found not one who advised me to use the money.

Louis Moss, a barber and a very particular friend of mine, met me on the street after he had heard of my having the money and said to me, quoting him in direct discourse, "Look here, Stradford, what in the hell are you going to do with that $1,000.00? Are you going to give it back to that white man? Did you ever have a thousand dollars in your life before?" I answered each question and told him that I was going to give it back to him. He replied, "You are the damnedest fool I ever saw. Take that money and use it, and when you have made sufficiency, come back to Indianapolis and build a swell hotel."

I had always had the greatest confidence in Moss's judgment in matters of importance. But not only Moss, all of whom I had talked to relative to the proposition, gave their views on the material side of the question, and only one agreed with me on the spiritual side, and that was my wife. After giving the matter very serious consideration, I decided that I would use the money to the very best possible way to bring about the desired effect. I had only one obstacle in the way to prevent me from using the money, and that was my wife. I was at a loss to find words to broach the subject to her. I knew her sentiment. She was bitterly opposed to the proposition, and I knew I could not reconcile her. And in order to settle the matter at once, I told her very firmly that I had decided to use the money in a way that I could get the quickest results. She said, "If you use it, I will not go up there with you." Then I said, "You and the children may stay here, and I will spend a day with you each month." So, I prepared to go to Alexandria, Indiana.

Before definitely deciding the kind of business that would be best to engage in, this question presented itself to me, "What will our group spend their money for?" First, for whiskey. Second, he will gamble. Third, he will spend his money on women, and fourth, he will spend his money for amusements. From experience, I knew that he would beat his room rent and board bill in order to buy whiskey to satisfy his thirst. I also knew that he spends everything he makes on Saturday nights, and Sundays and on Monday morning, he goes to work carefree and lighthearted and free. I knew too that they will gamble, recalling a record as a marble player in my youth, how I could beat all the boys and men who played the game, and now, I had established a business of selling marbles for eggs and had more eggs than the man who sold them out of his store. And, in addition to that, the reputation which I had made as a checker player, by beating a majority of the best players wherever I went, I was sure that if I put a checkerboard in the business and played for drinks, it would be quite a revenue. And I could have self-expression in doing something I delighted in doing. I was quite sure I would be able to cope with the situation.

After deciding to go to Alexandria, I sold my shop and left Indianapolis in quest of the pot of gold. After settling up my business affairs, I was in Alexandria several days, looking for a location. There was none to be found unless I bought a place. I found that the commercial hotel property could be bought. The chief of police was running the hotel. He had a lease on the building and agreed if I bought his furniture, he would transfer the lease to me. The price was $5,000.00, terms of $1,000 in cash and the balance in monthly installments of $150.00 with interest at six percent annually. I paid him his price for the furniture, bought the building and took possession in a few days. My boarders were all white people and were very congenial. They continued with me for several months. One of my boarders I had known for some time. He was a resident of Harrodsburg at one time but had made his home in Alexandria for some time, over a period of years.

His business while in Kentucky was a trotting trainer, and an all-around sporting man. He was connected with some of the best people in the country. His name was Sid Smith. He took sick while living in the hotel and did not have the money to pay his bills. I told him I would have to have my pay, or I would put him in the poor house. He besought me not to put him on the county, but said, "Write to my people in Harrodsburg and they will take care of my bills." I did as he requested me to do, but I did not get a reply from them. I continued to keep him in the hotel and saw to it that he was properly cared for. He grew worse every day for more than three weeks, and finally the end came. I notified his people of his demise and asked them what disposition should be made of the body. They said to bury it in the Potter's Field. I was never more shocked in my life. I was personally acquainted with his people in Harrodsburg. His sister's husband owned and operated the largest livery stable in Harrodsburg, and his family was considered wealthy. But they would not pay one penny for his keeping, and his remains were buried in the Potter's Field, according to their instructions.

In addition to the hotel business, I put in a barbershop which proved to be a lucrative enterprise. I did not go to Alexandria to run a barbershop or a hotel. I knew I would never make enough money to build a hotel from that kind of business. I went to sell liquor. At that time, before a license would be granted to sell or run a saloon, a person would have to be a citizen of the state and county in which he resided and was required to circulate a petition to the neighborhood with signers indicating their approval or disapproval of a saloon in that locality.

I employed a young man, William Lancaster, who was a citizen of the town, to make the application for license with the agreement that he would be the manager of the saloon with a stipulated salary. The white people in that neighborhood were bitterly opposed to it and said there should never be a saloon at that place, for it was the gateway to the residential section of the city. As soon as the facts were discovered, I went back to Indianapolis and reported the conditions to my benefactor. He asked me was that the only place in the city. He told me to go back to Alexandria and look for another location and he would come up and secure it for me.

 For several weeks after returning to Alexandria, I searched in vain for a place and had almost given up hopes of securing one. The real estate agent, whom I had employed to secure me a building, came down and informed me that he had secured a building for me, situated at 120 West Washington Street, two stories high, six rooms upstairs and a large storeroom on the first floor, 22 x 100, and the only stone-front building in the city. I at once notified my benefactor. He came up and bought the building for me with the understanding that if I succeeded in the business, I was to repay him the money he advanced me with interest. Everything was in readiness. I secured the license through Will Lancaster, my manager. My saloon outfit was furnished by the Terre Haute Brewing Company. I bought three pool tables, one cash register and a safe. The bar was 20 feet long. There were twin rooms and several card tables. On the opening night, my receipts were $350.00. Business was good and continued good for several years.

 During that time, I built a two-room brick apartment at a cost of $3,000 and rented them at $10.00 per month each. Everything was moving along in a successful manner, and I felt that in a short time, I would accomplish the desired object. My manager, after seeing that my business was so prosperous and having the license in his name, decided to eject me from the place and operate it himself. He felt that I was making too much money, and he might as well have it for himself. The day he planned to eject me, he got drunk and that evening I went to supper. When I came back from supper, he was behind the bar and had fired the night bartender. And when I started behind the bar, he pulled his gun and pointed it at me and said, "This is my place. Don't come behind this bar."

I looked him right in the eyes and asked him, "What do you mean?"

"This is my place and if you attempt to come back here, I will kill you."

Looking him straight in the eyes, I said, "Shoot," and walked straight up to him, snatched the pistol out of his hand and made him leave the room. Knowing that I could not run the saloon on his license, he decided to give all the trouble he possibly could. He employed a lawyer to institute legal proceedings to close the saloon. His lawyer advised him to compromise and let the saloon continue in business on his license the remainder of the year if I would pay him a certain stipulated amount of money. I agreed to the terms of the compromise, paid him off. And he left the city for Indianapolis.

Business continued good for several years. I not only kept all of my payments but made a great many improvements on the property, and my bankroll was getting quite large. At any rate, I was quite sure that it would only be a matter of time before I would be able to go back to Indianapolis and build my hotel. The natural gas flickered and went out, and the factories went out with it. Kelley's Ax Factory went to Charleston, West Virginia, and moved everything they had there. They even took the small dwellings with them. The Republic Iron and Steel Mill went back to Pittsburgh, Pennsylvania.

Chapter 9

All of the glass factories, with the exception of the Plate-Glass Factory, left the town. Some went to Chicago, some to Kansas and some to Oklahoma. Alexandria was a deserted village. One town of 10,000 inhabitants before the gas went out was reduced to less than 5,000 in one year's time. Property values depreciated 75 percent. Any person could get an icehouse to live in. All that was required was to pay the taxes and keep up the insurance. The bottom fell completely out of the town and all those who were buying property and had almost paid for it lost all they had paid on it and left Alexandria to start life anew in some other locality. It was a very pathetic incident to see old men and women who had worked hard for years to buy a home for themselves and children, lose it as they did. Such cases as these deserve the greatest sympathy and consideration, not only from the cities and counties and state, but also from our great philanthropists. I know quite a few men who are honest, industrious and economical, who have worked hard all of their lives to accumulate a home and a sufficient amount of living above want, only to lose all that they possess and have to start life all over again.

The doling of charitable and other welfare organizations of their sparing charitable gifts of a place to eat and sleep don't mean anything to that class of people. People who are ambitious don't want charity. All they want is a chance to show their value and usefulness to the community. It is the moral duty of the state and the United States government to restore them to the financial standard they maintained before the catastrophe. John D. Rockefeller has given millions for scientific research and millions to other deserving enterprises for the good of the public. Julius Rosenwald has given also millions to the YMCA and libraries for the same purpose. But in my judgment, if they would create a fund for the reimbursement of those deserving unfortunates whose earthly possessions have been taken away from them by means over which they had no control, there would be more real joy, comfort, happiness, inspiration and a demonstration of true manhood in one hundredth part of the money donated than there would be in all they have given for other programs.

I personally know several men who were wealthy, and after they had reached the age of near 60, they lost their property due to certain catastrophes. And they pass on through life buffeted, disappointed, manhood all crushed out, inspiration gone. Their friends give them the cold shoulder, and they are left on the mercy of cold charity. There are hundreds of such cases in this country today where men have been deprived of their property and are now at the mercy of the people.

When the gas went out in Alexandria, there was an encumbrance on my property for $5,000. The class of trade I had followed the factories to their new locations and tied crepe on my door. I was left without business enough to feed me and my family with the monthly payment of $115 to make on the mortgage. All of my other property was vacant, and I had no income at all to meet expenses. I put a barbershop in the building and found that it was not a paying business. I spent nearly all the cash money I had keeping up the payments on the mortgage debt. Finally, after an investigation, I found that the property was not worth the debt and that it was foolish for me to make further efforts to pay for it. I submitted a proposition to Mr. Eusley, the president of the Union National Building and Loan Association of Indianapolis. I told him that I had found it impossible to pay for the property and that I wanted to make a proposition relative to the disposition of it. I would give him possession of the saloon building on Washington Street, the note on the building on Gurney Street at a stated time that he would give me use of my residence for one year. At the expiration of that time, if I failed to redeem it, I would give him a quit-claim deed to all the property against which he held the mortgage.

During the time of my plight, there was an aged, white man who was very friendly to me, and always spoke encouragingly to me relative to staging a comeback. He spent a great deal of time with his daughter in Alexandria. The gas and oil were in their embryo in Kansas and Oklahoma, and the possibility of making good in Coffeyville was fine. And he advised me to go there with a determination that I could not fail. A great many of the glass factories had moved there, and also a great many of the glass workers whom I personally knew had gone there to work. I decided from his recommendation to go to Coffeyville and grow up with the oil and gas industry.

Among the many incidents which occurred while I lived in Alexandria, I will write in detail the two which I feel are worthy of mentioning. I had four children attending the public school there in whom I was very much interested. I visited the school every week to find out how they were treated and how they were progressing in their schoolwork. I found the teachers very fair to them, and to my youngest son, they were somewhat partial, on account of his superior ability. All of them treated him with the greatest respect. On each Friday, they had spelling bees, and the child who was the best speller would have a rosette pinned on his waist, indicating that he was the best speller. My boy just kept it all the time, and the teacher abolished the spelling bees.

The public school was one block west of my place of business. While I was sitting in my office one day, about 12:30, a lad came running in and said, "Mr. Stradford, the janitor is beating your daughter. He bumped her head against the brick wall of the schoolhouse and dragged her upstairs to the principal's room and locked her up."

I jumped up from my seat, put my coat and hat on in great haste, and started for the school. But after reflecting, I said, "I can't afford to interfere with my children's education." So, I took my coat off and sat down just as another lad came running in, out of breath, and repeated almost the same story which the first one had conveyed. I sprang up from my seat and said, "For what am I rearing my children? Not for a white janitor to beat." I grabbed my coat and hat and ran down to the schoolhouse. I went to the rear door and met the janitor coming down the stairs. I said to him, "Where is my daughter?"

He said, "Oh, she is not hurt."

I took him by the arm and forced him to take me to where she was. He carried me to the principal's office, and when we opened the door, my daughter was crying very bitterly.

I said to her, "Did he hurt you?"

And she said, "Yes, Papa."

I then proceeded to give him an unmerciful beating. I had a signet ring on my finger, and every time I struck him, the ring cut the blood from his skin until his face and eyes were swollen so much that he was unrecognizable. The fire alarm was turned on, and the fire department came down to put the fire out. I met them as I was leaving the building and got back to the office before the city marshal got there.

When he was informed who had caused the disturbance, he came up to my office and stood in the door and called for me. I asked him what he wanted, and he said, "Come up to court in the morning at 9:00 and stand trial for assault and battery on the janitor of the school."

I told him I would be there. I was there at the appointed time and was fined $45.00 and costs. Prior to the time I flogged that janitor, he was very prejudiced against our group of children and would not give them equal rights with the white children. My attention had been called to his mistreatment of the children several times, and I fully decided that if he ever did anything to one of my children, I would teach him how to treat all the children with the same respect and courtesy that he should. For more than two weeks, he was not able to come to his job, and when he did come to work, he was overcautious to treat our group of children more kindly, more generously, and, in fact, he was their best friend after that incident.

The chief of police, Cal Crea, was a man highly prejudiced against our group and felt that we had no rights he was bound to respect. He did not like to see us progressive and feel our importance as men. I was reported to him by one of my tenants upstairs over the saloon that I had ejected her from the room she had rented from me. He came down to the saloon, came upstairs where I was. He never asked me to state my side of the question, but began to abuse me and told me to consider myself under arrest. I told him that I was the police in my house, and if he wanted to arrest me to get a warrant and read it to me, I would submit. The following morning, he came with several other policemen, arrested me, put me in jail and kept me there overnight and would not let me have a bond. I employed an attorney to represent me in the case when it came up for trial. The fine was so trivial that my attorney advised me to pay it rather than appeal. Although it was unjust, it was cheaper to pay it than to appeal it.

Since I had fully decided to go to Coffeyville, Kansas, to start over again in the race of life, I wound up all my business affairs and proceeded to prepare to leave Alexandria, Indiana. I chartered a car for my furniture and loaded it. I left my residence, packed furniture of eight rooms for my wife and my children to use for the year. I had asked her to try to redeem it. I bade my family goodbye and boarded the train for Coffeyville on the night of the 31st of January 1904 and arrived in Coffeyville on the 2nd of February 1904. When I left Alexandria, the ground was covered with snow, and the weather was bitter cold. When I arrived in Coffeyville, it was typical spring weather. The birds were singing sweetly in the trees; the grass was creeping up silently under my feet, and the gentle zephyrs were blowing and all nature seemed to be aglow.

When I arrived at the station, quite a few of the citizens were there awaiting the arrival of the train. I met quite a few of them who were interested to know my business and also willing to give me all the information I desired relative to the business I had in mind. I found a lodging place, and then I went out to look for a location. I leased a building with the understanding that the rent was to begin when my furniture arrived in Coffeyville. It was 30 days before it came, and I had plenty of time to get acquainted with a great many of the citizens and also the city. The Dalton Boys were killed and captured in this city. The bullet holes in the face of the doors and windows of the bank building which they held up could be seen very plainly, and they are visible up to the present day.

I found most of our group progressive. They were engaged in businesses of various kinds—barbershops, restaurants, rooming houses, grocery stores, lawyers, doctors, and drugstores. Unfortunately, for our group, we have not reached that influential height where we can demand a sufficiency of capital to do business on a large scale. We have, among our group, men of superior business ability, capable of indefinite expansion in almost every line of endeavor who have not been able to develop or carry their ideas into execution on account of not being able to finance them. I know of several inventions which are the brains of our group, but the white man has succeeded in utilizing them for his own interests and takes the credit as the inventor.

As soon as my furniture came, I opened a place, a pocket billiard room with soft drinks, cigars, tobacco, and a two-chair barbershop, three pool and several card tables. Unfortunately for me, I secured a basement room under Robinson's Drugstore. It was an exceedingly wet spring, and since I was in a low basement, the water stood on an average of two feet in the room, and my furniture was floating on the water. The condition prevailed for several weeks, and my furniture was ruined. It was more than a month before I could secure another location as all the storerooms there were rented. Finally, I leased a lot on South Walnut Street and bought a building which was for sale and had it moved on the lot and fitted it up for business.

The business was as good as could be expected although in that location but was far from being sufficient to make anything to apply on my property in Alexandria, Indiana. I worked hard night and day to increase the business to a point whereby I could make enough money to have a bank account sufficient at the end of the year that I could go back to Alexandria and redeem my property if I found it to be to my best interest to do so.

During the summer vacation, somebody who had won the reputation of being the champion boy pool player of the gas belt of Indiana spent his vacation with me in Coffeyville. He was a very valuable asset to the business during his stay with me. He was quite small for his age. He had to get upon the table to make his shot. My customers—those who were good pool players—would beat me and jolly me and tell me I was a rookie pool player. I would tell them that my son would be here in a few days, as the case might be, and he would avenge my conquerors.

They would tell me, "When he comes, we will win this pool hall from you."

I said, "We will see."

As soon as school closed, he came directly to Coffeyville. I had talked so much of him that everyone who had heard me talk was desirous of seeing him play. He certainly was a big show, and everybody, men, women, and children, would come down to get a look at him. The pool hall would be crowded every evening to see him play. Those fellows who had been beating me came down to win my pool hall. I told my son not to win every game from them, but to let them win some of the games when the purses were small. When the purse was worthwhile, I would tell him to win. The first evening he was there, the hall was full of those good players who had said they were going to win the pool hall from me, and they were very anxious to play with him. One young man came in and said, "Kid, I will play you a game." He said, "All right, how much do you want to play for?" He suggested $2.00 per game of 50-ball, straight pool. Quite a few of his friends bet on him, and I was taking all side bets on my boy. A considerable amount was wagered on the first game, and we won. For three months, during his stay with me, he won every available dollar of pool money and all that came into the city from elsewhere. On account of his size and age, the pool players thought that they could beat him, and for three months, we failed to convince them that he could. But they paid dearly for their unbelief. And it increased my bankroll considerably.

In a short time, I had established a reputation for conducting an honest and on-the-square business, and everyone who played a game would say, "We will go to Stradford's place for he will not let anyone cheat in his games." The other joint, where they had games that were known as skin games and the one which had been operated for years lost most of its trade. He held a club over the chief of police and told him if he did not make me leave town or close up my place, he would squeal on him. I was not paying any protection but had all of the games worthwhile. The chief came down to my place one evening and told me I would have to cut out the gaming in my place or he would send me to the penitentiary. I told him that I had furnished the cards and checkerboards for the boys to play games in order to sell my stock, and when they played, I did not demand that they buy anything. When they lost, as a rule, they would buy a treat for each game they lost if they wished to. If not, they did not buy anything, and I did not compel them to. He said that it had been reported to him that I was running a poker game, and that he was coming down and raid my place and catch me gambling and would send me to the penitentiary. I told him, "If you come down to raid my place, bring a warrant and read it to me. If you come without one and break my door down, I will kill you." And with that statement, I left him. He laid his plans to catch me, but I was very careful. In fact, I cut out all games except the pool game, and my business depreciated to less than one-half in one month.

When vacation ended on September 1, 1904, I took my son back to Alexandria to school and brought my son, John, back with me to assist me in conducting the business. I got back to Alexandria on September 10th. At that time, the World's Fair was in progress in St. Louis. On my way to Alexandria, we spent several days attending it, taking in a great many shows on the Pike and visiting a great many places of interest, which I had never seen or heard of before. On the morning of the 5th of October 1904, I received a telegram from my son, Pinkney, saying, "Come home at once. Mama is dead." I was arranging to go and take my son, John, with me. And about two hours after I had received the first message, a second message came saying, "Not expected to live, come at once." My impression was that she had been pronounced dead from the second stroke of paralysis, but had been resuscitated, but was not expected to live. With this impression, we boarded the train that evening for Alexandria, hoping to see her alive. And I prayed fervently to God all the time I was on my way back, that I might see her alive once more in life.

When we arrived in Alexandria, we got off the train and in mad haste, we rushed home and into the house, thinking that we would find her alive. But alas, she was dead. The shock was very severe, but I was consoled by the fact that she had paid a debt which we all will have to pay sooner or later. After interring the remains and arranging for the welfare and comfort of the children for the winter, we returned to Coffeyville. Seeing the business there had been curtailed that I had no chance to make a fortune there, I began to look for another location.

I brought with me from Alexandria a carload of furniture which was in storage, and I was in a quandary to know what to do with it. I knew a man by the name of Wright, who had been employed for years in a furniture store and had acquired a knowledge of the furniture business. He could repair furniture and do upholstery work. He induced me to establish a new and second-hand furniture store and give him the job of manager. I took the matter under advisement and finally decided to open a store for him. I secured a room and filled it with second-hand and new furniture, employed a clerk and opened up for business. The furniture and fixtures were valued at $2,500 and I also deposited $500 in the bank, subject to his orders to buy additional furniture. The first few months, they had a land office business, and the business did fair to be a success. We sold furniture on the installment plan, and we bought for cash. In a short time, our books were full of accounts. The manager did not know anything about the business side of the question. He never investigated the character of those who applied for credit. Anyone could get the furniture on credit by making a small down payment. The clerk was a very unreliable man and as fast as he could make collections, he would play the money off in crap shooting. When the rent came due, they had no money to pay it. I was notified of the condition by my brother with whom I had left the $500 to purchase additional stock. I came up from Tulsa and found the stock depleted, bills uncollected and a general disagreement between the clerk and the manager. The manager accused the clerk of misappropriating the money and the clerk accused the manager of not having any business ability whatever.

During the time they were conducting the business, my losses were more than $1,000.00. I was so disgusted with the business that I sold it to a second-hand furniture man for $300.00, thus ending my experience in the furniture business. When I opened that store, I was living in Coffeyville, Kansas and busied myself in the business. When we had calls to go out to buy furniture from those who were leaving town or quitting housekeeping, we would go into those homes and set our price on the furniture, and we would never give more than 25 percent of the cost of it, and more often, 10 or 20 percent. I could see how second-hand furniture men could get up in the world so fast. I feel sure that I will have to answer to the Almighty for a great many deals I made with some of those unfortunates. I have a guilty conscience even now as to the small amount we paid some of them for their valuable sets of furniture when I knew and felt in my heart that I was not paying them a reasonable price for it.

After I had the argument with Nate Smith, the chief of police, I found it necessary to leave the town if I wanted to make a fortune. Oil and gas were in the first stage of development in Tulsa, Oklahoma. I went down there to look the field over, and I found that I had discovered the place where my dreams of riches would be realized. I returned to Coffeyville and moved my outfit to Tulsa, leaving my furniture store in Coffeyville. I arrived in Tulsa on March 8, 1906. The town of 500 inhabitants and I found these conditions existing, relative to our group. In the housing question there had been no provisions made for their housing. They lived in tents, in cellars, in barns, over garages, and any other place they could find to stick their bodies.

There was only one place of business, and that was a small restaurant. There were two rooming houses, a pool table room and a one-chair barbershop. Our group was rushing to Tulsa in great numbers with no accommodation. In seeking a room for my business, I had a conference with old Dr. Reeder, who had a vacant building which would have suited my purpose. He refused to rent it to me and said that our group should be segregated and not allowed to do business in a town where the whites lived. He offered to buy a tract of land about three miles from Tulsa and give me the agency of it at a certain percentage commission to lay off in city lots to sell to my group.

I refused his offer and told him that I could not see the wisdom of his scheme. I further said that I believed in a man buying property wherever he was able to buy, regardless of his color. I made an enemy of him, and he said to me, "You must think you are as good as white people." I told him I was as good as any man who had not done any more good than I had done and was better than any man that I had done more good than he had done. I told him that men, in my opinion, were graded like horses, good, better and best, regardless of color. For several days I tried to find a room, but to no avail. Finally, I decided to buy the restaurant if I could get a lease on the building. The lease secured, I paid the owner the agreed price and took possession of the building, which was a dilapidated shack. I put a tent on the rear end of it for my living quarters and moved into it. I had just enough room for two pool tables, a showcase and counter. My business went over the top from the beginning and continued so for several years. Since I knew that the prospects for making a fortune in the real estate and rental game in connection with my business were good, I embarked in the real estate and rental game. For my first venture, I bought three lots, 50 x 140, Numbers 6, 7, and 8 in the Turley Addition and paid cash for them, $750.00. Then I bought five portable houses. Three of them contained three rooms, and two of them contained two rooms. The three-room houses rented for $10.00 per month, and the two-room houses rented for $8.00 per month. They were rented at once.

Here's the paragraph broken out with better structure and dialogue:

The north boundaries of my lots were adjacent to the public-school property, and on the rear end of the lot facing the school building, I built a five-room house, and in the middle of the lot I built a two-room house. All of these were rented as soon as completed. I had eight houses on these lots, and the monthly rental was $85.00.

When my lease expired on account of the advanced improvements of new buildings, I had to move to another locality. The building was torn down and replaced by a new one, and I could not get a room in it. I had a hard time securing another room and had almost given up in desperation. The white people there were all opposed to renting to our group.

I went to see an old man by the name of John Thomas, who had a house which he had refused to rent to members of our group. He liked his whiskey very much and had been in my place several times. He was very friendly with a member of our group, and I was a friend to him. I induced his friend to get him to rent the house to me. He used his influence in every way but could not get him to let me have it.

As I said above, the old man liked his grog, and besides, he was an old bachelor. I got a friend to make an appointment at his house so we could go down and have a talk with him. I bought a pint of good whiskey, put it in my pocket, and carried it with me.

After the introduction, he treated me with due respect. He talked at length of the events of the day, and finally, he spoke of having a good drink of whiskey. To the surprise of my friend, and also our host, I took the bottle of whiskey out of my pocket and offered them a drink.

When the second drink was asked for, I began to talk about renting the house from him. He absolutely refused on account of his neighbors being opposed to it. I had also carried along with me a sufficient amount of money to tempt him. After taking his third drink, he began to feel very lively.

I said to him, "If you will rent me the building, I will pay you six months in advance." I took from my pocket $150.00 and laid it on the table and said, "Here is the money. Give me a lease on the building and take it."

He agreed, and I asked for a sheet of paper. I drew up the lease, and he signed it, and his friend witnessed it. After they had finished drinking the liquor, I left with the lease in my pocket.

In a few days after I had secured the lease, I moved my fixtures and all of my equipment into his building and began to do business again. His attitude toward our group was altogether changed. He treated me with the greatest courtesy and said that his opinion of members of our group had been formed from what experience he had had with those he had come in contact with around Tulsa and what he had heard others say of them.

Here's the paragraph broken out with better structure and dialogue:

When I went to Tulsa in 1906, it was in the Indian Territory and was ruled by the United States government. Instead of police, there were deputy United States Marshals, who were terrors to the law violators and would protect their prisoners with their lives. I never heard of a lynching during territorial days.

There were several deputies in Tulsa. One of them, by the name of Charles Petty, who was considered a bad and fearless man, was invariably given a bench warrant to bring in an outlaw who was wanted for some nefarious crime. He was ignorant, envious, and overbearing.

When I engaged in business in Tulsa, I tried in every way to gain his goodwill and influence, but to no avail. He was envious of my prosperity and kept my place under surveillance at all times and would advise my customers to stay away from my place or they would be landed in jail. Many a time he came to my place and took all of my tables and chairs out on the street and made a bonfire of them and claimed that I had permitted gambling to be carried on in the place.

He passed my place one morning; I called him and took him into the private office and told him I wanted to have a heart-to-heart talk with him. I told him that I came to Tulsa to make money and not to socialize. I further said that the other places of business were all making money, and no one was interfering with them.

I said, "I am making money, and I am willing to take you in as a silent partner in order to have your protection, and I assure you it will pay you at least $25.00 per week."

He said, "I don't want any interest in your building, and the best you can do is not to let me catch you gambling here. If so, I will run you out of town."

I knew it was an impossibility to succeed in that line of business when the police power was arrayed against me. I used all of my influence to have him lay off me, and when I found it could not be done, I decided to stop him, even to the taking of his life.

In a few days, he came up to my place again. He thought I was afraid of him, and by being so overbearing, he could make me leave town. When he entered the door, he yelled, "Trust, trade or travel. This is Charlie Petty, by God," and continued to come toward me.

I raised my left hand with my right firmly grasping my .45 and said, "Don't come any further."

He stopped and said, "You want to kill me?"

I told him that I did not want to kill him, but that he had, by his overbearing way, run a great many of my customers away from me, and I wanted him to understand that when he came into my place again, to destroy my property, to bring a warrant or catch me gambling or else, I would kill him.

In a few days, he came in again and brought another deputy with him. He wanted to take my tables and chairs and burn them, but the other officer told him he had no right to confiscate them. To tell the truth, I made up my mind to kill him and decided that if I did, it would have to appear to be self-defense, and it was up to me to bring about that state of facts.

Chapter 10

I rented the city hall to give a grand ball and had the bills printed in my son's name, as he was very popular among the dancers. Tickets were on sale for the ball two weeks before the date. We had handbills struck and advertised it extensively through the newspapers. Quite an interest was created among our group, and the night of the ball the house was crowded to overflowing. Financially, it was a big success. I was the doorman, and I sold and took the tickets. The people came in droves. Finally, Charlie Petty came to the door. I asked him for his ticket, and he pushed by me and went into the hall. At that time, several others came up. I sold them tickets, and when I had waited on all of them, I turned to Charlie Petty and said, "Pay your fare or go out." He said he would neither pay his fare nor go out, and at the same time, reached for his pistol. Being a little quicker than he was, I got my gun first, and being too close to shoot him, I struck him on the head with it, and he fell on the floor like a rock.

My son, John, came up and said, "Kill him, Papa."

I told him he was dead already. The ambulance came and took him to the hospital, and he lay in a semi-conscious state for nearly a fortnight, not expected to live.

After the assault, the chief of police came up on the scene and questioned me about the matter. I explained everything to his satisfaction with the exception of having my gun in my hand, and he said he did not think that I should have it so publicly in my hand. I changed the subject, and his mind was diverted from the gun for a short while. But he returned to the gun question again and said that I would have to put it away or give it to him. I told him I did not know how soon the wounded man might return or that some of his friends might want to avenge his injury, and if I gave him my gun, I would have no protection. He still insisted on my giving the gun to him. I raised the gun in my hand and said to him, "Do you see this gun? No man living or has ever lived can take it away from me. And if you think you can take it, be on your way." With that statement, no further demand was made on me to give up the gun, and he left me in charge of the dance hall.

At the expiration of my lease, which was for six months, I had to find other quarters on account of the owner selling the property to a brick firm to build a new business block. During the fall of 1906, I opened a law office in connection with my real estate and rental business. I practiced continuously for nearly one year and did not find the law business very remunerative. At that time, lawyers of our group had very little prestige at the Bar, and our group did not have much confidence in us. They had been taught that the white man was the ideal man with all the influence, and what he did or said was all right, and everything we said or did was all wrong. And there were not enough of those who believed in us to make the field very lucrative.

Before the late Civil War, the Indians owned slaves just the same as the white man, and when war was declared, they seceded from the Union and fought with the Confederacy. After the war closed, Uncle Sam found it necessary to make a treaty with the Indians, compelling them to give to each one of their ex-slaves a head right which consisted of 60 to 100 acres of land, depending altogether on the grade of the land. At the time of this treaty, all the territory of Oklahoma belonged to the Indians. Not an acre of territory belonged to the white man. As soon as this was known, the white man went into the territory and consorted with our group and the Indians until they were successful in getting possession of some of the property. When the treaty was ratified, the Indians and our group became wards of the government— the Indians, the master class, and our group, the servant class. Restrictions were placed on both the Indians' land and the land of our group. In other words, we were prevented from selling the land without the approval of Uncle Sam. Since we were incapable of transacting business for ourselves on account of our wardship, the government took this step to prevent unscrupulous men and women from defrauding us out of our property.

After the white man made his advent among us, consorted with our women, and made our race in Oklahoma God-Almighty's natural conquest, Uncle Sam took the restrictions off the Freed Man's land and left them to the mercy of the unscrupulous white men, who set their price on our group's land, and in a great many cases, defrauded them out of that amount.

In a short while after the restrictions were removed, 75 percent of the land owned by our group was in the hands of the white man. The natives, no sooner than they found out that they could sell their property, went wild to dispose of it, and the land speculator reaped a great harvest. The Glenn Pool Oil Field, the greatest oil pool in Oklahoma, was once the property of our group. Harry Sinclair and others made their millions out of the oil under the land which was acquired from our group. The maximum price paid for their head rights was $1,600. About the time the restrictions were taken off our group's land, I was practicing law and doing a real estate business in Tulsa, Oklahoma, and I was in a position to know the facts in the case. Many natives came to me and asked me to sell their property for them. I would not list it for sale and invariably would refuse them and advise them not to sell their property, for the reason that if they kept their property, they would be a factor, not only in politics but also in the financial affairs of the state. I made loans to several of them to tide them over until they could rent or lease their land, and they never paid me. Had I been selfish, I could have made thousands of dollars off them. They were eager to get that thousand or $1,600, and my advice to them fell on deaf ears, and a great many of them took most anything which was offered them for their land. Up to the present, the restrictions are still on the Indian's land in Oklahoma. They are still wards of the government. Their property has been safeguarded. They have reservations, their schools, and also the protection of the laws of the state and also the enjoyment of all the rights and privileges of any other citizen. Had our group's property rights been safeguarded and Uncle Sam had assisted us in the art of town-building and establishing sufficient public institutions to accommodate our needs, which was his duty to us—the blessing of life and liberty and the protection of the law—there would not have been any grandfather clauses in the Constitution of the state. No separate coach law, no law prohibiting our group from marrying an Indian whom we had associated with from time immemorial, and no law prohibiting the intermarriage of the races. And still, they preach to us loyalty to the flag, to our government, and to the Constitution. May I ask this question: what man of our group is loyal to this hypocritical government, whose motto is, "Down with our group and up with all the other groups of the world?"

It was impossible after my lease expired to find another location for my business. All the old houses were being torn down, and when the new ones were built, they would not rent them to members of our group. And I knew, on account of my scruples in the real estate game, I could not make a fortune in Tulsa, and so I decided to take a vacation for a few weeks and at the same time look for a location for a pool hall and cigar stand. I left Tulsa and went to Muskogee and spent a few days there with friends, left Muskogee for McCurtain in Eastern Oklahoma, where quite a number of our group were employed making coke, left McCurtain for South McAlester. Crowder City, a small town at the junction of the Fort Smith and Western and the Katy Railroad, was where I made connection to go South on the Katy to McAlester. I had to wait there three hours. While there, I walked up into the business part of the town. I passed a pool hall where there were several men playing and a few standing by the table. I went to the porch of the building to look at the players. There was a barbershop in the room also. I noticed three of the men go to the mirror and begin to adjust their ties. They were watching me, and finally, they came out on the porch and said to me, "Where are you going?"

I said, "It is not your business."

They said, "We will make it our business."

They went up the street and came back with the city marshal. I was still standing on the porch when they came up. The marshal said, "Captain."

I paid no attention to him. He called in the same way three times, and when he called the third time, I answered, "Are you calling me?"

He said, "Yes, come here a minute." I went where they stood, and he said, "Do you know that we do not allow your people in this town?"

I asked him was he not the city marshal and sworn to protect the rights of the citizens of the state. I told him that I was a citizen and demanded him to protect me. I would give him the Police Gazette for tomorrow and said that I was a United States Marshal myself.

The marshall then said that he would protect me and asked what my business was there. I told him I was waiting for the first train South. He told me the cause of prohibiting our group from landing there—a member of our group had attempted to assault a white woman there about a year before.

When I left him, I went down to the station to wait for the train. I sat in the waiting room for a few minutes, fearing for my safety on account of darkness. I went out of the room as soon as possible and concealed myself behind the car boxes until the train arrived going South to South McAlester.

In this fair land of ours, our group is not safe in traveling from one place to another, especially in the Southern states. I arrived safely in South McAlester on the following morning. I went out to get what information I could relative to the business side of the question and also the attitude which the city administration had regarding business of that kind. I remained there several days, but I was not much impressed with the town. And so I went to Atoka, which is about 10 miles South of McAlester. I found accommodations in Dad Hill's Hotel. I also met several men from Tulsa and other places who were good sports. As I had left Tulsa to have a good time as well as find a place where I could open a pool hall and sell liquor, we learned of a man by the name of Van Dements, who was running a draw poker game at Ward's Switch about 12 miles South of Atoka. The passenger train did not stop at the Switch. We had to get off at Caney and wait for a local which stopped at the Switch.

On the morning agreed upon, we left Atoka for Ward's Switch. We arrived at Caney and went into the waiting room to wait for the local train. I left the station to look for a place to get my breakfast. On my way, I met two men and asked them where I could find a good place to eat.

One of them said, "You go right down there to Mr. Jim. He is a good man and will treat you fine."

I went down to Mister Jim's place, walked in, and asked him what he had to eat. He said he had some chili. I had never eaten any chili, and I asked him did he have some kind of sandwiches.

He said, "No."

Then I ordered a bowl of chili.

Hearing a whistle which I thought was that of the local train, I went to the front door of the room to ascertain whether it was or not. I found it was not and went back to the rear of the room.

Just as I reached the counter, the cook said, "Your chili is ready."

An Indian was sitting at one end of the counter, and I sat down at the counter. I have never received such a cutting rebuke in all my life.

He said, "Niggers don't sit down there. Your chili is in the kitchen."

I arose from the stool and said, "I beg your pardon, son. I don't eat in my own kitchen," and started out of the room.

He followed me, and when we got near the door, he said, "You must think you are as good as the white people."

I replied that I was as good as any man who has not done any more good than I had done.

Just at that instance, he stepped behind the counter, picked up a hatchet, and said, "I will knock your G-D brains out."

In a flash, I drew my revolver and told him to drop it, or I would kill him. He dropped the hatchet, and I kept the gun pointed at him, and backed out of the door. I returned to the station without anything to eat. I found all of my companions there and told them what had happened, thinking they would defend me if anything happened.

After I left the restaurant, a mob was formed to do me bodily harm. In about an hour after the occurrence in the restaurant, the mob, headed by the owner of the restaurant, made its appearance at the station. I was standing on the platform with my back to it, my elbow on one of the trucks and my head leaning on my hand. Suddenly, my attention was attracted by footsteps and loud talking.

I turned and faced the mob, and one of them said to me, "You are the one who said that you were as good as any G-D white man."

I said that I did not say that, but I would show them the fellow that did say it. I went into the waiting room where those men were who came there with me. A great many of them followed me, and when I got into the room, I told them that not one of them had heard me say what they said I said, and not one of them dared to touch me. If they did, they would do it at their own peril. At that moment I pulled my pistol from my pocket and said, "Let me out of here." I went back out on the platform after they had all cleared the way for me to go. Then one of the mob represented himself as a deputy marshal and had a pair of handcuffs and told me to consider myself under arrest and started toward me.

I pointed my gun directly at him and told him, "If you make another step toward me, I will kill you. None of you can arrest me."

They were armed with bats, ax handles, and almost every conceivable missile.

One of them said, "A six-shooter play is what he wants, and we will give it to him." They dropped their missiles on the depot platform and started running away to get their guns. I see it in my mind's eye, just as plainly now as I did then. The leader of the mob was a man who looked to be around seven feet tall. He had come to the scene on a white-faced sorrel pony. He went to the pony and mounted it, and off he went. His feet were almost touching the ground. After they had all left the station, it was my turn to leave. I walked North on the railway from the station until I got to some freight car boxes.

One of the men, Nickle Billy, a guitar player, who had accompanied me from Atoka, came suddenly out from behind the cars and said, "Oh, Stradford, run for your life! I heard them say that they were going to kill you."

I continued to go north until I reached two section houses on the side of the track where members of our group lived.

I went to the first house and asked the tenant to let me come in so that I might have a little protection from the mob. She cried out, "Don't come in here."

I went to the next house and told them that a mob was pursuing me, and I wanted to go into their house in order that I could protect myself. John Williams, the tenant, said, "Yes, you can go into my house."

I went, and his wife, a noble, brave, and kind-hearted woman with a baby in her arms, followed me into the house, pulled the windows and shades down, and locked the front door. She gave me a double-barreled shotgun and said, "It is loaded good, and I want you to do your best."

I said to her, "Take your baby and get out of the range of the bullets." And she left me all alone in the house.

In a short while, the mob formed at the station and began to march up to the house where I was. I could see in the distance their guns. It seemed to me they were of every description, and every step they made toward the place where I was, was just one step less of time for me to live, I thought.

All of my past came before me, and feeling that the end would soon come, I said to myself, "If I could only see my children once more in life, I would die happy."

I thought of the boy who bought the tapestry from the peasant in the marts of Asia, the virtue of which was to lay it on the ground, get on it, and name the place you wanted to go.

And in the twinkling of an eye, it would land you at that place. If you have never had death staring you in the face, you have no conception of the feeling that possesses one who has.

I had almost given up hope. Just at that moment, a feeling of fortitude possessed me which seemed to say, "Be brave, you will see your children again. Do your best."

Just at this time, the mob came upon the scene. They went to the first house I went into first and searched it and frightened the woman, who was in a delicate condition, so badly that she ran from the house down a hill nearby and had a miscarriage. And I was told she died from the effects of it.

Then they came to the next house and said, "Who lives here?"

John Williams said, "I do."

They said, "Come and go in there with us. A six-shooter play is what he wants, and we're going to give it to him."

John Williams said, "There is the house. If you want him, go in yourself."

The house in which I was in faced south. It had two rooms with a door between them. The front door was left wide open, and also the middle door. I was stationed behind the partition of the door with several boards in front of me designed for a breastwork and had the gun resting on the board pointing directly at the front door. There were two steps to come up.

The two leaders of the mob carried in their hands a 45-caliber pistol. When they came upon the second step, I cried, "Halt," and they did. I said, "Get out from in front of the door," and they scattered like birds. There was an ex-deputy United States marshal by the name of Gabe, whom they got to act as a go-between. He came to the door and said that one of the men who had started into the house was a good and square shooter, and that he had come with the mob to see that I got a square deal, and it would be safer for me to let him and the other guy come in. I told him that they could come in and sit in the front room, but if they attempted to come into the room where I was, I would kill them. They agreed to this and came in and sat down near the door.

In the meantime, United States Marshal LaFlore had been called at Atoka and told that there was a "bad nigger down there who had made several gun plays," and they had him surrounded and to send an officer at once to take him. The house was surrounded by at least 500 people yelling, "Lynch the nigger," and others saying, "Burn him out!" The man on the inside with me stood in the door and remonstrated with them and avoided the catastrophe. The fast train, the Katy Flyer, was 30 minutes late, and on this train, the marshal was expecting the deputy marshal to arrest me. The house I was in was near the railroad track, and most of the crowd was standing on the track. The train approached, running at the rate of 60 miles an hour. The whistle blew, but before the crowd could clear the track, two men were struck by it. One was killed instantly, and the other was hastened to a doctor's office and died before he could get medical attention.

The north and southbound trains met at Caney. The officer came in great haste to the scene. He came in and said, "Give me your gun. I will protect you. Follow me; that train is waiting for us." We left the building, and just as I crossed the railroad track, a most ghastly object met my view. A dead man. His eyes burst out and hung down on his face, and his entrails were scattered along the track. As soon as we arrived at the station, we boarded the train for Atoka. When we arrived, I was incarcerated in the

County Jail. In the preliminary hearing, I was bound over to the district court and my bond was fixed at $500.00 and my case set for the October term of court. I remained in jail nine days before I could have bond arranged. My banker in Tulsa, where I had my deposit, sent the cash down to the court, and I was released. I went back in October on the day which the case was set for a hearing and remained there for several days. But it did not come up. For some reason, it was continued until the next term of court. I was there on that date, and still it was continued. I suggested to my attorney, inasmuch as the cost was so great to make so many trips down there, that I would plead guilty, provided the minimum fine would be assessed. The agreement was accepted, and I paid the sum of $45.00 and costs and was discharged for defending myself against a Georgia cracker.

I found it impossible to get a room in Tulsa in which to do business. The white people had entered into an alliance not to rent a business room to a Negro. Since I knew that the way to make money fast was in the recreation hall and club business, I decided to leave Tulsa. I first went to a small town in Oklahoma, Anadarko, put in a two-table pool hall, but found that the town was too small to support it. I stayed there for three months, and then I moved to another small town. I found business much better in Lawton than it was in Anadarko. For a while it bade fair to come up to my expectations. I had a three-table pool hall, cigar, cigarettes, tobacco, and a lunch stand, and I also sold soft drinks.

The Barnum and Bailey Show came to town. I secured a lot near the show ground for a lunch and soft drink stand. The agent for Pabst Brewery, Carl Schultz, agreed to sell me all the near-beer I needed for that day. I went out early on the morning and fixed up my stand for business. In that part of the state, there were a great many Indians from Fort Sill on the Kiowa Reservation, where Chief Geronimo was held as a military prisoner at Fort Sill on the Kiowa Reservation, four miles from Lawton. He had been transferred there from Alabama. He was allowed his liberty, and every Saturday and Sunday, he would come down to Lawton to have a good time, buying firewater, although it was an offense to sell it to him. There were a great many blanket Indians in the county, and on show day, they all came to town.

My tent was beautifully decorated with flags and different shades of crepe paper, which seemed to catch the Indians' fancy, and they all hung around my tent. I was selling near-beer, pop, sandwiches, and watermelons. I was doing a land office business, selling near-beer. The Indians were my best customers. They had plenty of money and spent it freely for what they wanted. I sold 40 cases that day, mostly to them, and it proved to be intoxicating, and they lay drunk around the tent until I closed the place, Geronimo and all of his followers. The agent for the brewing company had made a mistake and given me genuine beer instead of near-beer. Financially, this day was a grand success. I have often wondered how I escaped the clutches of the law after I had made so many of those Indians drunk on what I supposed was near-beer.

Lawton was the home of Al Jennings, the train robber, who in later years ran in the primary election for governor of the state. It was also the home of Jake Hammond, the millionaire oilman, who was killed by his private secretary. He was a power in politics in the Harding administration, and also, the home of the Chief of Police, Heck Thomas, who was noted for the number of notches he had filed in his revolver, each notch indicating one dead man, and his gun was almost full of notches. Lawton was one of the most prejudiced towns in the state. I went into the weekly newspaper office to call up a party. There were none of the attaches in the office at the time. But there was a white man sitting in the office. I asked him was he an employee of the office, and he said he was not. I told him what I wanted, and he said, "Use the phone: I guess there will be no objection."

I began to use the phone. Just at that time, the proprietor came in and in a gruff voice said, "Who told you to use that phone?" I told him. He said, "That man has nothing to do with this phone. Do you suppose I want to use a phone that a damn nigger's mouth has touched? Get out of here!" I obeyed orders and avoided an assault.

Another incident I will mention, which shows the attitude of the white man toward our group. In those days, saloons were flourishing all over the state. My place of business was near a saloon. One night, I went into a man's saloon by the name of John Russell and called for a glass of beer. He drew the beer and told me to come back to the rear of the saloon to drink it. I refused to do so and turned to go out. Just as I turned, he threw the glass and its contents at me and struck me in the back of the head. I fell forward to the floor, and when I regained consciousness, I got up and ran out. There were a great many soldiers in the saloon. They yelled, "Kill the damn nigger." In my dazed condition, I hid myself under some freight car boxes on the track. I could see them searching for me, but they did not find me. After they gave up the search, I went back to my place of business, bruised and bleeding from the effects of the blow. Many other incidents I can mention which occurred while I lived there, which show the cruelties and injustices which are perpetrated against our group, Negroes, not only in Oklahoma, but all over the Southland. In the evolution of things, I believe that there will be a day of recompense, and the white man will reap what he has sown.

Prior to establishing a business in Anadarko, I established a place of business in Enid, Oklahoma, which consisted of two pool tables, a showcase, and a counter and dispensed near-beer, cigars, cigarettes, and tobacco. After remaining there for several months, I sold it for $500.00 cash and went back to Tulsa. While there, I had a good business in my club room.

Booker T. Washington was billed to speak at Langston University, and our group would go from the remote parts of the state to hear him. Jim Rouse, a regent of the school, Pete Tyler, an attorney, George Robinson, and several others, all from Watonga, Oklahoma, were on their way to Langston City to hear him. They had to stop in Enid to make connections to go there. They arrived in Enid about 7:00 p.m. and had to wait until the following morning at 7:30 for the train going to Langston City. I was personally acquainted with Mr. Rouse. Since they were compelled to stay in Enid all night, they asked me to furnish some sport for the evening. Peter Tyler suggested a draw poker game with a charge of $10.00. They all agreed. I furnished everything for our pleasure, and we sat down to play and played all night. During the time we played, I never showed them a hand less than three aces. Every time they called, I would show them straights, flushes, full houses, and fours—fours twice, four aces three times. I won $500.00 that night and could have won as many thousand if they had it. I have never had so much luck in all my life in such a short space of time. I made an enemy of Jim Rouse. He said that he had always regarded me as an honest man, but since I had robbed him of his money, he had found out that he was wrong. I lent them money to finish their trip. This happened in 1906, and in 1927, I met him at the Elks' Convention in Chicago, and he had forgotten the past and retracted the statement that I was not an honest man.

The most important incident which occurred to me while living in Lawton was the meeting of my future wife, and how it happened that I met her. I was going from Oklahoma City to Tulsa, and we were on the same train. She was traveling in company with her sister and her sister's children on their way to Canton, Mississippi to see their mother. When we had gotten about 40 miles from Oklahoma City, we found that there had been a wreck of a cattle train, and a great many cattle were killed. The track was torn up for some distance and our train was delayed for six hours. I was a great lover of children, and by attention I paid to the little bright boy, I succeeded in making myself acquainted with her and her sister. I passed the time away very agreeably there during our delay. My first wife died in 1905, and from that time until I met this woman, I had not seen a woman whose appearance had appealed to me as a wife. She was fascinating, quiet, unassuming, dignified, and very loveable, and she made an impression upon me which was lasting. Before I left the train in Tulsa, I asked her for her address and the privilege to correspond with her.

In selecting a wife, it was necessary for her to have a reputation of morality and chastity and a soul which was pure and sweet. While she was in Mississippi, I made it my business to search

Middle-aged JB and his second wife

her record before I wrote to her. And I found her to be a woman of good moral character. Then I wrote to her with the view of making her my wife. The courtship lasted about six months, and at the expiration of that time, we were made man and wife. My happiness was made complete by the union. Her maiden name of Augusta I. L. Carmichael was changed to Mrs. J.B. Stradford, and she was quite an asset in helping in our business career.

The building in which I was located was leased by me from month to month. I received a notice to move on account of the building being sold. I tried hard to find another location, but there was none available. The same condition prevailed here as in Tulsa. It seemed that the real estate men and agents had entered into an agreement not to rent to members of our group, rooms in the business section of the town, and that is a great handicap to our businessmen. I had established a paying business and in less than 30 days, I was dispossessed of it and had to move somewhere or leave town.

I went to Chickasha, Oklahoma, and found a room there suitable and moved my outfit there. I promoted a pool tournament of 300-ball straight pool between a white pool player from Chicago, who had a great reputation as a player, and my son, who was at that time, 16 years old. I secured a large skating rink for the contest. The financial side of it was a failure, but my son won the contest, losing only the second string of the 100 points.

Chapter 11

In 1907, Indian Territory became a state, and the first acts of the legislature were to pass all the discriminatory legislation that was in existence in all the Southern states. Haskell, an Ohio man, was elected the first governor. He injected into the campaign the race question and in all of his speeches, he was vitriolic in his utterances against our group, which made it a very easy matter for him to defeat his Republican opponent, F. Frantz. The first act which was passed was the Separate Coach Law. The next was the grandfather clause prohibiting all of our group from voting whose grandfathers lived in the United States prior to 1861. Then the act preventing the intermarriages of the whites and the Negroes, and also the Indians and members. But the whites and Indians could marry at will. At the time these laws were passed, there were no restrictions whatever on trains, or voting, and a man could marry anyone whom he wished. The white man had been consorting with our group from time immemorial, and the Indian and members had lived together in family relations. When these laws were passed, they were not only repulsive, but they engendered hatred and ill will and a feeling of revenge on the part of our group for the white man who had associated with us until he had debunked and robbed us of our lands. Feeling the injustice of the matter, a great many of our people sold their farms and went to Canada, California and Africa to get away from the persecution. Those who remained had to grin and bear it. Others fought the laws in the courts of the state and also in the federal courts of Kansas and the Supreme Court of the United States.

On the first of June 1906, my son, Cornelius Francis Stradford, graduated from high school in Coffeyville, Kansas. At that time, I was residing in Chickasha, Oklahoma. I bought a through ticket from that point to Coffeyville, Kansas to see my boy graduate. Since I was an interstate passenger, I took the chair car instead of the separate coach compartment. The porter did not see me when I entered. When he discovered and saw me, he came to me and told me my coach was in the front and ordered me to go into it in a very dictatorial manner. I told him that I did not want to have any trouble with him, and the thing for him to do was to call the conductor and let him fight his own battles. He left me and sent the conductor. The conductor was a Swede, uncouth and uncultured. He came up and in a gruff voice said, "Get into your own coach."

I said to him, "This is my coach, and I am going to ride in it to my destination and the best you can get out of it is to call the law."

He left me and came back with the auditor of the road and asked me to show him my ticket. I gave him my ticket for inspection. He examined it and returned it to me. Later on, after the train left the station, he punched my ticket and things passed off peacefully until we arrived in Fallis, about 20 miles north of

J.B.'s son, Cornelius Francis Stradford

Oklahoma City. The mayor of Fallis and one of his commissioners boarded the train there and saw me sitting in the chair car and demanded my removal from the coach. The conductor told them that I had been ordered out of the coach in Oklahoma and had refused to obey orders.

Then they said, "We will throw him off," and started back to the seat which I occupied with the intention of putting me off the train.

I was sitting in the last seat at the rear of the train. When I thought they were near enough, I got up from my seat, pulled my gun, cocked it, and said, "If you make another step toward me, I will kill both of you."

The women screamed, and the passengers ducked down in their seats, and these two bad men went back to their seats, and the train kept on going.

At Pawhuska, 100 miles from Oklahoma City, a deputy sheriff eased himself into my seat and said, "I am an officer, consider yourself under arrest."

I submitted and said, "I refused to take that separate coach in Oklahoma City, where there is all the law, and they refused to have me arrested. And I can't see why you want to take the chance of arresting me and cause me a great disappointment."

He said that he had been called by the conductor to make the arrest, but if I would promise him that I would go into the car which the law provided for me, he would let me go. I thanked him and went into the Jim Crow car and got to Coffeyville in time to attend the graduating exercise. I remained in Coffeyville several days after the occasion, and then I took my two children with me to spend the summer in Chickasha.

When we boarded the train in Coffeyville, we took the chair car and remained in it without molestation until we crossed the Oklahoma line. After we had crossed the line, the conductor came to see us and said, "Your car is in front."

I told him that this was my car, and I would not be removed, and the thing for him to do to avoid trouble was to call the law. Wynona was the first city out of Coffeyville. He called the law there, and it refused to act. Dewey was the second stop, and he had called the law there. When the train pulled up to Dewey, there was a large, yelling crowd assembled there. They cried, "Bring him out here. We have a rope and will hang him."

The conductor stood in the doorway between me and the crowd, and the crowd clamored for me. I told the conductor that I would not get off there and asked him to take me to the County Seat, Bartlesville, or else there would be hell to pay in a holy minute. He carried me on to Bartlesville. When we arrived, there was an immense crowd awaiting me at the station. The sheriff came into the coach where I was and arrested me and my children and incarcerated us in jail. I had enough money to put up for bonding my children, but I remained in jail until the following morning when my case came up for trial before a Justice of the Peace by the name of Hull. In the meantime, I had secured a lawyer to defend me. The county attorney was a classmate of mine at Indiana Law School, and he knew of my sentiments relative to my rights. He had animosity against me and did all that he could to convict me. But Judge Hull decided that I was an interstate passenger and could not be held guilty under the interstate passenger law. The courtroom was filled to capacity during the trial, and when I was dismissed, the angry crowd threatened me and said to the conductor, "When he comes down to the train in the morning, we will be there. Put him where he belongs, and if he refuses to go, we will take charge of him."

While the mob was so threatening, my daughter cried out, "Oh, Papa, let's go out the rear door to escape their frenzy."

I said to her, "Don't be afraid. Follow me. No one is going to hurt you."

We pushed through the crowd and made our way into the street. For damages in this case, I sued Missouri, Kansas, and the Texas Railroad Company for $5,000.00 in federal court in Fort Scott, Kansas. After the case had been tried on its merits and from the evidence, we felt that we would get a judgment. The case went to the jury. Judge Pollock, in giving his instructions to the jury, said, "Gentlemen of the jury: When a black man comes into my court, I afford him all the rights and privileges of another man. But when it comes to the place where he wants to put himself on me in public places where the law forbids, I draw the line."

The jury was out for 15 minutes and came back with a verdict for the defendant in the case. I was so incensed by his instructions that if I had my pistol, I would have taken one crack shot at him. He made a reversible error, and I was advised by my attorney to appeal the case, but on account of the cost, I dropped it, feeling that there was no justice in this country for members of our group when our rights were denied us by the whites.

On the following morning, we went to the station and to avoid further trouble, we boarded the Jim Crow car for Chickasha.

My son remained with me until the latter part of August. I sent him to Oberlin College to pursue his master's degree, and he graduated from Oberlin College in 1912. In June 1915, my daughter married a man by the name of Samuel G. Toole. In the following year, she would have graduated from high school. I advised her against the union and told her I wanted her to finish high school, but he had made it plain to her that she could continue in school and finish the next year. And my advice to her fell on deaf ears. I told her that I had never refused her anything that she had asked of me, and that if that was her will, I would grant her request. I had also planned that after she finished high school that I would send her to the Conservatory of Music at Oberlin to finish her musical education. Her fiancé made her the same promise, and she believed him. And that was the end to all schooling for a couple of years. In one year's time, she was engaged in intensive housekeeping with a family of three.

I remained in Chickasha until October and then moved to Arkansas City, Kansas, and established a business there. It fell far short of my expectations in a money-making way, and so I was making inquiries of places where the prospects were rosy for making money. One of my acquaintances, who had been living on the Western coast, gave me a glowing account of Seattle and the possibility of a shrewd businessman of our group making a fortune there in a short time. The Panama-Yukon-Alaska World's Fair was to be held in Seattle in 1909. I decided to go, and he said that would be a good place to make money because there were a great many of our group living there. And on account of the Fair, thousands of them would be there from all over the country.

He further said that there were only a few places of business there operated by members of our group and that if I would go there early and get a good location in the right neighborhood, he was certain that I could make good. He further said that he was going to make the fair. He was a chief cook by trade and was going there for the purpose of going into the restaurant business. I began to get all the information I could about Seattle and the Fair, and I found that Seattle was a fast-growing city, and there was very little discrimination against our group. I started to make preparations to go to Seattle. I offered my place for sale at a very low price, but none of those would-be buyers had any money. So, I stored my outfit. Just before going to Chickasha to live, my wife and I visited my children in Coffeyville, Kansas. On our return to Lawton, we boarded the train in Coffeyville, and as there was no separate coach law in Kansas, we went into the chair car and took seats. When the train crossed the Oklahoma line, the conductor came to me and said, "Your coach is in the front car," and told my wife to remain seated. "This was her coach."

She told him that her coach was the same as mine. Then he said, "Both of you go into the separate coach."

I told him that we were going to remain in the coach we were occupying until we reached our destination; that we were interstate passengers, and the Jim Crow law did not affect us, and that we had been arrested and the case had been dismissed on the grounds that we were interstate passengers. He said that we could not ride in that coach and that if we did not take the coach the law provided for us, he would have us arrested. We refused to be moved, and at Dewey, he called the law to meet the train at Bartlesville. The sheriff's crew met the train, and we were arrested in Bartlesville and carried to a Justice of the Peace's office and put under a $50.00 cash bond each. I deposited $100.00 for our appearance for trial on a fixed date. On the date fixed, I returned to Bartlesville, but the case did not come up for trial and another date was set. I made another trip up there, and still, it did not come up. And I could get no information on when it would come up. When I demanded my money, I was told that the Justice was short in his accounts and had left the city, and so I was never able to collect my hundred dollars. That is the way our group is treated, as a rule, in all of his dealings with the white man, not only in Oklahoma, but all through the Southland.

While I was living in Arkansas City, I went back to Tulsa to look after my property. As I said before, there is no Jim Crow law in that state. I went into the chair car when I got to the train and was ordered by the conductor to go into the separate coach when the train crossed the Oklahoma line. I did not refuse to go, but before going, I asked permission to ask one question. Instead of granting the request, the conductor and brakeman both grabbed me and forcibly put me in the Jim Crow coach, and on the arrival of the train in Pawhuska, I was arrested and lodged in jail. On the following morning, my case was tried and I was acquitted. I then instituted a damage suit against the railroad for $2,500.00 in the Circuit Court of Pawhuska County, and the verdict was rendered in favor of the defendant. I appealed the case to the Supreme Court of the State, and the judgment of the lower court was sustained.

After a lengthy discussion of the facts in the case, the judge said, "We do not wish to understand as saying that the plaintiff in error is remediless. That question, not being before us, is not decided. The only question presented by the records is the liability of the railroad under the pleadings and facts. As has been seen, no liability is attached, and plaintiff is not entitled to recover. Having reached this conclusion, no good would be accomplished by the consideration of the other questions raised in the petition in error. The judgment of the district court of Osage County should be affirmed." Volume 36, Oklahoma Reports.

    In order to get to Seattle in time to get a suitable location for my business, I left Arkansas City in the latter part of April and arrived there about the first of May. The rainy season was about over. Seattle is a very beautiful city, and at that time, it was a very orderly one. I don't remember seeing any drunks there, although the saloons were flourishing. One of the most interesting objects was the totem poles on First Street. They were the most curious sights to behold. Another interesting, and, as I thought, most wonderful performance that I had ever witnessed was the washing down of those great high hills by hydraulic waterpower, filling up low places with dirt and making the city as level as a plane. I found in Seattle a very few of our group in business. The Japanese and Chinese had succeeded in getting all of the jobs which we were accustomed to having, such as porters, waiters, house servants, and barbers. There were a few barbershops run by our group, three or four saloons operated and owned by our group, and several club rooms run by our people. There was very little discrimination in a business way in restaurants, hotels, and inns, and on account of this condition, our group was not very clannish.

    After sizing up the condition, I decided to put in a four-table pool hall with cigars, cigarettes, tobacco, and pop and hire a girl to sell ice cream cones and be the cashier. I secured a room for business in the Florence Hotel for $100.00 per month. I was always a poor billiard pool player, and most everyone I played would beat me, but I would tell them that my son would be with me on about June 1 and would avenge my adversaries. I wrote my son a letter, enclosed $100.00 for him to pay his bills and come to us as soon as school closed. On account of my talking so much about him everyone seemed to know him when he came into the hall. He came in due time and after several weeks' practice, he took on all comers. He beat all of his opponents, and our coffers grew fat with filthy lucre.

His face was circulated up and down the coast as a great pool player. One evening, the champion pool player of Vancouver in the British came into my place, and the kid was practicing pool on the table. He said to him, "Kid, I will play you a game of pool."

The "Kid," as they called him, said, "All right." He then asked him how much he would play for. The Kid said, "Let your conscience be your guide."

The Vancouver man said, "I will play you 50-point line pool for $10.00."

The Kid said, "All right, put your money up in Papa's hands."

The man put his money up and picked his cue and began to practice. While he was practicing, the Kid came to me and said, "Papa, I can beat him."

A great many of the champion's friends had accompanied him to my place to see the game and bet on him beating the Kid. When my boy said, "I can beat him," I said in a loud voice, "Who will come along with him," meaning your bets are on. All of his backers came to me and laid their money on their friend. I took my notebook from my pocket and wrote the names of those who made bets and the amount opposite their names. After all the bets were made, a coin was tossed to see which one would win the break. The white man won the break, and after the break, he left a combination dead for the corner. My boy, on account of his height, did not see it. He then made a safe shot, and the ball, which was a combination, stopped right in front of the corner pocket. His opponent pocketed that ball, and the cue ball scattered the other balls all over the table. He then began his run. He ran the first 15 balls and then lined them up and began the second string. He played with so much accuracy and skill that I was sure that we would lose the game. When he pocketed the 23rd ball, I was standing on the opposite side of the room from my boy. My knees were shaking with excitement. My boy noticed my condition and came to where I was and said, "Papa. Don't be alarmed. All I want is a shot."

His opponent missed the 26th shot, and my boy's turn was next. In his masterly and skillful way of playing, he ran the 50 points. I ran to him, put him on my shoulder, and ran all around the pool tables with him, several times with frantic joy. Pandemonium reigned supreme for quite a while. Our group had bet on my boy, and all the white fellows had bet on their choice. Several hundred dollars had been wagered and lost by them.

After order had been restored, the Kid asked how much he wanted to bet on the next game, and he refused to play anymore and said, "You are too good for me."

Another game worth relating was played between my boy and Bojangles, the theatrical man, William Robinson. He and his partner were playing in the Orpheum Circuit in Seattle. Bojangles lost $75.00 that evening, which was all he had, and borrowed $5.00 of it back from me, and he still owes it. I am sure he would have paid it long ago, but I have never seen him since that night.

The World's Fair was a failure as far as attendance was concerned. The most business that I did, or in other words, the most money I made was what the Kid made playing pool. I had a three-chair barbershop in which I was the head barber, but it did not pay. I soon found that there was no big money to be made. I sold the place to two Japanese and went to Walla Walla, Washington, and opened a place of business there. Business was poor. There were not a great many of our group living there. I stayed there for only three months as I was not able to get a good location.

On the first of September, I sent my son back to Oberlin College and stayed in Walla Walla and remained there for about two months, sold out my place, and left to join my wife in Canton, Mississippi. Walla Walla is a beautiful city in the midst of a farming center. You can stand on the streets of the city and look for miles straight up on the hills until they seem to reach the skies and see wheat fields which produce 40 bushels of wheat to the acre. There is never a crop failure. The farmers know from a mathematical certainty just how much grain they can raise per acre. They have the irrigating system and know just how much water it will take to produce their crops. Socially, there was not much discrimination. All places of business were open to all our people. There were no Colored churches there at that time. All attended the same churches, schools, ate and slept in the same hotels and restaurants. There seemed to be a feeling of brotherly love among all of the people. I have never in all my life seen so little prejudice exhibited, even in Canada, as I saw displayed in Walla Walla.

The route I took from Walla Walla to Canton, Mississippi, was through Portland, Oregon, thence through California, Arizona, New Mexico, Texas, and New Orleans, from there to Canton.

My ticket called for two stopovers, one in San Francisco and one in Los Angeles. I spent a day and night in San Francisco, taking in Chinatown and visiting quite a few of the nightclubs. The sceneries along the route to San Francisco were most beautiful. One which is worthy of mention, and which created a lasting impression on me, was that of Mount Chastity. The train stopped there to give all the passengers an opportunity to take a drink of water which flowed down the mountainside, almost as far as you could see into the mountain. The stream was decorated with all colors of electric bulbs on each side of the stream, and it presented an unusual sight—grand, resplendent, and attractive. The beauties of nature combined with that of art is awe-inspiring and gives a feeling of such profound admiration that I cannot find words to express my feelings.

The next thing of great interest to me, which I think is worthy of mentioning was the ferry at Oakland, California. The train on which I was riding went into the ferry and many other trains also, and when it had finished loading its cargo of human and material freight and steered out into the water, it appeared to be a small city on an island. I was surprised beyond measure because I had never seen or heard of such a thing before. The greatest object I had in going the coast route to my destination was to see the Golden Gate in San Francisco. I had always fancied the idea that the gates were a colossal structure, hung on two huge golden posts which in company with the gates was kept shining brightly at all times so that anyone could see it far off. With what information I had, I started out to find the Golden Gate. The streetcar conductor let me off the car and directed me the way to find it. I followed his directions until I came in sight of the water. I saw no such sight as I had pictured in my mind. On the right-hand side, I saw a structure of stone or maybe it was a stone house. I was not close enough to see clearly, and opposite it on the left-hand side, there was another structure of the same kind. That was all I saw, and I have never been convinced that that was the Golden Gate. I cannot truthfully say that I have seen the Golden Gate.

The route over the Southern Pacific from San Francisco to Los Angeles was a scenic beauty. On the right side, I could see the broad, blue and mild Pacific, extending seemingly into the skies with the long waves rolling, shifting and washing the shores. On the left side, the beautiful fertile plains and woodland valleys presented the most beautiful appearance, making one feel like he was passing through the garden of the gods. Nearing Los Angeles, the scene was changed to grape arbors and for miles and miles, nothing met your view except those grape arbors. When I arrived in Los Angeles, I found that the grape industry was the principal product of that county. The station platform was packed with baskets of grapes and also the surrounding space for a block. I can truthfully say that up to that time, I had never had enough grapes at one time in my life. As there was no objection to anyone eating as many as he wished, I proceeded to get my fill. Los Angeles is a very beautiful city, situated on the Pacific Ocean.

While there I met a few of my friends who had left Oklahoma to escape Jim Crowism and segregation which had been legislated recently in Oklahoma.

The first incident that occurred after I left Los Angeles on the Southern Pacific for my destination, I went into the dining car to get my dinner. The head waiter seated me at a table in front of the car with my back to the rear of the dining room, and when he had taken my order, he pulled a curtain which hung behind me and shut off my view from the other part of the car. I did not see him when he pulled the curtain, and I sat there for some time waiting for my order before I noticed the situation. I jumped up from my seat and tore the curtain down and threw it on the floor and asked the head waiter had the train crossed the Texas border. He made no reply. My dinner was served without the curtain, and the next time I went in for lunch, I seated myself where I wished and there was nothing said or done to oppose it. The rest of the journey through Arizona and New Mexico was delightful. There was nothing to mar my comfort and happiness until I arrived at El Paso, Texas. I had never in my life entered a Jim Crow coach that I did not feel less of a man when I went out of it than when I went into it. As we approached the line of Texas, I could smell the fumes of persecution, discrimination and segregation permeating the air in the space before we reached the Texas line. We had a layover for several hours in El Paso and then started on our journey to New Orleans at the end of the line. The coach provided for our people was the smoker with one end partitioned off and six seats on each side of the car. In this coach, the Indians rode also. They were as filthy as hogs. They spit all over the floor. They were dirty, filthy and not worthy of the association of decent and respectable citizens. The separate coach law was passed for Negroes, and a separate boxcar should have been provided for the Indians.

 Along the line of justice, the legislature meted out in providing equal accommodation for all passengers, the basic principle of their government is justice to all of its citizens regardless of race, color or creed, and the inalienable rights of life, liberty and the pursuit of happiness are guaranteed to them. These high-sounding phrases and sentences don't mean anything to us. Every inspiration and every hope are fraught with opposition. Our manhood is being crushed out of us by the nefarious laws which have been passed by all the Southern states and by a failure of the Northern states and Western states to enforce the laws relating to our group. Fifteen million of our group, citizens of this republic are not loyal citizens of this government and can't be. They are awakening to a sense of their importance. The Day of Atonement is sure to come, and the oppressors will reap what they have sown.

When I crossed the ferry landing into the City of New Orleans, the first question I asked, "Where is the Gulf of Mexico?" To my surprise, I was told it was 91 miles South. I visited several places of interest in New Orleans, among them the YMCA. The secretary was a fine young man and was doing good work in collecting funds for a building. Dr. Burbridge was a director of the institution, and he entertained me by showing me the beauties of the city and inviting me to dine at his residence. That night I left New Orleans for Canton, Mississippi. I remained there for two weeks with my wife and her family. Canton, like all other Southern towns, has its peculiar characteristics relative to our group. They class all of us alike. One may be pure, wholly intellectual and as rich as a Croesus, but they say, "He is nothing but a nigger," and he has no right we are bound to respect. In support of this statement, I will mention an incident which occurred just before I arrived. A woman of our group did some laundry for a white woman in town and sent the laundry by one of her children to the white woman. She received the laundry and did not pay the child for it. When the child came home without the money, her mother went to the woman's house to collect it. She told the woman that she was a poor widow and had several children to support and they did not have any provisions at home and that she was expecting that money to buy something to eat for her children. She further said, "If you did not have the money to pay for the laundry, you should have told me, and I would not have done your laundry."

The woman said to her, "Nigger, don't you sass me. I will tell my husband of your impudence."

The laundress replied that she was not afraid of her husband and left the scene. In the evening when her husband came in from his business, she told him what had happened, and the following morning, he went to the Colored woman's home and severely beat her with his walking cane. She went before a justice of the peace and asked for a warrant for his arrest. The justice refused to issue it and told her to go home and behave herself and not to sass white people.

Another case happened while I was there. A woman of our group was working in service for a white woman who attempted to whip the servant for failing to perform some trivial duty, whereupon the servant gave the employer a severe beating. The servant was arrested and incarcerated in jail and on the following morning, her case was set for trial before the police judge. The husband of the plaintiff came to court with a cowhide, and when the prisoner was brought into court, he beat her unmercifully without the interference of any of the court attaches and her husband was a witness to the whole proceeding and was afraid to even voice a protest. After she had been beaten unmercifully, he assisted her home. That ended the trial. No further punishment was imposed. My soul was aflame with indignation against such persecution, and I cried out, "How long, oh, Lord, how long will such brutality continue?"

While in Canton, I was treated fine by our group. I was dined and wined. I visited several of the schools, private and public, and addressed all of the schools that I visited. In each address, I denounced the treatment which we received at the hands of the white man, and also the method employed to prevent us from voting in the elections of the state, etc. In each talk, I always warned the children not to tell Mr. George what I had said until I had left Canton. At the expiration of two weeks, my wife and I left Canton.

On our way to Tulsa, we stopped in Memphis, Tennessee to see Mr. Robert Church who was very hospitable and showed us quite a few places of interest. Among them was his park on Beale Street and the bank in which he was interested. Mr. Church was the wealthiest man of our group in Memphis and was very prominent financially and politically. Two of his children attended school in Oberlin while I was there. Molly, the older, graduated from college in 1884. Tom, better known as A.G., was a classmate of mine. I was very much attached to him and in 1915, I invited him to New York City.

We arrived in Tulsa the following afternoon. We did not get off the train but kept on to Coffeyville to see my daughter. We were overjoyed to see each other. I remained there several days and then returned to Tulsa, after three years spent in other places which I have mentioned before trying to accumulate a fortune. I did not have much success. I found conditions somewhat improved, along the lines of securing a place to do business. In the first place, I took over the agency of my property and engaged in the real estate business. I bought a building from a man by the name of Tom Gentry. The room was 50 x 80 feet and had six private rooms. I secured a charter for a social club. The six rooms were used as follows: first, president's office, second, reading room, third, dining room, fourth, kitchen, fifth and sixth, club rooms. The name of the club was "Marquette." In the large room, there were five pool tables and one billiard table on one side. And on the other side was the dance hall. Every Tuesday and Thursday, ladies were given the privilege to use the billiard hall. At that time, all lines of business were flourishing in Tulsa. Our group was very prosperous. The Northeast section of the city had been secured for our group and plotted into city lots with one business street running North through to the section line. We had all kinds of businesses on said street, hotels, rooming houses, grocery stores, wholesale and retail, garages, haberdashers, clothing stores, meat markets, drugstores, delicatessens, soft drink stands, barbershops, restaurants, pool halls and everything for our comfort and happiness. Carrying out the white man's ignorance in prejudice, we prohibited him from operating a business among us, and if he succeeded in getting a place among us, we could boycott him. We were very clannish along that line, so much so that we had members of our group as police officers and also justices of the peace. We had Jitney lines running out Lansing Street to accommodate the public. I had a wonderful business. On the South side of Tulsa was the residential section, and all the millionaires lived there in their magnificent structures. Each had servant quarters built in the rear and nearly all of them employed members of our group as servants. I don't think that I would exaggerate if I should say that at least 1,000 of our group were quartered on the South side. Some of them had as many as five or six servants and maybe more. Such men as Harry Sinclair, his brother, Earl, the Cosdens and many more too numerous to mention had made their millions, so to speak, overnight. This group of servants was well paid for their services and spent their money as freely as they received it. And every night, my place was filled with them, tripping the fantastic toe and enjoying themselves, partaking of all the wares I had to offer them in a lawful way.

Our charter gave us the right to have liquor for our revenue members which was quite a source of revenue. I was president and general manager. Each branch of the business had a man at the head of it. The man who had charge of the liquor reported that his supply was exhausted and asked me to get him a case. I told him I would try. There was a club up in town called, "The Mission Club," which had the reputation of furnishing such wares, and I decided that I would go up and try to get a case from them. I am simply stating this case to show the feeling those Southern crackers have for our group. I went upstairs. The bar was on the right, and as I approached the bartender, he said, "Take off your hat." The owner of the club was standing to my left at the bar. I turned and faced him and asked, "Mr. A, is this your rule for people to take off their hats when they come into this club?"

He replied, "Those are my rules, Stradford."

Looking all around me, I saw no one with his hat off. Then I replied, "If you fellows don't want to see me with my hat on, reach over here and take it off. Do you think that I would take off my hat in a dump like this?" And with my hand on my revolver, I backed down the steps in order to keep them from shooting me in the back.

A short time before this incident, one of our group was employed by a brewery company to deliver beer to saloons in the city and Oklahoma City. He went into the saloon to deliver a case of beer. When he entered, the bartender ordered him to take off his hat and when he showed no evidence that he was going to set the case of beer down and take off his hat, the bartender shot him dead on the spot. Remembering this incident, I went up there prepared to protect myself. Another reason, the owner of the club was considered a bad man. He had clubbed several United States Marshals with his six-shooter and more than once had ordered officers out of his place with his six-shooter pointed at them, ready to fire the fatal shot if they failed to obey his order. I have always been a casual observer of things and persons. I have always been deep down in my heart a lover and supporter of right principles, and I have lent a hand to those who I felt needed assistance as much as I could afford.

My dance hall was crowded every night with girls who were in service on the South side who had come from all sections of the United States, some bad, per se, and others good. They were all socially equal. They attended the same churches, dance halls, restaurants and other places of public accommodation, and went back to their quarters to perform their daily duties. I noticed quite a few of them who sat quietly through the evening entertainment without taking any part in the dance or accepting the attention of the young men.

On more than one occasion, I have gone to those girls and asked why they did not take a part in the entertainment and invariably, I would get the same answer, namely, that they had not been accustomed to going to such places and associating with that class of people. But their associates insisted on their going out with them, and as there was no other place to go for amusement, they went to please them. I asked them if there were any other places, such as a reading room or a library, would they spend their evenings in such places, reading good books and periodicals, etc. At that time there were no libraries or YMCAs in Tulsa for our people or for girls and young women. For humanity's sake I founded a library and reading room in Tulsa in 1915. I bought a frame building 20 x 30, had it moved on the lot of the Oklahoma Realty and Investment Company of which I was the president. I made a shelf 16 feet long and two feet wide.

Chapter 12

The height of it was 4-1/2 feet, and it was fastened to the wall with hinges. Our shelf was supplied with one daily paper and several weekly papers. I made a personal canvas from house to house, soliciting books to be used in the library. In a short time, I had collected several thousand books and a large American flag to hang out in front of the building, and a large dictionary, which was placed on a stand for the convenience of the patrons. Bookshelves were made for the books, a large stove, tables, chairs, and a desk were supplied as fixtures of the library. I had the building wired for electricity, furnished coal for the use of the library, and employed a young lady for librarian at a fixed salary.

For a long while, the library was a blessing to our group in Tulsa. I conceived an idea to make the library a bigger and greater benefit for our group. In order to do so, I called on quite a few of our big oil men and asked for donations. Among them was Harry Sinclair, who gave me $1.00 for its support. At first, I refused to take it, but he said, "Take it, Stradford, and come to see me again."

At that time, I was a member of the Republican City Committee, and I used my influence to have the city appropriate $1.00 per month for its support, and that threw the library into politics. When the next mayor was elected, being of a different political faith, he demanded me to turn over the library to the city or he would stop the appropriation. The matter was settled by paying me for the building and fixtures, and I donated the books to the city very reluctantly. I had become attached to the work, and my wife took great pride in it, and felt that she had lost a dear friend when we gave it up. I also turned over the list of subscribers so that the following librarian could collect the balance due on the subscription. Quite a few of the patrons had their mail addressed to the library, where it would be convenient for them to get it.

On one occasion, the special delivery man came into the library very abruptly. Quite a few patrons were seated quietly around the tables, reading. With respect for the place, he began to page in a loud voice, "J.B. Stradford, J.B. Stradford."

I raised my hand and beckoned him to come to me. When he came, I said to him, "Take off your hat." He said he came there to deliver a letter and not to take his hat off. I snatched his hat off, threw it back to the door, took him by the arm and put him out of the room, and threw his hat out to him. He came back into the room and asked me to sign for the letter. After I had signed, he left. At that time, we had two distinguished citizens from Boley, Oklahoma, Mr. Haynes and Mr. Leathers, town builders who had built several Colored towns for our group in Oklahoma. When they saw what I did, they left the room in an excited manner, saying, "Stradford was too radical, and he is going to be mobbed." Those are the kinds of spineless leaders who have done more to increase race prejudice by not demanding their rights as men at all times, even at the sacrifice of their lives. Although laws are passed by the States' legislatures discriminating against us as a group, and if we meekly accept the situation without a protest, we are doomed as a group who are not worthy of the respect of citizens.

My policy is to make men respect me as a man, and when one fails to do so, compel him to or else use your physical power in any way to redress the insult, even in violation of the law. You can hardly find a man so void of human principles that he does not know the rights and privileges of his fellowmen. Agitation along this line or persecution, even to the shedding of blood and not a little bit of it will crystallize sentiments in our favor, and in time, the old regime will have passed away, and the brotherhood of man will be installed. In all of the Southern states, the white man has taught our people their places, but in Oklahoma, up to the present, they have not succeeded. Our group, including the natives, knows that they have rights which must be respected and will fight for them, disregarding the discriminatory laws which have been enacted by the state legislature. All men desire to be free from oppression. In all my life, I have breathed only a few free days, tiring of persecution, which the statehood imposed upon me.

I began to look for a place where I could be a full-fledged citizen and enjoy all the rights and privileges of a citizen. My attention was called to Boley, Oklahoma, a town of about 5,000 Negroes exclusively. All of the city officials were Negroes. The railroad station agent, the telegraph operator, and the postmaster were all members of our group. They made their gas and electricity. It was a most wonderful town. Two banks were doing a good business. I decided, after I had obtained this information relative to Boley, to sell out my possessions in Tulsa and go there for a permanent residence. I also made an investigation relative to establishing a canning factory. I found that it would be a favorable enterprise. I went to Boley, sent a proposal to the Chamber of Commerce, that if they would give me a bonus of 10 acres of land on the outskirts of the city, that I would install a canning factory at the cost of $25,000. They refused the offer at that time, and referred it to the Finance Committee, and that ended my negotiations with them.

While I was there, I was treated with the greatest courtesy and felt like I was a free man. I had the pleasure to make several public talks and in each talk I was exultant. I could hardly contain myself. I was inflated with joy almost to the bursting point. Every office in the city was open to me, from the mayor of the city to the dog catcher. Every place or business was open to me. I had no fear of going to a drugstore and asking for a milkshake or a cold drink and being refused or going out on the street meeting a white man and being shot down like a dog if I failed to get off the sidewalk if he demanded me to do so, or meeting a white woman who did not like my looks and cry out that I insulted her and blood-thirsty mob would be formed to take my life and hang me to the first tree or telegraph pole.

My aspirations for true manhood were broadened, and my greatest desire was to spend the remainder of my life in such an environment. But alas! My hopes went glimmering. I had to return to Tulsa and withstand the conditions which had been provided for me by law.

I found business more prosperous in Tulsa. I bought several other lots and erected several other rental houses. I bought a very desirable lot in a white neighborhood. One of the neighbors by the name of Pender was opposed to me buying in that vicinity. He lived on the corner of Detroit and Dameron Streets. And I always passed his house on my way to and from my business.

One morning, while I was passing along in front of his house, he stopped me very abruptly and said, "There is no use of you niggers buying that property on Elgin Street because we white folks are going to take it away from you, and the best thing for you to do is to dispose of it for anything you can get for it as soon as possible." I asked him what he meant. He reiterated his statement.

I said to him, "If you want my property, put your money in your pocket and give me my price, and I will transfer it to you. But if you come up there with the intention of forcibly ejecting me from it, God will have mercy on you. I won't. I will fill you as full of holes as a slave."

He said, "Go on, nigger, you are not fit to talk to a white man."

A few nights after that, I dreamed that he assaulted me as I passed by his house, and during the night, his wife came out of the house and shot me in the stomach with a revolver. I relayed my dream to my wife, and she beseeched me to change my route, but I paid no attention to her entreaties and said I was not afraid to pass his house on the sidewalk.

At that time, he was putting in a basement under one of his small houses and had a pile of bricks stacked up on the outside of the sidewalk. When I passed along, he said to me, "I don't want you to pass on this sidewalk anymore." He was standing by the brick pile.

I stopped and said, "This is a public sidewalk, and I will use it whenever it is necessary." When I finished saying that, he grabbed two bricks from the pile and threw the first one at me, and it knocked the skin off the side of my face. When I saw him reach for the bricks, I started toward him in great haste. Before he could throw the second one, I was so close to him that he ran from the pile and left me in possession of it. I grabbed a brick and threw it at him.

Just at that moment, his wife came running out of the house with her hands under her apron and said, "Oh! Don't kill my husband."

I remembered my dream and said to her, "I will not hurt him, but I am going down and have him arrested." I went straightaway to the police court and had a warrant issued for his arrest. But the judge, being a Southerner, failed to convict him for assault, but I was not interfered with by him after that incident.

The majority of the citizens of Tulsa at that time were from Texas, Arkansas, Missouri, and Mississippi. They had settled there before statehood and had brought all their traditions, customs, and habits with them, and embedded them as firmly in Tulsa as in their former homes, although there was an influx of citizens from every state in the union. But the Northerner, as a rule, is just as hostile to our group when they go South as the Southerner. For an illustration, Haskell, the first governor of Oklahoma, was a native of Ohio. He was elected by injecting race hatred into the campaign and caused all the discriminating laws to be passed by the first legislature against our people.

Another incident which I feel is worthy of note. I bought two Stetson hats from a clothier in Lawton, Oklahoma from a firm by the name of Joe Wolfe, one for me and the other for my son, John. After we had moved back to Tulsa, a young man stole John's hat and cut the brim half off, all around so that no one would recognize it. The young man who stole it came into my place of business with the hat on and John recognized it and said, "Papa, there is my hat." I asked the fellow to let me see the hat. And I examined it carefully and decided that it was the lost hat. I asked the boy where he got the hat.

He said, "Dr. Smith gave it to me, and I will go with you up to his office and prove to you that he did."

I took the hat, and he got on his wheel and rode alongside of me, up to the doctor's office. His office was in the Egan Building on the second floor. He was not in, but the owner of the building was lying down on a davenport on the far side of the room. When we entered, he said, "What do you boys want?"

The boy said, "Mr. Stradford has my hat. Dr. Smith gave it to me, and I can prove it by him that he did give it to me."

Mr. Egan said, "Leave the hat here, and when Dr. Smith comes, he will decide whose hat it is."

I said, "No, I will not leave it. I am going to take it with me. I bought it and paid for it."

In the twinkling of an eye, he jumped up off his couch and began to fight me and said, "No nigger can talk back to me."

In a very few minutes, I had him firmly in my grasp and proceeded to give him a merciless beating. I blackened both his eyes, choked him until he was unconscious, and then searched him to see whether he had a pistol. Finding that he had none, I left the room and went back to my place of business.

Several days after the occurrence, about seven o'clock in the evening, about six officers, three of the sheriff's force and three of the police force, came to my place and called me to the front and said, "We have a warrant for you."

I said, "Read it to me."

When they had finished reading it, I said, "You must be mistaken."

When they said, "Get your hat and coat and come with us," I obeyed orders, and they carried me to jail and kept me there.

The following day I was released on a $1,000 bond for an assault with the intent to kill. I was prohibited from voting for Taft for president in 1908 by being incarcerated in the Tulsa County jail.

At the time I was in jail, there was a young Negro boy charged with the killing of a deputy sheriff, who was afterward convicted and sentenced to be hanged. He became very much attached to me, so much so that he gave me an invitation to witness his execution. The state law gives the condemned person the right to invite two persons to witness the execution. The time set for the execution was at daybreak on a Friday. I may forget the date, but I will never forget the incident. It was a memorable occurrence. The evidence upon which he was convicted was insufficient.

The newspapers had commented on the insufficiency of it, but the man killed, being white, and the killer being Negro, tried by a white jury, judge, and all the officers of the court, white, it was impossible for him to get a fair and impartial trial. We met promptly at the appointed time. The gallows was a gruesome-looking aspect which stood on a lot outside of the county jail. Everything was in readiness. We started our trek to the gallows. He ascended the steps until he reached the platform, and after a few preliminaries, the sheriff asked the convict if he had anything to say. His name was Frank Henson.

He walked firmly to the center of the platform and said, "I am not guilty of the crime for which I am paying with my life.

I admit that I fired the shot that killed the deputy, but I did not shoot until he had shot me." He then turned to ex-sheriff James Wooley and said, "You have sworn my life away. You know that you swore to a lie and just as you sow, so shall you reap."

When he had finished his saying, Sheriff Bill McCullough adjusted the black cap very nervously, after tying the rope around his neck. and said, "Goodbye, Frank," and at the same time, pulled the trap string and his body plunged into eternity. In a few minutes, the doctor pronounced him dead. The mandate of the law had been obeyed, and I left the scene with bitterness in my heart against the white man's treatment of our race.

The trial of the case for which I was out on bond did not come up for adjudication for five months. At the scheduled time, I was out of the city on business and did not appear before the judge. He forfeited my bond and issued a bench warrant for my arrest. Several days after the warrant had been issued, I was back in Tulsa. I arrived at about 7:30 p.m.

As I got off the train, an officer met me at the station who had the warrant. He said, "I have a bench warrant for you." I asked him for what cause. He said, "Go home and go to bed tonight and be in court at nine o'clock in the morning."

On the following morning at that stated time, I was in court. The judge was a particular friend of mine and permitted me to go on my own recognizance until the following day at two o'clock. At that hour, the case was called for trial. There were two witnesses for the plaintiff, Jim Egan, the principal, and the boy who stole the hat. I was the attorney for myself and demanded the separation of the witnesses. After the boy had been taken out of the room, the first witness was called to the stand. He told the court how I had come into his office and when he requested me to leave the hat with him, that I pulled from my pocket a large pocketknife with a blade six inches long and drew it on him and began to beat him severely and told him if he offered any resistance, I would kill him.

The prosecuting attorney asked him about my general reputation. He said that I was a bad nigger and was noted for fighting white people.

The boy was then called to the witness stand and, in substance, corroborated his testimony. The state rested. The judge asked me what I had to say. I asked to see the warrant and read it to the court. It charged assault and battery with intent to kill.

Having brought out clearly the lack of intent in both of the state's witnesses, I said to the judge, "You are the sole arbitrator in this case, and I am, indeed, glad that you are. I know you are a fair-minded man and are sensitively just in your decisions. I will tell you truthfully just what happened in that office. I went into the office with the boy to learn from Dr. Smith whether he had given him that hat. Dr. Smith was gone out on a call. Mr. Egan took it upon himself to act in the place of Dr. Smith and demanded me to leave the hat with him in order that Dr. Smith could decide whether he gave that hat to the boy. On my refusal to do so, he assaulted me just as I was leaving the room, and in my necessary self-defense, I gave him a severe beating. I never had a knife at any time during our engagement and never made any threats to do harm to him."

The judge, in rendering his decision, said that the preponderance of the evidence was against me, that two witnesses had already testified that I had the knife and drew it on the plaintiff. He further said that the evidence was conflicting, and in view of that fact, he assessed a fine on me for $42.50, which I paid and thanked the judge for his leniency and left the courtroom. Had the judge not known me personally, I would have gotten a term in the penitentiary for an indefinite period. Members of our group, for the least infractions of the law, are sent to the penitentiary.

Another incident which I will mention to show the real status of our group in the opinion of the white people. In 1912, I left Tulsa to attend commencement exercises at Oberlin College in Ohio. My son, Cornelius Francis Stradford, received his degree of Bachelor of Arts. When I attended that school, I knew I was black when I looked into a mirror. As far as my treatment was concerned, there was no discrimination against our group in any of the departments. Members of our group were connected with the Glee Club and were members of all the college fraternities. And I decided Oberlin was the garden spot of the world for Negroes. A man was simply a man. That was the teaching of the faculty, and it was strictly adhered to.

When I arrived, I found that those conditions had changed. We were barred from the Glee Clubs and almost all the college fraternities. Finding this condition, I was surprised beyond measure. And I sorely grieved for the reason that I had been an ardent supporter of Oberlin and had sent my son there on account of the fair considerations and treatment that we received there. When I found that the school had been southernized by the influx of pupils from the South and the failure of the faculty to enforce the rules as they were in President Fairchild's regime, I felt that it was necessary to complain to those old professors who were teaching when I was a student there. All of my old teachers, with one exception, were still teaching there, namely Professors Peck, Anderegg, Martin, and Kaskey. I went personally to each of them and stated my side of the case, telling them how I had been imbued with the love of that wonderful institution. For that reason, I had sent my boy there to enjoy the freedom and privileges of the school. I knew that the high ideals upon which the school was founded were not being carried out, and as members of the faculty, I thought they were responsible for that condition, and that I wanted them to see to it that our group was accorded all the rights and privileges of other groups.

The next year after I made the complaint to those professors, the bars were torn down, and our students were admitted to all the college societies, and I felt that I had been instrumental in removing the restrictions that prohibited our group from enjoying the privileges of any other group.

Upon my return home from Oberlin, I stopped in Cincinnati for a few days, visiting with friends. While I was riding on a streetcar, my attention was called to a large crowd on the street, our streetcar stopping on the corner of the street. Looking out of the window, I saw a Negro man lying on the street who had been apparently struck by a car. He was unconscious and was bleeding very profusely. This was one of our group.

Chapter 13

The car was filled with passengers. Two white women sitting in the seat in front of me looked out of the window and said, "Why doesn't this car go on? It is nothing but a nigger who got hurt or killed, as the case may be." That expression was only a mirror reflecting the prevalent sentiment of white people against our group. The white man has come from the South to the North and has brought our group with them and, regardless of law and order, accords them the same treatment in the North as they did down home. And their violations are condoned by those who have the power to see to it that the laws are enforced. In the South, the prosecutors and the justices of the peace will refuse to give a member of our group a warrant for the arrest of a white man who commits crimes and misdemeanors against our group. In the North, the prosecutors demand that the plaintiff deposit a sufficient amount of money to cover the cost of the trial. And if a conviction is secured, they agree to refund the money which has been deposited to cover the cost in the case.

    I can mention a great many other excuses which they give for not issuing the warrants. We are told that out of one blood God has created all nations of men, and we are His children, brother and sister, all. There are no privileged classes. Every brother and sister should enjoy his or her rights and privileges as a member of that family, and the head of that family sees to it that all of its members are given equal rights and protection of the law. The average white man has this conception of our group: "As long as he is a drawer of water and hewer of wood, they say he is a good nigger. But when he is elevated above that position and demands his rights as a citizen and is in pursuance of those rights, asserts his manhood as a citizen, especially his social rights, he becomes a nettle in the community and gives offense by even appearing on the street or any other place in the sight of the white man and is in danger of his life being taken, his property destroyed or being forced to leave the community by threats of being lynched or burned at the stake. If he fails to obey orders, the threats against him are carried into execution, and there is no redress for the aggrieved or the oppressed parties, and that is the measure of justice which is meted out to our group in the Southland.

In a great many instances in the North, especially in towns where our group has been shipped in as strike breakers and to do the most menial work in factories, the same conditions prevail.

Upon my return from my vacation trip to Oberlin, Niagara Falls, and Toronto, Canada, I decided to add more rental houses to my list. And in 1913, I completed a 16-room, brick apartment house, modern in every respect, at a cost of $6,000. I was very successful in all of my business undertakings, and always lending a hand to someone whom I thought was deserving, and the business he desired to embark in was a paying proposition.

A young man by the name of Franklin, who had some experience in the steam laundry business, induced me to buy a steam laundry outfit for him which cost me more than a thousand dollars ($1,000). After installing him into the business, he failed to be equal to the requirements and in less than six months, the place was closed on account of mismanagement and on account of the machinery not being modern. We could not dispose of it at any price. The investment was a total loss. I staked my son-in-law in a moving picture show which cost several thousand dollars. And that also was a failure. Other investments I have made for other men by staking them to barbershops, pool halls, restaurants, and club rooms are too numerous to mention. And in all of such investments, I have never made one which succeeded. In other words, all of them were failures. My experience has proven to me that it is bad business to invest money in anything unless you have personal supervision of it. To find a man among our group, capable, honest, proficient and with business acumen to discharge a business is like looking for a needle in a haystack.

After I had arrived at the point that I was neither a drawer of water nor a hewer of timber, my pathway was strewn with obstacles, especially from the ordinary class of whites who don't think our group had the right to live. If we tried to do something which will indelibly stamp ourselves in the community as men and women worthy of the respect and appreciation of all people, they will say, "He thinks he is as good as white people," or, "He is a sassy nigger and ought to be run out of the community." "And another reason he should be run out is that he has taught all the niggers in the community that they are as good as white people and every house of their group in a radius of a mile is an arsenal and ready for action at any time, and that the other niggers will do what he tells them to do." And those are a few of the faults which they find of the progressives of our group. I did all that I could to avoid contact with that class of white people, but the more I tried to avoid it, the more run-ins I had with them.

I had my watch repaired in the Boswell Jewelry Store. The watch repairer was a man who hated our group and was very abusive to members of our group whenever an opportunity presented itself. I took the watch out of the shop and paid the bill. It did not give me satisfaction. I took it back to him for adjustment and left it with him for several days so that he would have time to properly adjust it. At the expiration of that time, I returned to the shop for my watch. He gave it to me, but had not remedied the defect. I took it back to him and told him that he had not done anything to the watch, and I wanted him to either fix it or return my money.

He said, "Don't you tell me that I have not done anything to this watch. If you do, I will shoot your brains out."

I said, "I may be mistaken about that, but the watch is in no better condition now than it was when I brought it to you for repairs. And if you won't fix it, give me back my money."

Whereupon he laid my watch on the counter and said, "Take it and get out of here. I don't allow no nigger to talk back to me."

I demanded the money I had paid him for the watch.

He said, "I will kill you." He hurriedly went to his desk, pulled a 45 Colt revolver from the drawer.

Just at that time, a white lady customer was standing near me. I caught her by both of her arms behind her and placed her between him and me.

Just at that time, the chief of police came in, pulled his gun, and leveled it at the watch repairer and said, "Drop that gun, I am the man behind the gun."

After finding out the trouble, he made the repairer return the $3.00 which I had paid him for repairs. It was a very ludicrous sight to see a black man holding a white woman as a target to shield him from a murderous assault by a Southern cracker. I left the store in company with the chief of police, thanking God for my deliverance.

Another incident which I feel is worthy of mention here. I saw in the *Tulsa Tribune*, an evening paper, an advertisement, "Cooking utensils for sale," at one of the white restaurants on Main Street. I needed some cooking utensils, and my wife suggested that we go to the restaurant and buy some if we could find what we wanted. After supper, we went down to look at them. When we entered the room, one of the waiters asked me what I wanted. I asked to see the proprietor.

He then said to me, "Take your hat off."

I said, "No, thank you. I don't care to take it off." Just at this time, the proprietor came and I went back into the kitchen to look at the utensils. My wife remained in the front part of the restaurant.

One of the waiters said to the other one, "I will show him when he comes through here that he will have to take his hat off."

My wife heard the conversation and walked down near the door which led into the kitchen. And when I came out, one of the waiters ordered me to take off my hat. At that time, my wife caught me by the arm and said, "Come on out of here, Papa. Don't pay any attention to this poor white trash. They dare not touch you," and we walked out of the room without any further trouble.

I relate this to show how the average cracker treats our group. They put us all in one class and expect all of us to meekly submit to their treatment regardless of our rights or former environment. If we fail to submit, we are beaten, killed, lynched, burned at the stake, and no one is punished for it.

Another incident occurred in my place of business in Tulsa, Oklahoma. In company with several men sitting around a table in the rear of the room, playing whist, our attention was attracted by two city policemen coming into the place and running at full speed toward us. They demanded all of us to open our hands. All of us obeyed except me.

I refused to open my hands and said, "Why should I open my hands for you? You're not acting within the scope of your authority, and you have no right to come in here in such an abrupt manner." They still insisted on me opening my hands, and I absolutely refused to do so.

One of the players said, "Stradford, you know you are not guilty of violating any law. Why don't you open your hands?"

I still refused and said to the officers, "If I have violated any law, arrest me."

They said, "Consider yourself under arrest."

I said, "Let me get my hat and coat."

They grabbed me and forcibly ejected me out of the place after a struggle. When they got me outside, Officer Linkheart drew his large automatic revolver and pointed it at my face and said, "If you move, I will blow your brains out."

The other officer, John Patten, began to beat me up with his pistol. He aimed his blows at my head. In seeing them coming, I was able, by superior ducking, to keep him from landing a knockout blow on my head, although he hit me many a glancing blow on my head. For two blocks, he kept up his battery until I was as bloody as a stuck beer. During his beating of me, he said, "You black Ethiopian S.B., you tell a white man you won't open your hands. I will beat you to death."

They carried me to the station and locked me up, would not book me, and kept me there until the following morning. My wife came down with my attorney and had me liberated. I was in jail all night without medical attention. My head and eyes were swollen beyond recognition. He had struck me several times on the lower part of my back, and I could not walk. I was in a precarious condition. No charges were placed against me for any misdemeanor whatever. The doctor was called to my home to dress my wounds. I was disabled for some time, and while in that condition, feeling that my health had been impaired permanently, I took an oath that I would get revenge by taking my adversary's life and thereby planned to kill him.

During my convalescent period, I took a trip to Topeka, Kansas, to perfect the plans. I was there only two days before I received a telegraph message from my wife stating that I had a lawsuit coming up for trial the next day, and on the following day, I was in Tulsa to defend the suit. I considered the handicaps which are placed on our group relative to a crime of that character, and I failed to carry out my oath to kill the officer who had beaten me, although I had vowed from that time that no white man could beat me up and live for the reason that for 300 years, they had beaten, maimed, sold, and killed my ancestors with impunity. I have always felt that without the shedding of blood on our part, there will be no cessation of the custom. And I have been willing at all times to give up my life for the defense of that principle and have demonstrated it on diverse occasions.

Another incident along the same line happened in my place of business. There was a city ordinance closing business places (pool halls) on Saturday nights. This Saturday night in question, business was very good, and I forgot to close up at twelve o'clock.

At 12:15, the officer on the beat came into my place in a very rough and ungentlemanly manner and said, "What are you G.D. niggers doing in here playing pool this time of night? Get out of here, every one of you at once, or I will lock all of you up."

I said to him, "Mr. W., I own this place, and if I have violated the law in your view, arrest me. I won't stand for any man calling me a G.D. nigger."

He said, "Consider yourself under arrest."

I said, "All right, permit me to get my money out of the cash register, the day's receipts." I went behind the counter to go to the register. He followed me on the outside of the counter, and when I got up to the cash register, I pulled my pistol out of the drawer, cocked it, and pointed it at him and said, "Get out of here or I will kill you."

Looking down the barrel of my gun changed his mind. His face turned white as a piece of cotton, and he went out of the room as quickly as he could. I followed him to the door, and when he had gotten about half a block from my place, I called him back and told him that I would go with him to the station if he would do me no violence. He promised he would not, and he booked me on two charges: keeping the pool hall open after twelve o'clock and the other, resisting an officer. I put up a cash bond covering both offenses. On the following morning, the cases came up for hearing. I was fined for keeping the pool hall open after twelve o'clock, and the judge dismissed the case for resisting an officer.

A few days after this episode, this officer wrote an article which was published in one of the daily papers, giving the history of his service as a police officer and said that he had been an officer for many a year, and the only time that he had been in danger of his life was in a "Negro pool hall on North Boston Street. The proprietor, a big burly nigger, pushed a 45-caliber pistol in his face and ordered him out of his place."

I had the privilege of making the acquaintance of all of the lawyers practicing at the bar in Tulsa. One of them I knew personally. He returned to his hometown somewhere in Virginia and was away from Tulsa for about one year. After his return, I met him on the street one morning while I was talking to Mr. Williams, a real estate man.

He came up to us, shook hands with Mr. Williams, and then said to me, "Mr. Stradford, how are you?"

In reply, I offered him my hand in acknowledgment of the pleasure it gave me to have him back in Tulsa again.

Instead of shaking hands with me, he drew back his hand and said, "Oh! No, Mr. Stradford. I was born too far South for that."

It made me very indignant, and I said to him, "You are no part of a gentleman and would be better suited to associate with the savages of Horneo than to be associated with intelligent people."

He had an umbrella in his hand and raised it to strike me. I caught his hand and took the umbrella away from him. He ran around looking for something with which to strike me. I stood there waiting for him to make the assault. He could not find anything and left the scene in great haste and said, "Just wait until I come back."

Mr. Williams suggested that I should leave. He said, "He may return with a gun to kill you."

I left. I don't know whether he returned or not. This man, afterward, became City Attorney. This is the caliber of men who are chosen to mete out justice to our group in almost every locality of this country.

My business was very lucrative from the time I went back to Tulsa until I was forced to leave. I had amassed quite a fortune for a member of our group. I owned 15 rental houses, including one 16-room apartment, and a brick building. The rental value of $250.00 per month. The income from other sources was equally as much. I had a splendid bank account, and I was living on the sunny side of the street. I decided to realize my fondest hope, and that was to erect a large hotel in Tulsa, exclusively for Negroes.

The Santa Fe Railroad Company, desiring to build a passenger and freight depot in Tulsa, purchased city blocks of improved property for the site and advertised the buildings for sale. I selected several of the choice ones that had the kind of material which I could use in the hotel, wrecked them and hauled the material to the hotel site. I sold quite a bit of this material which was a source of profit. I secured 350,000 bricks out of the buildings and windows and doors too numerous to mention. The alley was paved with brick, 44 x 8 inches, and I had them dug up and used them in the foundation of the hotel. The dimensions of the foundation were 38 x 140, covering the entire lot. I did not contract the building foundation. I superintended it myself. The outside walls of the foundation were concrete. The middle walls were made of those large bricks. I am not throwing any bouquets at myself, but the building inspector passed it and said it could not have been done better. Then I employed a first-class bricklayer and paid him $0.25 per hour more than the other bricklayers to oversee the brick and concrete work. The North side of the lot, 140 feet long, was adjoining another lot on which foundation a blank wall was built 14 feet high and 13 inches thick. And the West wall was 14 x 38 feet. The South and West walls were made of concrete beams and pillars.

The next step was building the frames for the pillars and beams. I kept a carpenter whom I had given employment for quite a while that I thought was equal to the task. Before beginning to erect the building, I had an architect draw the plans and specifications for the job. I kept them displayed in my office in view of the public. Quite a few of my friends, after they had learned that I intended to give the foremanship of erecting the building to one of our group, said to me that they thought I was making a mistake, that the Colored carpenters and plumbers had not had sufficient amounts of experience to undertake a job of that proportion. They had not had even one job which was half as big as this job.

I answered them by saying, "Our carpenters and plumbers, etc., will never be proficient if we don't give them the big jobs. The white men will not give them their work on a large scale, and the thing for us to do who have big jobs is to encourage them to make themselves more proficient. As for my job, I am going to give it to them. And if they make any mistakes, they will profit by them, and I am willing to be the loser. Everything to be done in the erection of my building that they can do, they shall do it." And they did it with credit not only to themselves, but also to their art. Not a white man did one thing in erecting the building that they could do. We had no Colored roofers, tinters, tile setters or fire escape dealers, and that part of the work was done by white contractors. I regretted very much that we had none of our group engaged in those lines of business. The plate glass for the South and West side was put in by a white firm as there were none of our group engaged in that line of business. After the frames had been built for the pillars and beams and the proper amount of steel had been placed in them, the concrete was poured and nothing intervened from that time to halt the erection of the building until the roof was on.

An incident occurred while erecting the foundation that I think is worthy of mention. On account of my desire to avoid run-ins with the white man, I had secured a large amount of cement sidewalk, which I removed to my lot to mix with the cement. I had several laborers breaking it up into small pieces for that purpose. The weather was very hot at that time, and I was holding my umbrella over me for protection from the hot sun's rays.

The ice wagon drove up, and the ice man got out and asked me, "Why are you holding that umbrella over you? The sun can't tan you."

I told him that it did not cost him a damn cent to attend to his own business, whereupon he attempted to strike me with his ice hooks. Just as he attempted to raise it, I caught it, snatched it out of his hand, and struck him on the jaw, and down on the ground he fell. I stamped him with both feet and picked up a large piece of concrete to strike him, and just at that time, someone grabbed it and said, "Don't kill him, Stradford. They will mob you."

I let him go with this admonition, "Hereafter, don't meddle with other people's business."

After completing the shell of the building, I found that it was necessary to secure a loan to complete it. I took the matter up with my wife and told her it was necessary for us to secure a loan. She agreed to execute her part. The amount necessary to complete the building was $20,000. There was already a mortgage of $8,000.00 and we had to give a blanket mortgage of $28,000.00 to cover all of my property. I arranged with the loan man to make the loan, and my wife and I went down to his office to execute it. I went into his office first and signed the papers incident to the agreement. He called my wife and read the instructions to her, and she refused to sign it, saying she would not sign everything she had away; that I might fail to meet the payments and everything we had would be lost. I told her that there was no danger of losing our property. I explained to her how much our income exceeded the amount of $965.63, our monthly payments. I did all that I could to get her to sign the papers, but she stubbornly refused.

I said to her, "You have not contributed one cent to my fortune. When I married you, you had nothing. You have not done anything to add a dime to our possessions, only to be a good wife and companion. I don't think after not agreeing to sign the papers, you ought to stop the wheel of progress." I talked to her along this line for some time but could not get her to agree to sign them. Exasperated by her flatly refusing to sign, I told her that it was very painful for me to take the stand which I was forced to take. I said, "You have the option of two things. You will either sign that mortgage paper or you have no husband and I am leaving you now."

When I turned to go, she said, "Don't go. I will sign it." And so she did, and everything was lovely. She then went into the private office of the loan man, and he took her acknowledgment and gave me a check for $20,000.00 with which I completed the hotel.

The building was a very beautiful structure, trimmed in pressed brick above the windows and stone slabs at the bottom of the windows, 140 feet on Cameron, had large plate glass fronts which gave the building a beautiful appearance. There were six business rooms on the first floor, two on Greenwood, a drugstore and the lobby and four on Cameron, pool hall, barbershop, restaurant and the banquet hall. All of these rooms, except the lobby were leased at a good price before the building was completed. It not only took the $20,000.00 which I borrowed from the Tulsa Security Company to complete the building, but all of my income for more than one month and all of the cash which I had left when the roof was put on the building. After the completion of the building, I found myself without funds to furnish it. About 30 days before the building was completed, I ordered $5,000.00 worth of furniture from the Albert Pix Furniture Company and it had been standing on the track in a box car for several days, and I did not have the money to get it out.

After several days of manipulation, I succeeded in getting it out and putting it in the hotel. The terms on which I bought the furniture was one fourth on delivery and the balance in payments of $165.63 per month. These payments were kept up until the riot in June 1921. I owed one note then, and still owe and always will owe it.

Everything was in readiness, and on June 1, 1918, the hotel was opened in a very elaborate manner. The most beautiful chandeliers were hung in the lobby and the banquet hall. The bright lights were flashing, and the guests were enjoying the opening of the largest and finest hotel in the United States, owned and operated by a black man. All available space was taken up, and the business was a grand success from the beginning until the hotel was burned by a bloodthirsty mob on June 1, 1921.

Another incident occurred after the hotel had been completed. I had an attack of rheumatism and was advised by my physician to take the baths at Claremore, a town about 50 miles from Tulsa. Every morning, I would take the Frisco train at Tulsa and go to Claremore, take a bath, and return home in the afternoon. The train on which I rode was Jim Crowed; a part of the coach, which was used for smoking, was partitioned off for our group with about six seats on either side. Traffic for our group between Tulsa and Claremore was more than those seats would accommodate. Two of those seats were used for the conductor's office. He had his handbag locked to the arm of one of the seats, and the brakeman occupied the other. On the morning in question, I went into the coach and found the seats all taken. I took possession of the conductor's seat. When he came in, he asked me to relinquish my seat to him.

I asked him, "Is this not the Jim Crow coach?"

He said, "Yes."

I told him that he had no business in there and to take his paraphernalia and carry it into the white coach. I further said, "This is our coach, and I will not give up this seat."

He went out of the compartment in great haste and said, "When I come back, you will give it up."

I went to the door through which he went out of and propped it open so that I could see him before he entered the car. On account of the prejudice and animosity which the white man had for our group in Tulsa, I carried my gun as regularly as I carried my watch, ready at all times to protect myself regardless of the consequences.

He did not return, but instead the brakeman, a great, big man weighing at least 275 pounds, came in and said to me, "Why didn't you give the conductor his seat? You know that he uses those seats. You must be looking for trouble, you dirty puppy."

I said, "You are a dirty S.B." And just as I rose from my seat, he reached in his hip pocket, and my hand reached his pocket at the same time, and when it came out with his pistol, I had his hand firmly grasped in mine, and a hard struggle ensued. I rushed him back on the seat with our hands above his head, and for a few seconds, we remained in that position. He said if I would turn him loose, he would put his pistol in his pocket.

Just at that time, my friend, Wright, a druggist, pulled his pistol and said, "Turn him loose, Stradford. If he don't put that pistol up and get out of this coach, I will take care of him."

I turned him loose. He put his pistol in his pocket and left the coach, post haste, and did not return before we got off the train in Claremore. I made that trip every day thereafter, and I was never molested again. The conductor moved his things into the white people's coach, and we had our coach to ourselves.

With two years of phenomenal success, I had succeeded in having a nice bank roll. I was named as an alternate delegate to the Republican National Convention in Chicago in 1920 which nominated Harding for president. In company with my wife and chauffeur, we drove to Chicago. Before leaving for Chicago to spend the summer, I sent for my son and his wife who lived in

Chicago, to come to Tulsa and conduct the business for me in my absence. They came and I turned the hotel business over to them. I also had a pool hall which yielded an average of $500.00 per week. I left it in the charge of my son, John. I was away for months and during that time, I did not receive any income from it. He informed me that they needed money to pay doctor's bills, etc. The payment on the mortgage debts was $965.63 per month; on the furniture bill, which was purchased from the Albert Pix Furniture Company, $165.00 per month. During my absence, one payment on the mortgage debt was unpaid, and one on the furniture bill was delinquent. I was informed by my son, who had charge of the hotel, of the falling off of business.

In order to save what I had, I found it necessary to give up the business project which I had begun in Indiana and return to Tulsa. After arriving in Tulsa, I demanded an account of the business which he had done while I was away. He said, "Papa, I did not think you would demand an accurate account of the business from me." And to avoid further unpleasantness, I accepted his statement, paid him and his wife the contract price for their services, and they returned to Chicago.

The hotel had an enviable reputation for the manner in which it was conducted. Bootleggers, dope peddlers and sporting women were barred. No couple was permitted to register for lodging, especially those residents of the city, unless they produced evidence that they were married. Out-of-town guests without baggage were refused accommodations unless they could satisfy us that they were married. Young married couples would gladly take rooms in the Stradford because they knew that they would be protected from the insults which are usually prevalent in such places. Whenever we found women going into a man's room, we would call her to the office and check her out. We had several pathetic cases to deal with, but in each case, we enforced the rules of the hotel. The reputation of the hotel was established in Oklahoma, Missouri, and Kansas, and visitors leaving those places for Tulsa would invariably come to the Stradford for accommodations.

I recall an incident which occurred in 1919 on Commencement Day of the high schools in Tulsa. Quite a number of schools of the neighboring towns attended and the city had a gala day. The young girls were carrying curved-handled walking canes, decorated with a piece of blue or red ribbon, which was a fad at that time. I had particularly noticed two of those high school lassies that day coming in and going out of the lobby. They were quite attractive and very fascinating. That evening, after the commencement, about 1:00 a.m., they came to the desk in company with their supposed husbands to register for lodging for the night. My wife called me to the desk and asked me what to do about giving the people rooms for the night. They had signed the register. I asked them if they were married, and they said that they were. I asked where their baggage was, and they said that they were from Sapulpa and came over to attend the commencement exercises with no expectation of staying in Tulsa all night. But on account of the train being gone, there was no way for them to get back home tonight. I said to them, "I am not running an assignation house. You can find plenty of such houses in Tulsa. We are catering to the kind of people you say you are, and if you want to take the chance under these circumstances, to take those rooms, I will find out before morning whether you are married or not."

The porter showed them to their rooms. In a short time, the officer on that beat came along, and I called him in and told him I had two couples who had registered as man and wife upstairs, and I wanted him to find out whether they were man and wife. I told him the number of their room, and he said he would investigate it for me. He called in his associate officer and went upstairs to their rooms. Entering the first room, one of the officers took the young man out of the room and went down to the end of the hall, and there questioned him relative to his marriage.

Chapter 14

He told the officer that he was married in Oklahoma City. I don't remember the date he said he was married. The officer who remained in the room with the girl subjected her to the same question, and in their stories, they failed to agree. She said she was married to him in Dallas, Texas, and gave a different date from the one he gave of the time of marriage. After interrogating the other couple, they found that neither of them was married, and they asked me what they should do with them. I told him to take them out of the hotel. He took them to the police station and booked them for disorderly conduct. That night, they telephoned their parents in Sapulpa and told them of their plight. The next morning, before court convened, their parents had secured their release and took them back to Sapulpa.

One other case of this nature was reported, and the guilty parties paid a fine for their conduct. I never had any of those cases to contend with along that line, and such cases advertised the reputation of the hotel.

It is a custom in all cities and towns in the South to raid a member of our group's business at any time any police officer desires to do so without a warrant or any authority of the law. I have always resented any infringement upon my rights as a citizen, and for doing so, I have gained the respect of all who knew me.

While I was living in Indianapolis, I conducted a rooming house. We had one man roomer who had quit his wife against his will. He went back to the house where she was, and she refused to admit him, whereupon he stoned the house and broke several windows and smashed the door in. The police were called to arrest him. They ascertained that he was rooming at my house. They came directly to my house with the information that they had acquired concerning his room. They pushed my wife aside and rushed upstairs and went straight to his room, but he was not there. It frightened my wife into insensibility. She had just come to herself when I came in from my barbershop. I sat down by the bedside where she was lying, and she told me how the officers had abruptly come into the house and run upstairs to look for that man. They said that they would be back the following night.

On the following morning, I went down to the police station and reported the incident to the sergeant and told him what they had said relative to their return that night.

I said, "If you send them to my house anymore, give them a warrant. If they repeat the performance of last night, you had better send the ambulance, for I will kill them."

The sergeant asked, "Who are you?"

I said, "It did not matter a damn; you had better give them a warrant."

I closed my barbershop about one hour earlier in order to be at home when they came. After we had retired, the doorbell rang.

My wife was afraid for me and insisted on going to the door. I told her that I would open the door. I took my six-shooter and went to the door, threw it wide open, and stood out of sight of the officers and asked them, "What will you have?"

One of them asked, "Is Mr. Stradford in?"

I said, "I am he."

He said he had a warrant for a man by the name of Goings.

I said, "Read it to me." He did, and I said, "Come in." I took them up to his room, but he was not in. They thanked me and left the house.

Another incident which occurred at my hotel I will mention here. One evening, Glenn Shorter, one of my roomers, and I were in the pool hall playing pool. Two ordinary-looking white men came into the room, stood around for a few minutes, and then came to the table where we were and began to search Glenn Shorter. I objected to the procedure and asked them what they meant and told them they could not win a fight in here. They said they were officers and showed their badges.

I said, "Why didn't you show your badges at first?"

They said, "Consider yourself arrested for interfering with an officer while making an arrest."

I said, "Like hell."

He told his partner to hold us in the pool hall while he called the wagon. He went down to the hotel's office to call the patrol wagon. I followed him to the office and refused to let him use the phone. He went out, and in a short time, several of the police force, including Captain Elaine, came into the lobby of the hotel and said to me, "We want you."

I said, "For what?"

"For interfering with an officer," was the reply.

I said to them, "Wait a minute." I went up to my room, got my automatic revolver, and came back to the head of the steps and told him that I was not going with them.

He said, "You will go," and started up the stairs toward me.

I yelled to my wife to get out from behind the counter, out of the range of the bullets, and just before he reached the first landing, I covered him with my revolver and told him, "If you make another step, I will kill you."

He went back into the lobby and said, "I will take you to jail tonight if it takes the whole police force." He left the hotel and met one of the officers of our group and ordered him to arrest me. The officer told him that his life was just as dear to him as his was and that he wouldn't take a chance to lose his life when he knew that I had not committed an offense grave enough to even be arrested. I remained at the head of the stairway on the second floor, awaiting the return of the police. I had firmly decided to sell my life at the highest possible cost, if they came back and attempted to take me.

In the meantime, news of the incident spread all over our section of town. The Knights of the Pythias Lodge was in session at that time, and my friend, Ed Howard, the Chancellor Commander, closed the meeting. He, in company with those fearless, race-loving members, came immediately to the hotel prepared for the fray.

Ed Howard patted me on the shoulder and said, "Stradford, I glory in your spunk. We have come to protect you at any cost and to see to it that if they take you to jail tonight, it will be over our dead bodies. If we had a few more such men as you in this town, it would be much better."

They remained with me in the lobby of the hotel until the wee hours of the morning, and said upon leaving, "If they return, you know my phone number."

The following morning, I went to see my lawyer. He advised me to go to the police station and make bond, and he went with me. I took a sufficient amount of money to deposit for cash bonds. My son, John, was arrested that night for backing me up when those two hicks attempted to arrest me and was in the holdover. I went to the bank and drew out $500.00, and we went to the police station. My lawyer went to the desk sergeant, stated my case and also that of my son, and said he wanted bond fixed for our appearance.

My son had already been booked, and his bond was fixed at $100.00. I gave the sergeant a hundred-dollar bill, and John was released. Two charges were preferred against me, and the bond was fixed at $100.00 in each case. Just as I was handing the sergeant two one-hundred-dollar bills, Captain Elaine came up to me and said, "If it had not been for your wife, they would have been using that money for your burial this morning."

My lawyer said, "Don't say anything to him, Stradford," and we left the station. Our cases were set for trial the following morning, and the court dismissed us.

Captain Elaine was considered one of the most dangerous policemen on the force. On the Saturday before he came to my place, he killed a white man who resisted an arrest. He was one of that class who not only believed in the saying that our group has no rights that a white man is bound to respect, but he felt that all of us would be better off dead. But when he was going to step up on the landing and looked into the barrel of my automatic, it changed his mind, and when I ordered him to go back down the stairs, he very dutifully obeyed orders.

Fifteen millions of our group with pent-up indignation against the white man of this country on account of mistreatment, mob rule, burned at the stake, hunted like wild beasts of the forest, shot down like dogs, segregated, discriminated against in public and in private, and also in the courts of justice in this supposed land of the free and home of the brave, without any visible signs of getting better, can't last always. It will only be a question of time before this menacing proposition will come to a head unless something is done to avert it. If not, this pent-up indignation of these 15 million will burst forth like the Johnstown Dam and shake the foundation of this government to its depths.

In 1872, the Brazilian government emancipated their slaves and made them citizens. They marry and intermarry freely. There's no segregation, no Jim Crow, or discriminating. The color question in Brazil is a negligible quality. There are no special privileges; equal rights for all and exclusive privileges for none; a government of the people, for the people and by the people, a union of hearts and a union of hands, a union that nothing can sever, a union cemented into the hearts of Brazilians, a Brazilian union forever.

In this country, from their earliest existence, children are taught to disregard the rights of our people by calling our group niggers, and are too degraded to respect our citizens. When the lowest type of foreigner comes to this country, they have been taught, from some source, that we are some kind of animals and not worthy of their respect and association. They fall in line with American citizens in their treatment of us. Our rights to equal accommodations in traveling are denied all over the South, and the judges in some states where the Civil Rights bills are on the statute books have ruled that a common carrier has the right to fix the places for the passengers. We pay first-class fare and get third-class accommodation, and have no redress for the insult. We have borne these insults for more than 60 years, and instead of conditions getting better, they are growing worse, and no remedy is in sight.

The rich and the poor are at daggers point in the economic situation of this country. The rich are getting richer and the poor, poorer. The rich are encircled by everything that embellishes civilized life. The poor are struggling to keep body and soul together and making a very poor job of it, and they are pleading for a chance to make a decent living, but it falls on deaf ears.

News comes to our ears from diverse places that Communists are teaching revolutionary doctrine and are teaching children to sing Communist songs, and that the communities in which this revolutionary doctrine is taught are asking for a federal investigation. This is a fertile field for our group, and in many localities, it is espousing the cause of the Communists, for there is plenty of testimony to prove that Communism has no respecter of persons, and our group is willing to accept anything which is in opposition to the caste system which is practiced in this country. Into every country in which the American white man goes, he takes his prejudices against our group along with him. Two of them went to Russia and became citizens. They were very much displeased with the manner in which our people were treated and gave vent to their feelings by assaulting a worker, and for their actions, they were deported back to the United States of America with the understanding that a man is a man in this country.

The prohibition question is another menace which has separated the people in a bitter conflict within, and I can't help but think that the Japanese question is the most serious of all. When the Japanese whipped Russia and Roosevelt was called in as an arbitrator to settle the contention, he said, in substance, to the Russians, "You have been licked. Go home and tend to your crops. See to it that you raise a good crop." He then said to the Japanese, "You are good fighters. You have given the Russians a good beating. Go home and take care of your crops and many industries." The Japanese said to Mr. Roosevelt, "Don't we get something?" and he said, "No." This, in so many words, was Roosevelt's decision.

The next controversy between the Japanese and this country arose over the segregation of the schools in California for Japanese children. This question was arbitrated, and the Japanese were defeated. The last controversy, which took place between the Japanese and this country, was the Alien Land Law, forbidding the Japanese from owning any land in California. This country proposed that the question be arbitrated, but the Japanese said no arbitration would go on, and the question is resting as it was before the court's decision. It is my opinion that the Japanese are just as much displeased at the discrimination against them now as they were then and are only awaiting an opportunity to avenge their grievance. To my mind, these are all signs of the beginning of an end of imperialistic, proud, haughty, blatant, and avaricious government.

We started on our trip to Chicago. At the time, the roads were bad, and I had a chauffeur who thought he knew the roads to Chicago and was too obstinate to inquire about the right road to take, and we drove more than 100 miles farther than was necessary. Many a time, we found ourselves 10 and 15 miles out of the way. My speedometer registered 1,300 miles. At any rate, we had a very pleasant trip, driving in the day and at night. We could not get accommodations on account of our race. We stopped in several towns in the nighttime and could not get any place to sleep or eat. No hotel accommodations whatever for our group, and we would then proceed on our journey by night. The roads in Missouri were horrible, the hills were high and rough, and it was dangerous for cars to go down those steep hills. After leaving one of the towns where we could not find hotel accommodations, we traveled about five miles, and we agreed that we would stop on the side of the road and remain until morning. We stopped in front of a farmer's house. About twelve o'clock that night, we heard a voice coming from the direction of the house, ordering us to move on, that he was afraid for us to stay there.

I replied to him that there was no need of being afraid, that no harm would come from us, and I further said, "You have a comfortable bed, and we are out here in our car, very uncomfortable."

He said, "You had better drive on."

I said, "We will not."

My chauffeur said, "Let's drive a short distance down the road," and I agreed to it.

We drove down the road about 20 rods from his gate and camped there for the night. The following morning, just after daylight, my attention was attracted by a gang of men coming from every direction toward us. Some of them had guns on their shoulders.

The chauffeur, who had experience of that kind, said, "Those men are after us."

My wife cried out, "Oh! What shall we do?"

Just at that time, one of the men called one of us to come over to where they were. I told the boys that I would go. My chauffeur said that if I went, he would leave me on the road and make his getaway. I had never learned to drive my car, and I had to yield to them in this case. He further said that I would have to let him do all the talking, for he knew if I said anything to them, I would mess up the party. All agreed.

The boys went over to where they were. They questioned them relative to our business and who I was. They told them that I was a rich hotel man from Tulsa, Oklahoma, who was on my way to the Republican National Convention as an alternate delegate.

They said, "You will have to drive back to town," a distance of about 10 miles, "to be investigated. Follow that car. It will take you back to town."

We turned our car around and followed the designated car. Several cars followed us. We reached the town at about six-thirty. The Justice of the Peace was still in bed, and they kept us waiting for several hours before he came. When he took his seat, I was ordered to appear before him for questioning. He asked me a thousand questions. I had some papers in my pocket, and a letter of introduction from James McBirney, President of the National Bank of Commerce of Tulsa. I showed that to him. I also had a cashier's check for $1,000, and he asked to see that. I asked him if I had to tell him the history of my life, to which he took exception and said, "Don't get mad, nigger." He then ordered me to open my handbag and to take everything out. I laid them on the table for his scrutiny, and I had satisfied him that I was not a bandit. He released me and we started for Chicago.

About 15 miles out from this town, we were arrested again and carried to another town about five miles out of the way to answer to the same charges. When they stopped us, I told them that we had been arrested by the officers in the town through which we had just passed and objected to go with them. But they forced us to go. Then they telephoned back to the place where we were first arrested and were informed that they had investigated us and to let us go. I started on my way, not rejoicing but humiliated by the gross insults which had been heaped upon my wife and me by the violations of our rights as American citizens.

After five days of travel, pleasure and displeasure, we arrived in Chicago on the day of the opening of the convention. Our purpose when leaving Tulsa was to make preparations to find a location where we would make our future home, knowing that our lives were unsafe in Tulsa, and our property was transient. My wife had pleaded with me very earnestly to sell our property and go someplace where we would be safe from the Ku Kluxism, grandfather clauses in the Constitution, and Jim Crowism on railroad trains and being discriminated against in all public places of accommodation. In pursuance of that pursuit, while in Chicago, I busied myself trying to find a suitable location. I visited several towns which had been recommended to me as good towns for the hotel business. The most favorable of them all was Indiana Harbor. I went there and organized a hotel company with a capital stock of $50,000. We secured a charter and were negotiating for the purchase of a lot upon which to erect the hotel. We were proceeding with the project very nicely, and just at this time, I was notified by my son that the hotel business in Tulsa was slow and that he had not been able to meet the payments on the mortgage note or the furniture. I found it necessary to abandon my undertaking and return to Tulsa.

During our stay in Chicago, we had a very enjoyable time with our friends and relatives. My wife visited her mother in Canton, Mississippi, and remained with her for several months before returning to Chicago in time to accompany me back to Tulsa. I gave my automobile to my son, C. F. Stradford, and $129.00 to have it repaired. After attending to some other minor details relative to returning to Indiana Harbor the following year to complete the hotel, I left Chicago for Tulsa and resumed the running of my business.

In the following month, I caught up on delinquent payments on the mortgage note and also the payment on the furniture note that was delinquent. The loan business in which I was engaged was very profitable. Our group was very prosperous, and it was a hard matter for Negroes to borrow money from any of those white loan companies. So, I busied myself in making loans on their automobiles, household goods, jewelry, diamonds, guns, and anything of value. I had notes amounting to $5,000.00 deposited in my safe, ranging in amounts from $5.00 to $900.00. Every one of them was destroyed during the riots of Tulsa.

After a period of 45 years, the Ku Klux Klan organization appeared in Tulsa and began to carry on its nefarious violations of the law. They mobbed one of our group, took him from jail with the failure of the sheriff executing his duty, and hanged him without a judge or jury. And the verdict of the coroner's jury was that he met death by unknown hands. At that time, I have no doubt there were more than 100 rooming houses which had Negro porters that stood in front soliciting roomers. In quite a few of those houses, the porters were accused of being intimate with some of the women roomers, and, in fact, they would bring some of them to our dance halls to enjoy the dances, etc. The Kluxers would take the porters of our group out at night and severely flog them and make them leave. I remember one beautiful white girl, who used dark powder on her face, said how she wished she were a member of our group. On one occasion, when in court defending herself against being caught in company with a porter, she swore that she was part-Colored and was ordered to leave town.

Because this outlaw organization was so insistent that all the laws be enforced, an investigation of the vice and political corruption of the city was made. When the subject of miscegenation came up for investigation, it was found that it was very general in those rooming houses. Testimony was produced that one of our group had one of those inmates as his mistress and, on more than one occasion, had beaten her and made her give him her money. A man by the name of Judge Oliphant, who appeared to be a friend to our group and very much interested in our uplift, would attend our churches. And when any of our prominent men came to lecture to us, such as Du Bois, Sutton, Gregg, and others, he was always given a seat on the rostrum as one of the distinguished guests. He happened to be on the Investigation Committee and heard this testimony, and when questioned by a reporter relative to what he thought of the case, said, "That nigger ought to be hanged." I read what he had said in the evening's *Tribune*. I was very much mortified. I immediately called him over the phone and told him that his attitude toward our group was far from that which I thought it was, and I could never have dreamed that he would have made that statement. I further said, "Such a statement from you at this time is liable to precipitate a riot." He made no apology for the statement and added that hanging would be too good for him. After the investigation, feelings were bitter against us. Every now and then, the Ku Klux Klan would take one of the porters out for a ride and give him a flogging, and tell him to leave town. The city commissioners passed an ordinance prohibiting the porters from standing out in front of buildings, and also in the stairways for the purpose of soliciting business. The city administration was Republican and every mother's son of them was Ku Klux Klan. And the same feeling which existed against the Negroes during the days of Reconstruction was revived, and it was necessary for our group to prepare to protect itself.

Orders were issued by the chief of police to question all of the women of our group whom they suspected to be of the underworld class. The officers had no respect for any woman of our group. They arrested a great many of our good women and took them to the police station and searched them in a very indecent manner. Some of our wives were subjected to the same treatment, which aroused the indignation of every race-loving citizen in Tulsa.

Our group called an indignation meeting, which met in the lobby of the Stradford. At that meeting, the mayor, chief of police, and one of the councilmen were present. The purpose of the meeting was stated, and several bitter speeches were delivered against such violations of our women. The most bitter denunciation of the actions was made by the Reverend James A. Johnson, Pastor of the Avenue Baptist Church.

He said in part, "The order given by the police to arrest and search any Colored woman is a relic of ante-bellum days, and that no officer had the right to trespass on the rights of any citizen, regardless of color or previous condition of servitude. If we stand passively by and suffer such insults, what will be our condition in this town? Are we men and stand for such violations of our rights? No great cause has ever succeeded without the shedding of blood. I have a wife who is as dear to me as my life, and I love her with the fervor of my first love, and I am willing to die for her. If any police officer shall arrest her as a suspect, I will take my gun and go to find him and at sight, I will kill him. It matters not what the consequences will be."

Several other vitriolic speeches were made by members of our group denouncing the order and the chief of police. After giving vent to our feelings, the mayor addressed the meeting and, in his speech, guaranteed that there would be no arrests of any woman of our group unless the officers were absolutely certain the party arrested was a street-walker soliciting for her business. The chief of police and the commissioner both addressed and expressed regrets for what had occurred.

The meeting had this effect: Although officers were natives of the Southern states where they had been accustomed to treating us as chattel and thought that we should submit to the same kind of treatment, after listening to our protests and threats to kill any officer who would dare to misuse our wives, it embittered them against our group, although they were very careful not to search any other woman of our group. This feeling showed itself very clearly on the part of the police force when they precipitated the riot a few months after that meeting.

During the time I lived in Tulsa, I was prominently engaged in politics, not for money, but for the good that I could accomplish for my people. I was elected Precinct Committeeman, appointed Election Inspector, and served in that capacity for several years. I was also elected as a delegate to the state convention. I never sought any kind of appointive position. I paid my campaign assessments. I would not accept any office but was in a position to name the parties whom I wanted to fill positions which were available for our group.

On the morning following my first election to the office of City Committeeman, I was called over the phone by the chairman of the committee, asking me to resign for the reason that there were some white people living in my precinct and that he did not think that a black man should be in a position that a white man would have to go to him for any information whatsoever, and if I did not resign, he would prefer charges against me and present them to the committee and cause my expulsion. I asked him what objections did he have to a member of our group going to a white man for information. "We have members of our group who are better prepared on any subject to give information than you are, men who have brains, more money, and men who can whip you. You are ignorant and prejudiced, and where ignorance is bliss, it is folly to be wise, and when I meet you on the street, I will make you apologize to me for the insult." Fortunately, I never met him. True to his threat of bringing charges against me, he brought them, and they were thrown out. Afterwards, this same man became a candidate for nomination to the United States

Senate, and our group, to a man, voted against him, and he was defeated.

Prior to this time, two bootleggers, Geronimo, a Negro, and Joe Baker, a white man, were engaged in bootlegging for a drug company in Tulsa. A quantity of the liquor which they had equal charge of was stolen. The white man said that Geronimo had taken it, and when Geronimo came to work that evening, the owner of the whiskey accused him of taking it and told him that Joe Baker said that he had stolen it.

The owner had great confidence in Geronimo because he had worked for him for a number of years, and during that time had found him honest in all his dealings. And he had never come up short in the amount of liquor allotted to him for disposal before. In answer to the accusation, Geronimo said that Joe was a damn liar and told the owner where Joe had disposed of some of the whiskey and had him go to the man who had bought the whiskey from Joe.

After finding out that Geronimo was innocent of the charges, the following morning, when Joe came on duty, the proprietor told Joe that Geronimo had said that if he said that he had stolen the whiskey, he was a damn liar and that he knew where he had sold it. Joe became very indignant and said, "No damn nigger who calls me a damn lie can live in the same town with me, and I'm going to kill him at sight," and went out of the drugstore to get his gun.

In the afternoon, when Geronimo came to work, Joe had just left the store. The proprietor told Geronimo what Joe had said and told him to prepare himself for the worst. Geronimo said he was not afraid of Joe, and if that was his game, he was ready to play it.

On the following evening, when Geronimo came on duty, Joe Baker was sitting on one of the stools at the soda fountain with his back toward the front door.

Someone said, "There is Geronimo."

Joe Baker turned on the stool quickly, and as he rose, he reached for his gun. Geronimo shot him before he could get his gun out of his pocket. He emptied the contents of the gun, five bullets, into Joe Baker's body. Each bullet entered the body not more than three inches apart. He fell to the floor and died instantly.

At the time of the tragedy, there were quite a few people in the store, and for a time, pandemonium reigned. After the smoke from the gun had cleared away, no one was in the store, not even the proprietor. And then Geronimo left the store.

The sounds from the revolver attracted the police on the beat. He came in haste, and after getting the information and the direction Geronimo had taken, he followed in hot pursuit. He overtook him and struck him on the head with his gun. Geronimo grabbed his hand and said, "If you attempt to strike me again, I will kill you. You may arrest me. I will not resist, but you can't beat me up."

The officer carried him to the police station, and the chief of police transferred him at once to the County Jail for safety. Passion ran high among the whites against Geronimo, but that night passed without any violence.

At the preliminary hearing, as he was bound over to the Grand Jury without bond, he was indicted and charged with murder in the first degree, found guilty, and his punishment fixed at death. His lawyer, knowing that he did not get a fair and impartial trial, appealed the case to the Supreme Court. The verdict was set aside, and a new trial was granted. His lawyer was a man who had always been fair to our group and believed in equal protection. He said that his client would never hang, and if it cost him everything he had, he would see to it that he would get justice.

After a new trial had been granted, Geronimo was admitted to bond in the amount of $10,000. The lawyer secured a bondsman, and he was released. For some reason, the case did not come up for trial at the next term of court, but the following term, the case was called. Geronimo had departed for lands unknown, and he never came back so far as I know.

Chapter 15

Another incident: there was a white woman who was running a rooming house by the name of Jo St. Claire, who was caught violating the liquor law and was lodged in jail in default of an $800 bond. Her attorney, Janay Hartindale, made a specialty of such cases, securing bonds for his clients. He came to me and asked me to make the bond for his client, saying that all of his resources for furnishing bonds were exhausted, and so were the woman's. The woman had been living in the city for a number of years. He would assure me that there would be no danger of her hopping it. I signed it, and when the case came up for trial, my ward had gone to parts unknown. The bond was forfeited for several months. I employed a detective to locate her. He finally located her in Danville, Illinois. Armed with proper authority, he went to Danville and brought her back to Tulsa. Before incarcerating her, she begged the detective to take her to see me. I asked her why she had hopped her bond. She said that she was advised by her attorney to hop it and that he told her that she had no chance to beat the case, and the only chance she had was to leave town. She said that she told him that she would not be treating me right.

He said, "Your bondsman is a rich man, and he will never miss the $800.00. In a short time, you can make enough money to repay him."

Upon his advice, believing that she would be able to, in a short while, repay me, she left town. I asked her why she did not tell me of her intention, and she said that she was afraid that I would have her put in jail again. The scene was very pathetic as she pleaded with me, with tears running down her cheeks, not to put her in jail. I told her that she had my sympathy, and I would be glad to yield to her desires, but that once loss of confidence was once too often to ever be regained, and with regret, I told the detective to put her in jail. He did so, and I was released from the bond, although it cost me several hundred dollars to bring her back to Tulsa and deliver her to the custody of the jailer.

My reputation as a hotel man had been established, and I was in demand in a great many cities to promote the erection of hotels for our people. There was a hotel company organized in Kansas City, Missouri, with a capital stock of $500,000 for the purpose of building a hotel of 125 rooms, and I was elected president of the company. I subscribed for 1,000 shares of stock at $10.00 per share, and I also agreed that on the first of June 1921, I would take up my duties as promoter and builder of the prospective hotel with a commission of five percent of the cost of the building, which five percent was to be a mortgage on the building when complete. After arranging all minor details, I returned to Tulsa, awaiting with great expectation for the time for me to enter upon my new duties. My wife was overjoyed at the thought of having me leave Tulsa on account of the hostility and prejudice against us. Many a time she had begged me to leave Tulsa before the crisis came, but I was doing so well financially, I ignored her pleas.

On May 31, 1921, a riot started between the whites and blacks and ended on June 1, annihilating all of the property owned by our group, which consisted of 42 blocks, and many a life were lost. Since the time I returned to Tulsa from Chicago, my business was very prosperous. I had contracted to buy Lot 9 in Curley's Addition to the City of Tulsa, which was located in the rear of my hotel. I had also bought a 10-room dwelling house, which was to be moved on one of my vacant lots. We had also planned to purchase a Marmon Touring car on June 1st, the price of which was $5,500. My wife and I would go down to the store where the car was on exhibition every night to look at our car or the one that we called ours. With joy and expectancy, we were satisfied that we would be the happy possessor of it in a few days.

On this day, a messenger boy of our group went into the Drexel Office Building on an errand for the firm by which he was employed. He entered the elevator and ascended to the eighth floor. After he had attended to the business, he again entered the elevator, and in doing so, accidentally stepped on the elevator girl's foot. She flew into a passion and began to scratch and strike the boy in the face. He caught her around the waist and, with his other hand, he lowered the elevator to the first floor and ran out of the building.

At the time of the incident, the city editor of the *Tulsa Tribune*, a daily paper, was on the elevator. Being one of those who wished to see our group exterminated in Tulsa, he went directly to his office and put a large headline on the front page of the paper: "A Negro Assaulted a White Woman in the Elevator in the Drexel Building." This headline aroused the wrath of the Ku Klux Klan, and they said that they would mob him that night.

The sheriff telephoned the *Tulsa Star* office, a Negro paper, and told the editor that he expected that an attack would be made on the jail that night to get the boy, and that he was going to need all of his power to prevent it. If he found that he could not cope with the situation, for us to get together, and he would call us to help protect him.

My wife and I remained in our apartment every evening until nine o'clock. We had not read the evening *Tribune*, nor had we heard anything about the incident.

About nine o'clock, a young man by the name of Jimmy Starr came up to my apartment and told me that they were going to mob the boy, and he thought that I ought to know it. I asked him where he got his information. He then asked me if I had not read the evening papers. I said that I had not. He said that a meeting was in progress in the *Tulsa Star* office, and he had been requested by the editor to notify me.

I hurried as fast as I could. The editor, A. J. Smitherman, stated the object of the meeting and also what the sheriff had said. Excitement was running high. After the editor had taken his seat, calls were made for me to speak. I hesitated at first, for the situation was a very perilous one. I advised the boys to be sober and wait until the sheriff called for us. I further said that I had expected something of that nature to happen long before this on account of the bitter feelings against our group, and I said then, as I had said before, that the day a member of our group was mobbed in Tulsa, the streets would be bathed in blood.

"If I can't get anyone to go with me to resist the mob, I will go single-handed and empty my automatic into mobbists and then resign myself to my fate."

The members of the meeting refused to abide by my advice and said that they would not remain up there and let the mob get the boy. When they decided they were going down to the jail, and if it was necessary for the sheriff to have assistance, if need be, they would be on the ground to assist him. The opinion of the majority prevailed, and I said, "I will go down." And every member of the meeting offered to go.

The editor of the *Star*, A. J. Smitherman, rose and said, "Mr. Stradford, I will go for you. You are of too much importance to go. We need men of your caliber on the outside to help those of us who are unfortunate enough to get into the clutches of the law."

All agreed for me to stay away from the scene, and I went back to the hotel. After the meeting, the boys began to fill up on moonshine and furnish themselves with guns and ammunition. A great many automobiles were owned by them. They got into their automobiles and went down to the courthouse and parked their cars about two blocks from the courthouse.

Among them was a young man who had seen service in France. He lined them up in marching order and said, "March!" They marched three abreast until they came to the courthouse. They found at least 5,000 white people there demanding that the sheriff turn over the boy to them.

The leader of our group, as they advanced, said, "Stand back, white men, there will be no lynching here tonight."

A white officer knew one of the boys who was among the marchers and went to him and tried to take his gun. That was the beginning of the fray. Our boys shot into the crowd, and a number were killed and wounded. That murderous crowd, which had assembled there for the purpose of mobbing that innocent boy, scattered like birds. Our boys went back to the cars and drove back to our part of the city.

As soon as the white man awoke to the danger he had to face, he prepared for the fray. Our section was the northeast part of the city. The thoroughfare to our part of the city was through Boston and Cincinnati Streets to Archer. Detroit, Elgin, and Greenwood Streets were closed south of Archer Street. The Frisco Railroad was between Archer and First Streets and was located in the center of Boston Street. The railroad was the dividing line between the main part of the city and ours, and it made it necessary for the white men to come either down Boston or Cincinnati Streets to get into our part of the city.

Knowing that they were coming over in our section, the boys concealed themselves behind boxcars and houses, and when they attempted to cross the line, they would shoot. Finding that route was almost impregnable, they sought another way to attack us. Our boys were on the alert and met them when they attempted to enter at other places. The firing was furious from about 10:00 to 12:30.

I can't find words to express the intensity of the shooting. So to illustrate, if you have ever attended a public park like the Congress in Saratoga Springs, New York, or Riverview Park in Chicago, when there is a display of fireworks, and when your sensibilities are benumbed from the sounding of the report of guns of all calibers and the earth seems to tremble from the report, and you will say, "How wonderful are the works of man."

At about 12:30, hostilities ceased. In some way, I can't tell how, the chief of police communicated with our group and informed us that they had had enough of the fight and for us to go home and take our rest, and the next day, the matter would be adjusted fairly. As soon as we ceased firing, the chief of police telephoned all the nearby towns and called for reinforcements. Freight cars were used in transportation. He furnished the guns and ammunition, not to keep the peace but to kill a nigger. Several testified against him in his trial for removal from office on the ground of incompetency.

It was agreed that at five o'clock the following morning, the sound of whistles of the large factories would be the signal for them to come over into our section and kill, burn, and riot. The Boy Scouts accompanied them. Each one was furnished a can of kerosene oil and matches to set fire to each house after they had removed the occupants. Some of them were allowed to move their goods out on the sidewalk before they set fire to the house. Houses that the tenants had deserted would be pillaged, and the furniture removed from their homes. Quite often, men of our group were caught in their homes by the rioters. They would throw up their hands and beg for mercy, but there was no mercy to be found. They were shot dead on the spot.

The practice was continued until 42 blocks of our property were laid to waste in ashes, and 10,000 of our people were left homeless. After the conflagration, an order was given to arrest everyone in our group and confine them in the Convention Hall or the baseball park, and those who were wounded were put in churches, and the dead were placed in the morgue. I was confined in the Convention Hall.

After the meeting at the *Tulsa Star* office, one of our group was shot just in front of me. One was shot in front of the hotel and lay on one of the benches in front of the hotel, and one was shot in the arm just after leaving the hotel. When I returned to the hotel, my wife had the lights out, and the hotel was dark and gloomy, and all the guests were filled with fear and distress. I turned the lights on again, and with two trusted companions, we pledged ourselves to protect the hotel with our lives. I furnished them with all the ammunition I had, so to one I gave a Winchester shotgun, and to the other, a .45-caliber Colt pistol, and I had an automatic pistol. The lights in the lobby were left burning. Those on the second and third floors were out. We went up to the second floor and I assigned one of them to watch the East side and the other the West side, and I took the North side. No assault was made on the hotel that night.

We never slept one minute during the night. I gave permission for some to go to the roof of the hotel. All were armed with rifles and sawed-off shotguns. The fire walls made a breastwork, and from their concealed position, they did some very effective work, according to a report by a deputy sheriff. About nine o'clock that night, I had a telephone call from Muskogee, Oklahoma, saying, "We are informed that you are having a bloody riot. If you need us, let us know. We have 50 men who are ready now to come to your rescue. We have our cars parked, ready at your command." I told them that I did not think it necessary, that I thought we were able to cope with the situation. I received another telephone call from someone, from members of our group, offering their assistance in case we needed them. At the time their messages came to me, I had no conception of the gravity of the situation.

If I had, I could have had at least 50 or more to help protect our homes and lives.

During the time of cessation from fighting until five o'clock the following morning, our group went to sleep and was awakened by the onslaught of that infuriated mob.

Beginning at the north section, they began to burn and destroy all of our belongings, and also to kill and maim, and plunder. For several hours, they kept up their burning and killing until they had come within two blocks of my hotel. I was sitting in the window of the lobby looking westward. I saw an airplane approaching the hotel from the west. I can't say whose plane it was. At that time, there were only two planes in Tulsa, one was owned by Harry Sinclair, the oil magnate, and the other one was a government-owned plane. It was sailing like a huge bird in the direction of the hotel and about 200 feet above the ground, and just before it reached the hotel, it swerved a little and shot several bullets through the transoms and plate windows. One shot a man running through the lobby. He went upstairs and pitifully called for a doctor, but there was none to be found.

At that time, there were at least a dozen people who had remained all night, as conditions were very perilous. The women had become hysterical, and the scene was very pathetic. The wife of the man who had pledged himself to die with me in the defense of the hotel pleaded with her husband to leave the hotel, go out, and meet the mob and beg mercy from them. He yielded to her entreaties and came to me and said, "Stradford, I am going to leave you. My wife's entreaties have caused me to leave you feeling that if we are trapped here, all of us will be killed. If we leave now,

The Stradford Hotel, Tulsa, Oklahoma, 1921

we may have a chance for our lives. Here is your gun and shells." Then he said to the others present, "Who wants to go with us?"

After a short parley, all agreed to go, with the exception of the other man who had agreed to defend the hotel.

My wife cried, "Oh! Papa, let us go, too."

I told her that I intended to protect my hotel with my life, and if she wanted to go with the crowd, to go, that I would remain and see the results.

She then said, "I will stay, and if necessary, I will die with you."

Then my pledged defenders said to the bunch, "Let's go." They all left the hotel and went north.

At that time, a machine gun was stationed on Standpipe Hill and was trained on the hotel, shooting out the windows on the west side of the hotel. There was a porch on the second floor of the hotel, which extended to the full width of the building, and a door leading out on the porch. The man, who had pledged himself to defend the hotel with me, and I went and stood in this door, not realizing the danger. And he was shot down by my side. There were about six men in the hotel who had been shot and were calling for medical attention. I can't say whether they died or not.

A short while after, the man who had left the hotel came running back to tell me that he had met the mob about two blocks from the hotel. They stopped him and asked from where he had come. He told them from the Stradford Hotel. They asked how many men were in the hotel. He told them that he had been in the hotel all night and that there was no one there besides him. They thought I had a regiment of men in the hotel, to give them battle when they showed up.

"Go down to the hotel and tell him that we have come to take him to a place of safety. It is not safe for him to remain in the hotel."

I sent word to the leader that if they would guarantee that my hotel would not be burned, I would go to the Convention Hall with them. He returned to me with the assurance that they would not burn the hotel.

In a few minutes, they came. I opened the door to admit them, and just at that instant, a man was running across a lot, southeast of the hotel, trying to make his getaway. One of the rioters fell on one knee, placed his revolver against the pillar of the hotel, and began to shoot at him.

I yelled at him, "Brute! Don't shoot that man!"

The leader of the group said, "Don't shoot in that direction. You might hit one of the soldier boys in that yard."

The Militia had been ordered out to take charge of the affair, but instead they joined the rioters.

When I opened the door, the leader said, "I know you, Mr. Stradford. We came to take you to a place of safety. It is not safe for you to be here."

I said, "If you guarantee that my hotel will not be burned, I will go with you."

He said in reply, "Your hotel will not be burned. It will be used for a place of refuge."

A great many women and children were standing on the outside, and he said to them, "Come in here. This will be a safe place for you, and your wife may take charge of it until you come back."

Then he said, "We have got to round up a few more fellows. You may remain here until we come back, and then we will pick you up."

Just as I was getting into the automobile, the raiding squad arrived on the scene. They broke open the drugstore and appropriated cigars, tobacco, and all the money in the cash register. The perfumes, they sprinkled over themselves. Most of them wore only a pair of pants, a shirt, and a belt to hold the pants up. Their shirts were filled with silk shirts, handkerchiefs, and fine socks.

While I was there, they did not enter the hotel. On my way to the Convention Hall, about a half a block from the hotel, I met a great many of my folks being marched to the hall with their hands above their heads, and every time one of them put their hands in any other position, the guards would jab them with their guns and make them throw their hands up. The guards acted like wild men. It is incredible to believe that in this civilized age, that a white man could be so void of humanity and so brute-like in his nature. Oh! If you could have seen them jumping up and down and uttering words which were too obscene to be printed, striking and beating their prisoners, I am sure you would be surprised beyond measure.

After leaving the hotel, the car in which I was riding was stopped about one block north. Someone in the crowd said in a gruff voice, "Take off your hats!" All of the occupants in great haste took off their hats. I was a little slow in getting mine off, and one of the rioters struck at me with his six-shooter. Happily, he missed his aim, and the auto started on its journey. We went out Eastern Avenue. There, I owned a block of tenement houses. As I passed, the flames were leaping mountain high from my apartments, and I was afraid to even make a protest. But in my soul, I cried for revenge and prayed for the day to come when I could personally avenge the wrongs which had been perpetrated against me. When I arrived at the Convention Hall, a ghastly scene met my eyes. First of all, I saw the remains of two men from our group in a truck outside the hall. The hall was designed to seat 5,000—filled to capacity. Women were giving birth to children. The lame, the blind, and the deaf were all crowded into that space. I saw a teacher who taught in the public school crossing the stage. I yelled to him to sing, "My Country 'Tis of Thee." Someone cried out that I had better keep quiet or they would mob me.

I saw one of the women left in the hotel with my wife, and I asked her where was my wife.

She said, "In a short time after they took me away, the marauders came in and took possession of the hotel and arrested everyone in the hotel." She said that my wife went back into the hotel, and she did not see her come out. And after they had gotten several blocks away from the hotel, it was in a light blaze.

Knowing my wife's temperament, I felt that she had decided to die in the hotel. And I was greatly alarmed. I found Mrs. Carey, the private ex-secretary to the ex-mayor, and explained to her my uneasiness over my wife. She said she would go immediately and try to find her and bring her to me. She came back without her. I told her that if she had any human sympathy, she would go again and search for my wife and not give up until she found her.

In her first search, she told me that my hotel had not been burned, and that gave me some encouragement that my wife had not met a violent death. I pleaded with her to go again. On her second trip, she went to the Baseball Park, had a man with a megaphone page her, and have her come to the office where she was. In a short time, she came to the office and found Mrs. Carey waiting. Mrs. Carey put her in her automobile and brought her to me. When they arrived, I was paged and went immediately to the office, and to my delight, I was standing face-to-face with my wife. My joy was beyond measure. I kissed her, I wept, and I laughed, and it was some time before I could compose myself.

Chapter 16

A short time after I had been incarcerated, we were addressed by one of the white ministers of the city, who said that we need not fear any violence from without, that the city authorities were having badges printed which would give us police protection and that any white man who would sponsor for us could secure badges at the office and pin them on the lapel of our coats and could take us out. Every member of our group in the city of Tulsa was restrained of his liberty. Not one could be seen on the streets. The police had gone into the homes of the rich on the South side and had taken their servants and put them in one of the two places of confinement, and it created a very bitter feeling against the administration. When the badges were secured, there was a rush of that class to get their servants out in order that they could go back to their work. It was a very bitter pill for me to ask some cracker to stand sponsor for me in order that I might get out of that hell.

My son, John, and I were confined in the same place. While he was standing on the stage, he overheard a conversation between an ex-representative of the state, a State Senator, and several citizens of Tulsa. They said, "We will get Stradford tonight. He has lived here for 15 years and has taught the niggers that they are as good as white people and every house of theirs in a radius of a mile is an arsenal, and he is the cause of it. No nigger can live in Tulsa who will fight and talk to a white man like he does. We will truly give him a necktie party tonight." My son told me what he had heard. I am a good checker player, and it was my move. George Mowbrey, an undertaker, whose campaign for commission I had conducted in my precinct, passed and saw me and said, "What can I do for you, Mr. Stradford?" I told him to get a police protection badge for my wife and me, and take me out of that miserable place. He said that he would gladly do it, but public sentiment was so strong against me that if I were seen on the street, anyone would be liable to kill me, and he did not want to be a party to the killing. He said, "You are safe here, and I advise you not to leave here, for your own good."

The second man I talked to was a deputy sheriff. He said, "Your hotel was a strategic point for your group to shoot from. There were more than 150 men—dead men lying on the streets of Tulsa this morning, and the men shooting from the roof of your hotel contributed largely to that number." I was greatly surprised and said that it could not be. He said, "There is no use to deny it; we know from where the shots came." What he said spurred me on in my endeavor to get out of that place, for I felt sure that unless I did, they would carry out their threats. Looking over the crowd, I saw a man whom I considered a good friend of mine. He was the proprietor of the hotel on the Northeast corner of Boston and Second Streets. I can't recall his name. He came over to where my wife and I were. He grabbed my hand and in a fervent voice said, "Mr. Stradford, what can I do for you? I will do anything. I saw those brutes when they burned your hotel." I said to him, "Go and get me a police protection badge and take us out of here. We are not used to such treatment, and I am sure that you care for us until we can make another start."

This man and I had been on the most friendly terms. We visited each other in our hotels and freely discussed business interests. He said that he would get me out that night and reiterated that public opinion was so strong against me that it would not be safe for me to be seen on the streets. I insisted on his getting the badges at once, and he would leave his car by the side of the hall so that we could get into it without being detected and make our escape to Sand Springs, a distance of seven miles from Tulsa. But he would not take the chance, but said he would take me out that night. He gave me his solemn promise that he would do so that night and left me.

No sooner than he left, another man with whom I had business relations for 15 years came over and said, "Hello, J.B., what can I do for you?" I told him to get a police protection badge for me and my wife and take us out of this place. I explained our discomfiture to him, and it seemed to touch his heart. The name of this man was A. W. Brink. He said, "I will take you out. I would take you to my house, but my wife died a few weeks ago, and I have been so upset that I have decided to rent my house." He went to the office, got badges for us, and backed his car down the alley on the west side of the building to the side and said, "Come on, get into the car." We got into the back seat and he told me to hide myself as much as possible. I sat down on the floor, rested my head on my wife's lap. He backed his car out onto the street and started for Sand Springs to the home of one of our friends. He carried us there at a terrific rate of speed. When we arrived, we found guards patrolling the road. They stopped our car and inquired about our destination. We told them that we were going to the home of Professor William Lane, who had charge of the city schools. I showed them our police protection badges, and they let us pass. Mr. Brink took us to the residence of Professor Lane and left us after offering me whatever aid I needed. I told him that we did not need anything at that time, but would call upon him later.

When I left home, I had only my pants, shirt, shoes, and hat on. My wife had on a skirt over a coat. Everything else had been burned in the hotel. I was anxious about the contents of my safe, especially the money and the notes. I sent Professor Lane to Tulsa to look after my interests there. He found that the safe had been broken open and the contents taken out, and a great many of my papers were scattered all over the ground. The money, which amounted to $1,400.00, had been taken. Five hundred dollars ($500) of it had been deposited by one of my roomers, Hattie Hannifin. The other $900.00 was my own. When Professor Lane made it known that he was there in my interest, he was assaulted and ran away from the scene. He told me how bitter the feelings were against me and advised me to go out in the open and stay all night, for he was sure it was not safe for me to stay in his home. I thought differently and remained there until two o'clock that night, and the police guarded me to the station, and I left for Kansas.

Two hours after I left, several automobiles filled with men came to his home looking for me, and he could not convince them that I had gone until the police told them that they had given me protection to the train which left for Independence, Kansas, at two o'clock. I arrived in Independence at seven o'clock, June 2, and remained there with my brother until the next day. In the meantime, orders were issued by Attorney General Barrett for my arrest and were sent to Independence with instructions to the chief of police to pick me up.

On the following morning, about eight o'clock, the chief of police went to my son's place of business and asked for me. He told him that I was staying with my brother on Waldsmith Street, and as soon as the officer left the place, he called me over the phone and told me that the chief of police was looking for me. Before I could dress, the chief of police knocked at the door and inquired for me. My brother told him that I was there and called me. I asked if he had a warrant for me, and he said he did not. I told him that if he wanted me, to go get a warrant for me. He said that in a case of this kind, he did not have to have a warrant and that it was his duty to pick me up for investigation. He started to come into the house. My brother advised him not to go in, but I said, "Don't stop him. If he makes another step in this direction, I will kill him," whereupon he asked me to come to the door so that he could explain. I went to the door, and he told me what his duty was. I pronounced that as soon as I had my breakfast and attended a business matter at the Western Union, I would go to Tom Wagstaff's office, an attorney, and telephone Bill McCullough, the Sheriff of Tulsa County, and if he said he wanted me, I would submit to an arrest. He said, "All right," and left. I ate my breakfast, and then we went to the Western Union office.

My son had wired me $50.00 to come to Chicago at once. I got the money and went directly to Tom Wagstaff's office. When I got there, they had Bill McCullough on the phone, and the chief said to me, "You may talk with him," and handed me the receiver. I said, "Hello, Bill." He said, "Hello. Is this you, Stradford?" I said, "Yes. Has an order been given there for my arrest?" He said, "Yes, and Adjutant General Barrett has issued a warrant for your arrest. Will you come with extradition papers?" I said, "Hell, no!" and hung up the receiver. I then turned to the chief of police and said, "I am your prisoner." He incarcerated me in the County Jail.

I immediately notified my son in Chicago of my arrest, and as soon as he got the news, he boarded the first train for Independence and arrived there about twelve o'clock Saturday night and came to the jail to see me. The jailer permitted him to come into the jail where I was. When he came in, he had his gun on him. I asked him if he was not afraid to have that gun in his pocket, and he said, "No." He spoke comforting words to me and said, "Don't be alarmed, Papa, I will have you out of here in a few days." The following day was Sunday, and nothing could be done on that day. On Monday, he instituted habeas corpus proceedings, and I was released on $500.00 bond on account of the authorities in Tulsa not sending the warrant charging me with inciting a riot. Fearing that at any time, the warrant would reach the court, as soon as I was admitted to bond, my son said, "Let us leave here at once." We caught the Interurban car and went to Cherryvale, Kansas, and from there, we took the train to Chicago.

I have often heard the saying, "It is no disgrace to run when you are scared," but I never got scared until I began to run. The patter of feet behind me made me think that someone was after me. Every man I met looked like a lawman. I went into mortal terror to think that at any time I might fall into the clutches of the law. I had been fighting men all of my life up until this time, but the fighting spirit had died within me. If a little child had told me he wanted me, I would have tamely obeyed his command. Of all men, I was the most miserable.

After arriving in Chicago, I went into hiding, but not for very long. I immediately sought out financial contacts from our group in Chicago to present them with the same idea for a hotel that had worked so well in Tulsa. Their reception was anything but encouraging. One of the leading men said, "Your ideas about the hotel business are exaggerated." I said to him, "When Columbus conceived the idea that the world was a sphere." He said, "Damn Columbus! How much money have you got to invest in a hotel?" I said, "I have none." He then said that if I wanted to go into the hotel business to get some money. He got up from his seat and opened the door for me to go out. At that time, they were the three leading men, financially and politically in Chicago in our group. Men who had achieved prominence and experience by accident, men who were too selfish to give succor to a deserving one, men without human sympathy, and who had never acquainted themselves with the story of the Good Samaritan. They knew that a few months before I approached them, I was a successful businessman and had amassed a fortune, and was surrounded by all the luxuries of life. They knew that my condition was brought about by no fault of my own, and in the face of these facts, they turned a deaf ear. Charity in the world is cold. When you have money, friends are plentiful, but few friends can be found when you are broke and struggling for existence.

A few days afterward, I was riding on a State Streetcar, and my attention was attracted by a light tap on the shoulder. To my surprise, there stood a very dear friend of mine, the Reverend A. J. Smith, a former pastor of the Presbyterian Church in Coryville, Kansas, a man whom I had learned to revere on account of his Christian integrity and his moral characteristics and dignity, and I highly respected him on account of his ability to play at the game of checkers, although I was his superior at the game. He was a man who believed in the brotherhood of man and the fatherhood of God, and he practiced it in his church services to the chagrin of some of his members. The meeting was a very agreeable surprise. He had heard of my calamity and expressed regret. He gave me his card and said, "Come to see me. I may be able to help you in your undertakings."

I learned of an opening for a barbershop on the West side and a pressing and cleaning shop. I bought the barber chair and mirror, tools, and a heating apparatus, and opened a one-chair barbershop and remained there for one month. During that month, I did not take in enough to pay my room rent. I changed to a more favorable location where I had room to have tables to play cards and checkers, for drinks and cigars. Business increased rapidly. My son, John, who had been living in Omaha, came to live with me and insisted that I open a pocket billiard parlor. I secured large quarters and in connection with the barbershop and bathroom, we had a lunch stand and three pool tables. In six months, I had $1,700.00 in the bank. I was induced by some of the group to open a cabaret. My place of business was 2048 Ogden Avenue, and the room next to me, 2046, was for rent. I secured it and fitted it up at a cost of $1,000.00 as a first-class cabaret. I employed a white man and his wife to manage it, and a girl from our group as a ticket seller. We did a land office business for a season. We were in the heart of an Italian settlement. We had an excellent orchestra, first-class entertainers, and the place was filled with the most beautiful Italian girls who delighted to dance with members of our group, and, of course, the boys of our group were more than delighted to have the pleasure of tripping the fantastic toe with those dainty dolls.

The men did not like to see their girls dancing on such familiar terms with members of our group. Several protests came to me about it, but there was nothing that I could do or wanted to do to stop it. In the first place, it was a source of revenue for me, and in the second place, I have always believed in people doing just what they wanted to do and having just what they wanted to have, so long as they did not violate the rights of others. And I must say, it was a great pleasure for me to conduct such a cosmopolitan business.

On Arbor Day, 1925, my place was bombed at 12:30 a.m., just after the crowd had dispersed for home. I had retired to my bedroom in the rear of my pool room and barbershop at 2048 Ogden Avenue. The report from the blast greatly excited me. The windows in both buildings were broken, and also the windows on the other side of the street in half a dozen houses were shattered. In a few minutes, the fire department was on the scene, and divers, policemen, and the street were crowded with thousands of people. I remained on the inside of the room until I was satisfied that the danger had passed, then came out. I was questioned by the police relative to the bombing. They investigated it but were not able to get even the slightest clue. I repaired the damage done to the building and also my fixtures, and in a few days, I began the operation of the business again, but without success.

The people were afraid to attend and said that the perpetrators of the bombing were only awaiting the time when the room was filled with patrons, and then they would kill all of them. For more than six months, I kept this place open for business. I kept my orchestra and entertainers employed at their regular salaries at a great financial loss to me. Seeing that it was impossible to get people to attend, I had to get a new location.

I secured a building located at 1544 Lake Street. After repairing and decorating the room for that purpose, we gave the grand opening of the "Shuffle Inn." We had a very successful opening financially, and for several weeks, everything boded fair to be a great business success. This was during the Dever administration.

One evening during our performance, the place was raided. The officer found no liquor and nothing going on in violation. After they could not find anything on which to make an arrest, they asked me for my license. Under the Thompson administration, I did have a license. The Dever administration was bitterly opposed to cabarets, and he pledged himself that his first official act would be to clean up the 2nd and 3rd Wards and rid the city of the black and tan cabarets. I told the officer that I did not have a license, and he cited me to appear in court the following morning. I appeared before the judge at the designated hour and was fined for running a cabaret without a license and not having money with me to pay the fine. I was incarcerated without them giving me an opportunity to even notify my son or a lawyer, and I was told to close the place. While I was in jail, my cabaret was broken into and a great many of the fixtures were stolen. Among the articles stolen were four Westinghouse 20-inch blade electric fans, a lot of chairs, and all of our stock. That was the termination of a business that had cost me more than $2,500. I could find no sale for the outfit, so I put it in storage.

About the same time, some officers were raiding a building in the rear of my pool hall, and they said that they saw some boys shooting craps on one of the pool tables. They came to the front door of the pool hall and knocked. I opened the door and let them in, and they carried all of us to the station and booked us for gambling and revoked my pool hall license. After entering the place, they sought diligently to find some evidence of gambling but failed, and I was convicted by the testimony of an officer. Once more in life, I am broke.

Another incident occurred to me while I was on the West side. I had a room for my barbershop at 1940 Polk Street, in which I had installed a water heating apparatus for the barbershop. It was connected to gas, and there were no pipes to carry the fumes of the gas out of the room. In this room, I slept and cooked. The room was not sufficiently ventilated, and the burnt gas fumes were very strong at times, so strong that I had to open the door and keep it open for some time after turning the gas on.

Chapter 17

On the night in question, I had closed up the shop, and being very tired from work, I prepared my bed and lay down to sleep. The following morning, I arose and began to clean up the shop. Just as I began to clean, a man came in and asked for a haircut. I told him to take a seat in the barber's chair. After adjusting the haircloth, I began to cut his hair. Just as I was finishing the job, dizziness came over me, and I said to the customer, "Excuse me for a minute! I am a little dizzy." I sat down at the end of the shop and became unconscious at once, and for two hours I remained in that condition. They could get no sign of life in me and pronounced me dead. When I was resuscitated, the room was full of people, doctors, and a white nurse, who had reported that I had attempted to commit suicide. My son had been notified, and he came and brought a physician with him. When I came to myself, the first question I asked was, "Why are all of these people in here?" The next question was, "Where is my pocketbook?" I thought I was playing a game of checkers and said, "It is your move." After I had been fully restored to normal,

I asked what was the cause of my peril and the doctor said that I had been overcome by the fumes of the gas from the gas heater. A lady nurse, who was the first to serve on my case, said that I had attempted suicide. Several other theories were advanced relative to my condition. I am not in a position to say what was the real cause of my condition, but I can say without successful contradiction that suicidal intent was not the cause.

Just a thought—relative to the hereafter, and its consequences. In the midst of life, there is death. Just before the incident, I was enjoying life with a goodly portion of its attributes. All of a sudden, I became unconscious, and for several hours, I lay lifeless on a couch, and as far as I was concerned, I was dead to this world, and the word "finished" had been written.

Without pain, sorrow, or grief, I entered into the spirit worlds miles away. I learned nothing of that fairyland that I could tell of on my return. On one occasion, gas was administered to me for the purpose of extracting a tooth. Just before I became unconscious, I heard the doctor say, "Hold his hand." Just then, a terrific pain, and I felt the separation of life from the body. While lying there, lifeless, my tooth was pulled, and after the operation had been performed, a gentle tap on the shoulder and a voice saying, "All right," brought me back to consciousness.

If death is a dissolution of the body and soul, brought about suddenly, either by accident or otherwise, why should we have such a horror of it? Science has proven that there is no literal hell. The body is only subject to pain, and the spirit goes to the God that gave it, so we can see there is no suffering after death. The spirit is safe, abiding in the realms which have been prepared for the departed.

At the age of 64 years, I found myself broke again, disgusted, and despondent on the road looking for a new location. I decided to go to Indiana Harbor.

As I said before, in 1920, I incorporated a company to build a hotel there. One of the incorporators was a wealthy real estate operator who was very much interested in the project. I thought of him and felt that he would help me to make another start. I went to his office to see him. He had heard of my misfortune in Tulsa and greatly sympathized with me. I told him what I wanted him to do for me; that I wanted to start a business there and had no money to pay rent for a place in which to do business, nor did I have money to have any fixtures moved from Chicago to the Harbor. He not only told me to look for a suitable location but also instructed two of his agents to find a location for me.

Several days passed, and we could not find a suitable place. Just about this time, I had given up hope of finding a place, when I went to a grocery store run by a member of our group, which was an ideal place for my business. I stated my business to him, and he offered to sell his place to me and give me possession at once. I had no money to buy, so I referred the proposition to Mr. Saric, who told me to buy the place and he would furnish the money. I gave the owner the wholesale price for his goods and fixtures, and he gave me possession immediately.

The rent for the building was $50.00 per month. The cost of drayage from Chicago for my fixtures was $50.00. The amount of the stock and fixtures was $250.00. Mr. Saric paid all of those bills for me and also the decoration of the room, and I was installed in business once more. The place consisted of two storefront rooms. One was used for a barbershop and the other was for my cabaret.

The cabaret was elaborately fixed up. I had a sign, 12 feet by 18 inches, electric, hung across the street with the name of the cabaret on it, the "Shuffle Inn." We sold pop, cigarettes, cigars, tobacco, and lunch. At night, it was utilized for a cabaret. Our future for business was very promising. We made good for a short time. There was not the class of people in the Harbor to support a business of that kind. I was in the business for big money, and I soon found that the business was not sufficient to pay for my time. I decided after giving it a thorough test by staying with it for more than a year, long enough to pay the man who had advanced me the money to open up the business. In addition to the cabaret and barbershop, I opened a recreation pool hall and a gymnasium and furnished it with the necessary equipment for the boys, such as punching bags, dumbbells, jumping ropes, and an 18-foot ring. I had the management of one good boxer who fought a 10-round battle in the Armory with a white man to a draw. He was a very promising boxer and the better of the fight when it ended.

While in the Harbor, I had some very pleasant things happen to me. I had a son living in Dayton, Ohio, whom I had not seen for several years. Two of my other sons came over to the Harbor and took me on a motor trip to Dayton to see him. The trip was a very enjoyable one, and I was delighted indeed to see him, so much so that I had him come to the Harbor and turned my business over to him and his wife. From Dayton, we went to Cincinnati to visit a friend of mine who was a classmate at Oberlin College in 1893. He was very prominent in politics. He was also an editor of a newspaper and the author of a book. He had a financial rating of many thousands of dollars. He gave me an excellent reception. Mr. Dabney was known as one of the greatest guitar players of all time. The strings of music which he produced from that instrument were most wonderful and had the effect of making me feel that his soul was floating on the waves of his sweet music. Mr. Dabney brought his guitar with him when he came to Oberlin, and at that time, he was a very charming performer.

We left Cincinnati for Indianapolis, my old hometown. I met a great many of my old acquaintances and friends. Among them was a lady whom I had known, who was considered wealthy. Ever since I first met her, I have retained a grassy spot in my heart for her. She was a widow looking for a good husband, and I was a widower looking for a good wife.

Since 1921, everything on which I had embarked had been a failure, and after due consideration, I decided to enter the matrimonial field for profit. So, I called upon her and told her I had come to make her my wife.

No sooner than I made the proposal, she said, "What is your holdback? Let's go."

I am not positive that she meant it, but as my time was short in Indianapolis, I told her that I was not quite ready at that time, and that there would have to be some time spent in considering what would be required of each of us.

As soon as I returned home, we would enter into correspondence with each other relative to the terms of our agreement. I had only one ambition, and that was to be established in the hotel business once more. I felt that Indianapolis was a good field for the business. Twenty-eight years before that time, I had attempted to erect a large hotel there. She knew what my ambition was and assured me that my fondest hopes would be realized. She gave me her card and said, "Be sure to write," and with a fond good-bye and a kiss, we parted, and I left for home. That kiss of affection lingered with fond love and devotion for several months.

After my trip to Dayton, Ohio, Indianapolis, and Chicago, I went back to Indiana Harbor and prepared to move to Muskegon, Michigan. Glowing accounts had been circulated relative to the chances of making big money there. It was said that it was an automobile industrial center, and the foundries all employed members of our group. And they were all running full-time. It was also said that members of our group were earning from $5.00 to $12.00 per day.

I went to Muskegon to investigate the report. And I found that it was a good field to make quick money if I could get a proper location and get the patronage which was necessary. I also found that little or no attention was paid to the conduct of our group. The work which they were employed to do was the most menial. The white men could not do the work, and Campbell Wyand, Gannon Foundry Company, had agents on the road making shipments of our group laborers into town daily. I also found that there was no place of amusement for them, no club rooms, no barbershops, no YMCAs, and no pool halls.

When the shipments came into town, they were quartered in three different rooming houses with very inadequate accommodations, and each of them had an average of 50 men. Some of them had bunks with upper and lower beds. Another had a large tent in connection with their residence, which could accommodate, in a very unsanitary way, a great many of them. There was not a public place in town where a respectable member of our group could get accommodations. Seeing their conditions, I called on the president of the foundry company and laid the matter before him and insisted on him building a place for the workers of our group and to give me the management of it. All that I could induce him to do was to donate a lot upon which to erect the building, and when he sent me to his lawyer to draw up the contract, he served a clause in the contract whereby, in such a length of time, he would have to be paid for the lot.

I had induced a member of our group to invest a thousand dollars ($1,000.00) in the enterprise, and I had agreed to invest $500.00. He accompanied me to the lawyer's office to invest the money but said that until a deed is given in consideration of $1.00 and a clause stating that if the house was not erected, the lot will revert to the donor, he would not invest one cent in it, and the negotiations failed.

Determined to use every effort I could command to secure a location, I remained in Muskegon for several weeks. I went to a rental agent, Mr. Cook, who told me that he had a barbershop that I could buy. The owner was sick at that time, and he had a man running it for him, but he could give me possession of it immediately. The man who owned it, Mr. Pepper, sold the place to me. I had the City Attorney Palmer to write the bill of sale and paid the owner the agreed amount with the understanding that I was to have possession on May 1st, 1926. I went back to Indiana Harbor, closed my business there, and had my fixtures sent to Muskegon Heights. I arrived in Muskegon on the night of May 1, 1926.

About 1:00 a.m., I went to the place I had leased and found that the man who was running the place was still there. I had employed a transfer man to truck my outfit to Muskegon, and I came along with him in the truck. I knocked on the door, and at first, I did not get a reply. I continued to knock and finally a voice from the inside asked, "Who are you and what do you want?" I told him, and he said, "Get away from that door. You can't come in here." In the meantime, he called the police and told them that I was a robber and was trying to break into his place. Several policemen answered the call and found me there, demanding entrance. They came up to me in a very insulting manner, demanding to know why I was disturbing the peace and quiet of this man.

After I had related the circumstances to them, they told me to drive the truck to the police station and park there until morning, and then I could do what was necessary to get possession of the place. The man in possession of the place was the man who had sold the shop to the men from whom I bought it. The owner at that time had a very bad spell of rheumatism and had left the former owner to sell the business for him and to remain in the building until he sold it or until he was able to take charge of it. The former owner, Reverend John Phillips, occupied one part of the building for a barbershop, and the other side was used for non-denominational church services.

The next morning, I went down to the place and demanded possession. He said that I could take the things out of the room at any time, but he would not give me the room. I went to see the lawyer who had drawn up the agreement for me, and he explained to him how he had relinquished his rights to the lease when he sold his shop to Mr. Pepper, but he refused to give up the place. To avoid a lawsuit, we went to Mr. Pepper and asked him to use his influence to have Mr. Phillips move out. He said that the lease had been transferred to Pepper when he, John Phillips, had sold the shop to him, and John Phillips was a trespasser. He went down to the place with us and told Reverend Phillips to move out or he would put him out. Finding that he was going to be put out, he asked for a little time to secure a location. We gave him one week, and at the expiration of that time, he moved.

I had the room repaired and decorated, and then moved my outfit into the place, and in a few days, we had our opening. We had a two-chair barbershop, two pool tables, and a club room. The business was indeed lucrative; our receipts were on average $300.00 per week in profit. The building was located on the corner of 6th and Broadway. One house was a mere shack with thin board walls and about 10 feet high. It was on the principal thoroughfare of the city, and if you should drop a pin on the inside, you could hear the report on the street. That class of our group who work around foundries, mines, and oil and gas belts, is very noisy and would attract the attention of passersby who protest against it. Oftentimes, they would stand on the outside in front of the building and obstruct the sidewalk, although I used every effort to keep them quiet and to keep them off the sidewalk in front of the building. On account of the fact that there was no place of recreation for our group in the city, except this one, the chief of police was very indulgent towards us. Many protests against the place were made, and one of the councilmen came with the chief of police down to the place and demanded him to order the place closed. He refused to order me to close it, saying that it was not the only place that protests were made against, and he would give me a chance to try to keep the boys quiet and also from obstructing the streets in front of the building.

The business steadily increased, and if I could have remained there for an indefinite period, the object of my going to Muskegon Heights would have been realized. The place was not so bad, but there were so many Ku Klux Klan in the town at that time that had taken oaths to do everything in their power to keep our group from prospering and knowing that one of them had a place which was conducive to good business, and also four out of every five protests came from them. The chief of police lived one half block south of my place and passed by it going to his lunch six and seven times a day. And he said he had seen or heard nothing which would justify him closing the place. But the damned Ku Klux were so determined that the place should be closed. The chief came to me and said that for his interests and for my own good, it was best for me to get another location, and he would give me 30 days to find one.

One evening after I closed the barbershop, I went into the club room. The boys were playing checkers for treats, and others were playing cards. The window shade was up, and anyone could see in from the outside. I told the attendant to pull the curtains down, that a policeman from our group had been appointed, and I was not acquainted with him, and I did not want him to see any money passing over the table to pay for the treats. One of the boys said, "Mr. Stradford, meet Mr. Wells, the new officer."

I acknowledged the introduction by saying, "I am delighted to have the pleasure of shaking your hand, but I have never been more greatly surprised." He said, "Don't be excited. You are conducting an orderly place, and so long as you conduct it in this manner, you will have no interference from the police department."

Business continued to be good, and I did not make any great effort to find a location for I knew that there was no other place suitable that I could get. I had decided that when the month was up, to try to get another extension of time. When the chief ordered me to move, he said he would help me find a location.

Early one morning, he came to my place and told me to come and get into his car, and he would help me find a location. We went to several places on the outskirts of town, but none of them were suitable for the business.

Finally, he said to me, "You can't stay where you are, and you must select some place where you may go and build up a business." He then took me to a storeroom on the corner of Hovey and Temple Streets, which was for sale. He advised me to buy it and move as soon as convenient.

I went to see the owner of the building, and we entered into a contract for the purchase of the property. The terms were purchase price, $1,600 with interest at 6% per annum; monthly payments $25.00. A loss clause was put into the fire insurance in my favor. I paid the $300.00 cash on the contract and took possession of the building. After making some needed repairs, I moved in.

The place was eight blocks from the traffic on the main road. I gave a grand opening and started out with a good business, but that was on account of the extensive advertisement for that night. After that, there was no business of any consequence. I barely made expenses. Determined to make the business pay, I built a six-room, two-apartment building, furnished it, and rented the apartments for $5.00 per week. By so doing, I brought several families into our part of the city, and this was quite a financial help to my business. Several other families bought property in the neighborhood, and that added more financially to my business. I added an addition to the building and used the room for a restaurant. Business was on the increase. Although I knew that it would never come up to my expectations, I had invested my money and intended to stay with it until I could get it out.

Just at this time, I had an attack of rheumatism, and my physician advised me to go to Mount Clemens and take a course of baths. Before leaving, I arranged my business so I would not have to close it while I was away. I left it in charge of William Camack, whom I thought was an honest and trustworthy man. On the morning of May 1st, I left Muskegon Heights for Mount Clemens, Michigan.

On the second day of May, about 12:00 a.m., someone set fire to the building and completely destroyed it and all of its contents. I was at once notified of the fire and was advised to return home. When I returned, I found myself homeless and all of my personal property destroyed by fire.

The fire insurance adjuster and the State Fire Marshal called to see me and took a written statement of the losses and other matters incident to the fire, and when I had finished the statement, I signed it and asked the insurance adjuster when I could expect a settlement. He said as soon as the fire marshal made his report to the company. Then they left me with the impression that the claim would soon be settled.

I went to the insurance agent's office several times each week, inquiring when they were going to settle, and they would say, "We are looking for a settlement every day." Matters drifted in that way for more than two months. Feeling that they did not intend to settle, I put it into the hands of an attorney for collection.

The house was insured for $1,500. The policy on the house was in the name of the seller. She brought suit against the insurance company for the amount of the policy. The court allowed her the equity in the policy, which was $1,125, but to the present day, I have not been able to collect my equity in the policy, although I had employed an attorney to collect it for me.

My furniture was insured for $1,000. After I found out that they did not intend to pay it, I employed a lawyer to bring suit against the company. The case was tried in Judge Vanderwerp's court, and he decided it in favor of the defendant on the ground that the defendant never waived his rights of demanding a notice of the losses.

In those 200 or more clauses in those policies, one of which reads: "The insured must, within 60 days after the fire, make a list of the articles lost with the cost attached to go before a notary public and swear to it and send it into the company." Being ignorant of that clause, I failed to comply with it. My lawyer contended that the statement, which I signed before the adjuster and the state fire marshal, was sufficient proof of loss.

We appealed from the decision of Judge Vanderwerp to the Supreme Court of the State of Michigan, and the Supreme Court affirmed the judgment of the lower court.

Having considered myself a bungler in my efforts to succeed in a commercial way to get the money and retain it, I decided to commercialize matrimony for a profit. Having secured the plans, specifications, and a large photo of the hotel building and all arrangements having been made to safeguard my interests at home, I decided to go to Indianapolis to look my intended wife over and see whether or not she would, in other words, whether she would make it possible for me to have employment.

On the 27th of October 1928, I arrived in Indianapolis to make a thorough investigation of the subject matter. I went to her home, and she received me with open arms. I have never been more royally treated in all my life. I was made to feel that I was at home and that everything that I wanted would be supplied. I was given the choicest room in the house and all the courtesies that could be afforded. My bride-to-be was a young woman in looks, full of vim, vigor, and vitality, and was as gay as a lark. She believed in following all of the fashions and at all times keeping herself neat, tidy, and charming.

On the next afternoon, she gave me a pencil and a notebook for the purpose of taking a list of her property and the income thereof. First, a two-story building on Indiana, which contained four storerooms on the ground floor and a rooming house on the second, which contained 26 rooms. The rental value of the first floor was $140.00 per month. The rent from the rooming house was $300.00 per month.

On the following day, she took me over on California Street, where she owned a large double house with seven rooms on either side. It rented for $45.00 on each side. On the same lot, in the rear, she had a six-room house, which she rented for $20.00 per month. Further up on Indiana Avenue to the 700 block, she owned several houses on one lot, which brought in $84.00 per month.

On the next day, I went in company with her to the city park for our group, and about two blocks from the park, she owned two beautiful 50 x 100 lots. These two lots were the property she owned, which was not mortgaged. Before returning home for the evening, we visited the park and also the evening services of the church she attended and then went home. I found, upon investigation, that the rental value of the property was $694.00 and the total value was $65,000.

I then asked her was the property encumbered, and she informed me that it was all in the building and loan company. The life of the loan was 10 years. Some of the property had been in the company for seven years, and the other not so long. I then asked her would she convert the property to money so that we could start the hotel. She said that she would rather wait until the time expired, and then she would turn it into the hotel project. I then asked her how much money she had to invest in the project, and she said that she had very little. She also said that I could take charge of her business and make it very much more profitable than what it was, and when she had paid off the mortgage, we would be in good shape to build the hotel. After the conference, I went to bed to dream over the situation, very much disappointed. It may have seemed a wonderful chance to some, but I could not see it that way, and I decided not to take the fatal leap.

On the following morning, after breakfast, we went into the sitting room where we privately talked the matter over. I told her that in view of the facts connected with the proposition, my pride would not permit me to marry her and depend on her for my living. And if she could not put me in business according to the agreement so that I could make a living for her and me also, for the time being, we would not consider the proposition further.

Although it was very painful to me and no doubt, more so to her, I think it was in the best interests of both of us. My plan to erect the building was to incorporate a hotel company with a capital stock of $250,000 and have her as secretary of the corporation and have her deed this property to the company. And then we would go out and sell stock to raise money to finance the building, but she flatly refused to take an interest whatsoever in the project. Undaunted by the disappointment, I decided to do all within my power to build a hotel.

Proposed hotel in Chicago

Chapter 18

I took my plans and specifications and made a canvas of all the leading men of our group in the city of Indianapolis and solicited them to take stock in the enterprises. I secured a certain number of names who were to act as a board of directors. They had subscribed as much as $1,000 in cash. I called the Secretary of State's office to find out just what was required to incorporate a company with a capital stock of that amount. The main point was that the company must deposit 25 percent of that amount with the Secretary of State before we could sell any stock for the company. It is needless to discuss the other requirements for the reason that we could not comply with Requirement No. 1. He also suggested that we reduce the capital stock to $100,000 and secure some property for the location, which was worth $25,000, and deed the property to the company. Then he would grant the charter. Several days after I had been informed what was necessary to be done to secure a charter for that purpose, I met an old friend who was a customer of mine and a practicing attorney in the city. I told him my business there and he informed me of one of his clients who owned some property on New York Street which was a suitable place for the hotel, and, in fact, he had been trying to erect a hotel on the lot for our group. He said he would take the matter up immediately and arrange a meeting for us so that we could talk the matter over.

On the following day, we met in the attorney's office in the Lempic Building. After discussing the proposition, he agreed to deed the property to the company for a consideration of $40,000, and he was to be the secretary of the company. Our attorney, John W. Bowlus, prepared the Articles of Agreement between us. Afterward, we went to the Secretary of State's office to secure the charter. We presented our security to him after discussing the terms of our agreement. He said that before he could grant the charter, the property would have to be raised, and he would send the state appraiser over and have him appraise. He further said that the next day at two o'clock, he would be ready to pass on the question of leasing the charter.

We met him the following day at the appointed time, and he refused to grant it on the grounds that the property was not worth enough to justify it; that the property was not worth one-third of the price agreed upon.

At that time, there were several men of prominence who had offered to assist in erecting a large hotel for our group. Among them were ex-Governor McCray, and also the Honorable Thomas Taggart, a former hotel man, whom I knew personally. I called him over the phone and told him I had a matter of business which I wanted to discuss with him and would like for him to fix the time for me to meet him. He told me to come to his residence the following morning at nine o'clock. I took all of my paraphernalia for the erection of the hotel and promptly, at the appointed time, I rang the doorbell and was escorted to the sitting room by the butler. In a few minutes, Mr. Taggart came in and shook hands with me, and after renewing our old acquaintance, I began to talk of the hotel business with him. He was in very good humor and listened attentively to me.

After I had finished my statements, he said, "I know a hotel of that size in Indianapolis for your group will be a paying proposition, and I am in favor of such a hotel. Your people have been my friends; they have always proved true to me, and I feel that I should do something for them that would be a lasting monument to me and them when I have passed into the beyond. At present, I am sick, and I am going to Florida for my health. But you can rest assured that as soon as I return, I will see to it that your group will have a hotel which will not only be a credit to your race, but a monument to the memory of him who appreciates in the greatest degree the loyalty they have shown to me."

I thanked him for his cordial reception and the interests which he manifested in our group, and I told him that God would bless him for his kindness of heart and his generosity of purpose.

When I left him, I felt very much encouraged and redoubled my efforts to get subscribers who were interested in the proposition. Of all the citizens I solicited, I found only one who would advance one cent to promote the enterprise and become a member of the Board of Directors, and that man was the Reverend Pope of Bethel AME Church. He deposited $25.00 with the treasurer, which amount was refunded to him on demand.

I am free to confess that when I left Muskegon Heights, Michigan, to go to Indianapolis, Indiana, my finances were quite limited. I had left my property in the hands of one of my tenants to collect the rent, which was $40.00 per month and send it to me so that I would have money enough to pay my current expenses. I was depending on it solely to meet all of my expenses. On the day that he had been sending the money, I received a letter from him stating that he was leaving town and that he had left the property in the hands of a reliable man and that he owed me $25.00 for two weeks' rent. He was on his way to Buffalo, New York, and as soon as he got there, he was going to work and would send me the money. My room rent and board bill were due, and I was broke and at the mercy of the landlady. Not knowing in what shape he had left my property, I decided to leave for home immediately. I left the plans and specifications in Indianapolis, as I was expecting to return by the time Mr. Taggart came back from Florida so that I could help in any way he suggested to begin the erection of the hotel building.

When I arrived home, I found that all of the tenants were paid up two weeks in advance, but being at home, I had sufficient credit to carry me for two weeks. I had been in Indianapolis six months and each day, except Sunday, I met and talked the hotel business to someone who I tried to interest in building a hotel for our group. I have some pleasant memories of my stay in Indianapolis and also some regrets. I went to church every Sunday morning during my stay there.

In the church which I was a deacon for a number of years, I met a great many of my brothers and sisters in the Lord, and we had a joyous meeting. I also met a few of my checker-playing friends and also a few barbers who were barbering there while I was operating a barbershop there. Twenty-five years make quite an epoch in the life of a man after he has reached the years of maturity. Quite a few of my friends and acquaintances had passed into the great beyond. Others had grown old, feeble, decrepit, and the vigor of youth had departed from all of them. And it seemed to me that I, alone, had retained my youth, vigor, and vitality, and I yearned for the association which I had when I was making my permanent residence, but it had fled.

I found our group there to be non-progressive. The height of its ambition seemingly was to run barbershops, restaurants, pocket billiard halls, club rooms, and to sit passively by and submit supinely to every infringement of their rights which the white man wanted to impose on them. As a result of this non-combative feeling, they have separate schools, parks, discrimination in restaurants, hotels, public inns, lunchrooms, moving picture shows, theaters, and several objectionable signs were displayed in windows in full view of the public reading: "Negroes are not allowed in here." We also have a class of our group who feels that the white man has rights which we must respect and we have none which they are bound to respect. The fact is that the rank and file of our group are afraid of the white man. The fire department of our group have a white man for captain, who is their boss and goes to every fire which occurs and bosses the job.

Our firemen are so stuck on their jobs that they are afraid to make a protest on account of losing their jobs. I had a personal talk with one of the firemen, who told me that their liberties were abridged and some of the firemen would tell the white man everything that was going on among them, and to hold their jobs, it was necessary to be very careful what they said or did. In expressing a denunciation against those conditions, I was warned several times by members of our group not to let the white folks hear you talk that way, that is the kind of talk which will cause trouble and is liable to precipitate a riot.

We have several members of our group who hold appointive positions in the state house who are just as afraid for their jobs as the firemen are for theirs, and are only puppets in the hands of their superiors, with no initiative of their own. The preachers as a rule, professional beggars, are afraid to take a stand for the rights and privileges of our group as citizens, on account of being afraid that he will lose some donations which he wouldn't get if he would interest himself in the political and social advancement of the race in Indianapolis. What Indianapolis needs is a few race men who are tried and true and loyal to our group, to organize the member of our group into societies for the protection of our rights as citizens and combat every infringement on them in public and in private and to employ men of our race who are fearless that will go into those places where we are discriminated against and demand our rights, and if refused, pass out quietly and go to the court. But if any violence is ordered, be ready to repel force by force, if necessary, to the extreme. Employ a first-class lawyer to represent us and in a short time the dockets of the courts in Indianapolis would be filled with cases against those who refuse to accord to us the same rights and privileges in their places of business that they would afford all other citizens.

We should use our votes as we would use a club to break down prejudice against our group. Unless we use all of our efforts to better our condition as citizens, we will forever be the group which will be deprived of its rights as citizens in this, the land of the free and the home of the brave. The Constitution of the

United States guarantees to every citizen the right of life, liberty, and pursuit of happiness. The Civil Rights Bill of the state of Indiana reads: "than no person shall be discriminated against on account of color, race or creed, in hotels, restaurants, inns, moving picture shows, theaters or travel by land or sea or in jury service and the penalty for each offense is a fine of $100.00 or 30 days in jail or both at the discretion of the court." All we want is the enforcement of the laws which are in the statutes of the state.

Why should we not organize? Our organizations would be within the law. The Ku Klux Klan, an outlaw organization, was organized 59 years ago for the purpose of keeping members of our group in their places, and after having been killed by mobbing, burning at the stake and shooting them down in cold blood, intimidating and coercing more than the number of men killed in the late Civil War, after having taught those who were left their places, by the lash and persecution, they ceased to function until 1917, when they reorganized and began their nefarious practices again. They charged $10.00 for members' fee. They paid their officers lucrative fees and salaries for the purpose of circulating such propaganda that would engender race hatred and create such enmity in the hearts of the poor white trash against our group that it is not safe living among them

The wealthy people of our group should maintain such societies for combating every infringement of our civil rights and not only our civil rights, but also our political and social rights. If I could arouse them to support such an organization, paying their presidents' and other officers' salaries, commensurate with their services, I feel that it would be the beginning of a new day for our group in this country, and I would feel abundantly rewarded for the interests which I have taken in the matter.

When I arrived in Muskegon Heights from Indianapolis, I found myself without a place to sleep. Having had a lot of burned lumber, I decided to build a room for my residence on the lot, and in a few days, I had it erected and had it furnished. Therefore, it was not necessary to put any of my tenants out of the apartments in order to have a place to sleep. I also decided to build a small store on the site of the building which was burned so that I could conduct my business. The dimensions of the building which I intended to erect were 16 x 24 x 8. I assembled my lumber and began work on it, and in several weeks, I had completed the framework of it. That part of it I could not do, such as plastering and building the chimney, I hired it done. Upon completion of the building, I furnished it with such things as was needed to operate the business. I then rented out my one-room residence, furnished, for $5.00 per week. My weekly rentals were $20.00. Besides, I had a place to conduct my business, to sleep and eat. Business was fairly good for a season until I had paid off the debts which I had made in building it, and then came the depression.

Another incident which I feel will be of interest to my readers, I will relate. Just before I moved to Muskegon Heights, I employed a drayman by the name of Claude Echols to move my fixture to Muskegon for $100.00, $75.00 to be paid as soon as the goods were in transit and the remainder to be paid on our arrival in Muskegon. We left Indiana Harbor and arrived in Gary, Indiana without any mishaps. Leaving Gary, we proceeded on our journey for several miles, and then we had a blowout. He did not have any tools to work with—no jacks or wrenches. His tires had several boots in them to prevent blowouts. He stopped several cars as they were passing and tried to borrow a wrench. He went to several houses along the roadside and tried to borrow a jack, without success. He then decided to return to Gary and get the necessary things to use for repairs and also to buy a new tire. So he flagged the first bus going to Gary and left me with the truck.

I stayed on the job all night and the following morning, he returned stating that he could not get the things he wanted that night, and he had to wait until morning.

The night in question was exceedingly cold for the time of the year, and during that night, I thought I would freeze. I ran and walked up and down the road all night to keep from freezing. He repaired the tire, and we were off again. We traveled as far as Sawyer, Michigan, and then we had another blowout. I stayed in Sawyer that night at the hotel. The next morning, before we started, he said that the load was too heavy and it would be impossible to complete the journey with me, and suggested that he leave it in Sawyer, and he would come back and get it the next day. I agreed to his proposal, and we took a part of the cargo to our destination. I have already told of the reception which I received when I arrived there.

After storing that part of the furniture, we started back to Sawyer the next morning to get the remainder of the furniture. When we reached South Haven, we stopped at an oil station for water and oil. I got out of the truck to buy a cigar. I went into a cigar store several doors from the oil station, and while I was in the store, he drove away and left. To my surprise when I came out of the store, he was gone. I inquired of the station agent which way he went. I thought perhaps he had gone someplace in town and would return for me in a few minutes. In the meantime, a man drove up to the station from the direction we were going, and

I asked him did he meet a man of my group driving a Chevrolet truck. He said yes, and that he was driving at a terrific rate of speed and that he was at least five miles away from us. I told him that if he would overtake him for me I would pay him $5.00. He accepted the offer. I jumped into his automobile and the race was on. He drove his car at a terrific rate of speed for nearly an hour before we overtook him. We drove in front of him and ordered him to stop. He did so reluctantly. I jumped out of the car and got into the truck as he drove off. I demanded that he stop so I could pay the man for catching him for me.

When he failed to stop, I pulled my knife from my pocket, caught him by the head, and told him that if he moved another foot, I would cut his throat. The man who caught him for me became greatly excited and sped away as fast as he could without getting one cent for his services. He evidently thought that a tragedy was imminent, and there would have been if the fella had shown the least resistance.

We continued on our journey until we reached the town north of Benton Harbor. He said, "I am afraid of you and will not ride any further with you." He stopped the truck and got out. I remained in the truck. He called the sheriff and told him that I had assaulted him in his truck and that I had refused to get out of his truck and asked him to come and arrest me so that he would be able to proceed on his journey. And he emphasized the fact that I was a bad man.

The sheriff and his deputy came out to where we were post haste and found me. I was sitting in the truck when they came up. Echols pointed me out as the bad man and proceeded to tell them what I had done. When he had stated his side of the question, the sheriff asked me what I had to say. I explained everything in detail. I told him what our contract was, that in consideration of $100.00, he was to move my fixtures to Muskegon Heights and that I had paid $75.00 of that amount and that he had claimed the load was too heavy and had unloaded a part of the furniture in Sawyer and we were on our way there to get it to bring it to Muskegon Heights. I told how he ran away and left me about 20 miles north of us and how I had offered to pay a man $5.00 to overtake him. And we caught him a few miles north of that town. I admitted that while in a passion, I had threatened to kill him if he did not stop the truck.

After hearing both sides, he ordered both of us to get into his car and carried us to Benton Harbor and put him in jail. After he had been incarcerated for several hours, I used my influence to seek his release by not signing an affidavit against him. They released him, and he left that night for Indiana Harbor, and I returned to Muskegon Heights. I had to employ a truck driver to go down to Sawyer and bring the remainder of my furniture and fixtures, and I had to pay him $75.00. The man whom I had engaged to move my outfit was a dishonest fellow of the lowest type, who was the most unscrupulous fellow I have ever known. The truck he owned was no good. All of the tires were filled with severe boots each, and that was the condition of the truck, which he used to haul my furniture 170 miles. And it took two days to make the trip one way. We left half the furniture on the road, and I had to pay an additional $75.00 to have it brought to Muskegon Heights. This is the class of businessmen of our group who have caused our group, in many instances, to fail to give our businessmen their full patronage in all of our business endeavors.

They fail to give their customers value for their money. They want tribute for their goods. If you are running an account with them, they will pad it; things you never got will be added to your bill and then they have the gall to say that our group won't patronage each other in business.

Regardless of what they say, I advise our group, whatever it needs, if it is a truck to haul your goods, get one which will do the work and get the work done at the lowest possible price, from a man who has established a reputation in the community for honesty and integrity. It makes no difference whether he is a man of our group or of some other group. When all things are equal, I give my group the benefit of every doubt.

In concluding this autobiography, I will give you an account of my social and political activities, and the feeling which those of the Nordic group have for our group and the enforcement of the laws which are on the statute books of the state relative to our group. As is my custom, I busy myself in politics wherever I make myself a citizen.

My first activities were assisting to elect a mayor of my political faith, who was fair in his dealings with our people, although at that time, there were not very many substantial citizens of our group residing in our city, Muskegon Heights. Prior to his election, the Ku Klux Klan had elected their entire ticket in the city and, as usual, had done everything they could do against us. On account of being refused service in a Greek restaurant, I went to the prosecuting attorney's office and demanded a warrant for the arrest of the proprietor. The prosecution refused to issue it unless I got his name and found out who the person was that owned the restaurant and also the number of his license.

Feeling that was more than I could accomplish, I asked him to issue a "John Doe" warrant, and he refused. I found that quite a few of the restaurants and moving picture shows made a practice of discriminating against our race. And I vowed that I would use all of my influence to remedy those conditions. In the following election, I selected two candidates to support. One was Joseph M. Sanford for prosecuting attorney and James McLaughlin for Representative to Congress. I had several conferences with Mr. Sanford relative to our rights as citizens and those particular cases which had come to my knowledge. He pledged that he would enforce the Civil Rights Bill of the state of Michigan. He further said that whenever any cases came up to be sure to have two witnesses, and he would issue warrants for the violators of the law and prosecute them to a bitter end. On these pledges, we elected him. After the election, he told me that heretofore, it had been the custom for the plaintiff in the case to deposit $15.00 for cost in the case, but by having two witnesses, I would not be required to put up the cost in the cases.

A few days after his election, the City Commissioner attempted to pass a segregating ordinance. Our group arose in their might to oppose the ordinance and organized a society known as the Greater Muskegon Citizens' League, and I was elected its president. The purpose of the league was to combat every infringement of our rights as citizens, and by cooperation, secure as many jobs for our group as possible and see to it that Negro names of members be put in the jury box in order that we, those who were unfortunate enough to fall in the clutches of the law, would have members of our group to sit as jurors on their cases sometimes. Any violation of our rights was reported to me. I would then investigate the case and decide on its merits.

The first case which came to me was the refusal of the management of the Regent Theater to admit two ladies to the main floor of the theater building. Somewhat doubtful of the report, a day after, in company with these ladies and another man, we went to the theater. I bought four tickets and started to go into the main floor of the theater.

The usher stood in front of the main door and said, "Go up into the gallery," in a gruff voice.

I said to him, "Get out of the way, boy. Don't you think I know where I want to go?"

He jumped aside, and we went into the main floor. They offered no resistance, and we went in and found seats.

There was an objectionable sign displayed in an Italian restaurant which read, "Negroes are not allowed to eat in here." When that was reported to me, I said, "That sign will be taken down from there before the sun goes down tomorrow night." That night, I took two members of the organization and went into that restaurant. I went to a table and pulled out the chairs and told them to be seated. We gave the waiter our orders and he served us. While we were eating, I remarked that I did not see the sign which I had heard was displayed here. One of our group pointed it out to me. I then remarked that that sign should not remain there until the sunset on the following day.

On the next morning, I took the matter up with the prosecuting attorney. I demanded him to order it taken down on account of it being in opposition to the Civil Rights Bill of the state of Michigan. He said to me that the law did not say anything about objectionable signs and that my remedy was a civil action. I read the Civil Rights Bill to him stating that no person shall be discriminated against on account of his color, race or creed, in public places, hotels, restaurants, inns, etc., but he stood firm in his position and reiterated that my remedy was a civil suit and that he would not do anything in the premises. But in a few days after that meeting, the sign was taken down. I am satisfied that he caused not only that sign to be taken down, but also theaters to cease their discriminatory attacks against our group.

    The next discrimination against our group, three members of our group went into a restaurant on Western Avenue for lunch and were refused service. The waitress said that they did not serve Colored people. On the next day, they brought the complaint to me. In company with the complaining witnesses, we went to the prosecuting attorney and demanded a warrant for the arrest of the proprietor of the restaurant. I told him I had two witnesses who would testify against him. He then said that to institute a suit of that kind, it would be necessary to deposit $15.00 for cost of the suit and that if the defendant was convicted, our money would be returned.

CONCLUSION

A Sudden Ending

In the introduction to my great-grandfather's memoir, we noted that he never brought his story to a formal conclusion. We do know that he left Indianapolis without successfully building another hotel, and as he moved toward the end of his life, he chose to spend his time with family. Back in Chicago, he still found time to continue writing his memoir, which he left with his oldest son, Cornelius, and his daughter, Anna Toole. They have since shared it with descendants, including Laurel and me. John Baptiste Stradford—educator, lawyer, and defender of his race—passed away on December 22, 1935. In the pages of his memoir, he invited the nation and the world into his life with all its struggles, never succumbing to obstacles, and always maintaining an unyielding determination to be a successful entrepreneur and leader of his people. He did his best and played his part in bringing the race up the "rough side of the mountain," and his efforts, like those of others, have made life better for subsequent generations.

His memoir stands as a testimony to what can be achieved when men and women are determined to succeed. Let his story encourage everyone who has read and enjoyed it to use it as a catalyst to move on to bigger and greater things. That was his purpose in taking the time to write about his life. He made this quite evident on the very first page of the memoir when he wrote: *"If this story encourages any member of our group to greater faith in his ability to demand his rights as a citizen and to give his time and talent in the prosecution of this principle, I shall feel amply repaid for my labor and pain."*

THE CURATORS

Laurel Stradford received her master's degree in Interdisciplinary Arts from Columbia College in Chicago, Illinois. She was Muhammad Ali's personal photographer and also served as a White House photographer under the Carter Administration during the negotiation of the peace accords between Egyptian President Anwar Sadat and Israeli Prime Minister Menachem Begin. She later became Revlon's International Ethnic Hair Care and Cosmetics Marketing Manager for the United Kingdom and Africa. Laurel is also an entrepreneur, having created What The Traveler Saw, a boutique shop in Chicago's Hyde Park neighborhood. She presently resides in Chicago.

Dr. Leslee Stradford attended the School of the Art Institute of Chicago, where she earned a Bachelor of Fine Arts, a Bachelor of Art Education, and a Master of Fine Arts degree. She received her Doctoral Degree in Educational Administration from Illinois State University. She was selected for Chicago's Artist-in-Residence program, creating visual arts for the city's permanent collection. For seven years, she taught art classes at Norfolk State University, a prestigious HBCU. She later served as Dean Emeritus at Berkeley City College and Laney College in California's Bay Area. Dr. Stradford also lectured at Oxford University in England. Though now retired, she continues her abstract artistic career and is publishing her family and personal history. Dr. Stradford has traveled widely, especially to Paris, France, and currently lives in Sag Harbor, New York, where she was the Artist-in-Residence in 2023.

www.ingramcontent.com/pod-product-compliance
Lightning Source LLC
Chambersburg PA
CBHW060349080526
44583CB00012B/239